"*To tell the truth,
there is no fraud or deceit in the world
which yields greater gain and profit
than that of counterfeiting gems.*"

From the 37th Book of Historie of the World
by the Roman historian, C. Plinius Secundus

Published in the year 77 A. D.

GEM
IDENTIFICATION
MADE EASY

A HANDS-ON GUIDE TO MORE
CONFIDENT BUYING & SELLING

ANTOINETTE L. MATLINS &
A.C. BONANNO, F.G.A., A.S.A., M.G.A.

GEMSTONE PRESS
Woodstock, Vermont

Matlins, Antoinette Leonard.
    Gem identification made easy : a hands-on guide to more confident buying and selling / Antoinette L. Matlins & Antonio C. Bonanno.
        p.   cm.
    Bibliography: p.
    Includes index.
    ISBN 0-943763-03-7 : $29.95
    1. Precious stones—Identification.   I. Bonanno, Antonio C.
II. Title.
QE392.M33   1989
533.8—dc19   89-1611
                                                                               CIP

Cover photograph courtesy of
Frank Bonham, G.G.

Book design by James F. Brisson
Illustrations by Kathleen Robinson

Some of the material in this book appeared originally as articles in *National Jeweler*.

10   9   8   7   6   5   4   3   2

Manufactured in the United States of America

Published by GemStone Press
A Division of LongHill Partners, Inc.
Sunset Farm Offices, Rt. 4, P.O. Box 237
Woodstock, Vermont 05091
Tel: (802) 457-4000
Fax: (802) 457-4004

A SPECIAL THANKS

To each of you who participated in our
pocket instrument workshops across the country,
whose excitement and delight with each discovery
affirmed our belief in the need for this book
. . . and gave us the extra support and
encouragement to make it
a reality.

To Ruth Bonanno,
who since our writing of
JEWELRY & GEMS: THE BUYING GUIDE
still has nothing—and everything—
to do with it

and
Stuart M. Matlins
Without whose confidence, support
encouragement, and endurance
this book would not have been written

✦ *Books by Matlins & Bonanno* ✦

Jewelry & Gems: The Buying Guide
*How to Buy Diamonds, Pearls, Colored Gemstones, Gold & Jewelry
with Confidence and Knowledge*
3rd Edition
GemStone Press

Engagement & Wedding Rings:
The Definitive Buying Guide for People in Love
GemStone Press

Gem Identification Made Easy:
A Hands-On Guide to More Confident Buying & Selling
GemStone Press

Contents

List of tables

List of color plates (following page 110)

Preface

The great transition of gemology from an art to a science is little more than 50 years old. "Exotic" tools, such as the microscope and refractometer, were both unknown to jewelers and unused in jewelry stores just a few decades ago. Merchants tended to take the word of salespeople and jewelry suppliers about a gemstone's species or quality. Common distinctions, such as a species (a division that indicates a single mineral) and a variety (different colors and types within a species) were unknown to those merchants. Identification and quality grading was based on the personal and primitive investigations of a few, the superstitions of some, and the ancient customs and beliefs of many.

As with all new concepts in any field, gemology as a science has been a slow and difficult one to take hold. In ancient times, some of the gemstones we wear today, such as tanzanite and tsavorite, were unknown. Had they been known, tanzanite would probably have been called sapphire and tsavorite, emerald. It was generally held that if a stone were blue it was sapphire, if it were red it was ruby, if green, it was emerald, and so on. The primary criteria used to identify stones were hardness and color. And since the hardness test was a "destructive" test (putting a scratch on the gem would certainly mar its beauty), color was relied on almost exclusively where jewelry was concerned.

Furthermore, imagine if you will how baubles, bangles, and beads were traded and regarded in ancient times. It was of little consequence if the gemstones were imitation or precious. Imitation lapis-lazuli was known and used in ancient Egyptian times and regarded with as much devotion as the genuine material. It was, after all, the color that was the most profound reason for owning a stone. Color had a deep personal and emotional impact on the psyche and most ancient people ascribed both magical and medicinal powers to gemstones based on their colors. Color, the ancient tradesman understood, was the way to separate one gem from another and any technology that might aid in such separation was left to the alchemists.

Innumerable mistakes resulting from identification based on color alone have been made throughout history, even into the 20th century. Bearing witness to this is the Black Prince's Ruby set in the Imperial State Crown of England. This jewel, according to jewelry historians, found its way to England and into the hands of the Black Prince in the 14th century. It was later worn by Henry V on his helmet when he crushed the French forces at Agincourt in 1415 and later by Richard III. It was lost in the disposal of the Crown Jewels by the Puritans. As fate would decree, the Black Prince's Ruby was bought by a jeweler for a mere £15, and later sold to Charles II after the Restoration of the Stuarts in 1660. For centuries, that matchless stone was believed to be a priceless ruby, until modern technology made separation and exact identity possible. It was found that the Black Prince's Ruby is not a ruby, but, instead, a large ruby-colored spinel of great beauty. A red spinel is another lovely red stone, often indeed a true "gem." But it is not a ruby. Given its size and beauty, were the Black Prince's Ruby truly a ruby, its value would be beyond imagining.

The story has its parallel in today's antique jewelry, lovingly carried to a jeweler for appraisal and sometimes repair. Often the stones set in antique jewelry are not what the owner thinks they are. Unfortunately, when the owner learns that the stone is an imitation such as glass, a doublet, a synthetic, or some altogether different gemstone, the jeweler's skill and honesty are questioned because the owner doesn't know whom to believe. For after all, didn't this belong to grandmother or great-grandmother?

Credibility problems often arise because few within the jewelry trade or among the general public are aware of the many types of imitations that exist, or that imitations have been made for thousands of years. Even synthetic stones have been around for almost 100 years! In 1885, near Geneva, Switzerland, small pieces of synthetic corundum of good ruby color were fused together into larger stones. Between 1885 and 1903, these "Geneva Rubies" were often sold as natural rubies. Some of these stones may well have been set in jewelry and reached the showcases of fine American jewelry firms. At that time, jewelers knew very little about gemstones and relied on their suppliers, wholesalers, and manufacturers for factual information. Relying on erroneous information themselves, they might easily have *mistakenly* sold them as natural ruby.

Information was so scant and technology so new that almost anyone's advice on testing was considered scientific. The following was written by an author known only as Charubel and comes from his book *Psychology of Botany*, published in 1906. The advice is for testing a genuine ruby:

Get a round goblet glass free from cuts or marks of any kind. Place your stone within the bottom of the glass, at the centre. Then fill the glass with clear water; allow the daylight to fall on the glass, and keep it clear of the shades of outside things. Also, keep clear of direct sunshine. Your stone will now be magnified so as to enable you to see such marks in it as you could not see otherwise, as the magnifying power will be equal at all points. If you find your stone laminated, and a haze at some point, you may infer it to be the true Ruby. The paste [glass] one cannot be made to contain these characteristics; consequently the paste will appear more brilliant than the true stone, but, more glassy.

The world of gemology in the United States remained largely rooted in primitive techniques until 1930 when a young visionary named Robert Morrill Shipley began to teach and call for professionalism in the jewelry trade. Mr. Shipley, with an encyclopedic knowledge of gemology and newly graduated from the National Association of Goldsmiths in London (now called the Gemmological Association of Great Britain) and Paris, went to California in 1931 and founded what became the Gemological Institute of America. After Shipley decided that he would learn how to detect fake and fraudulent gems and distinguish them from natural ones, he became the evangelist who brought the gemological gospel to the jewelers of America.

Over the past 50 years, the creation of gemstone synthetics has accelerated concurrently with gemological technology. It has been stated by experts that every gemstone—except garnet and peridot—has now been synthesized and is available in the marketplace. This includes lapis-lazuli, malachite, coral, and turquoise. Even a limited number of small "fancy" yellow diamond synthetics and some gem-quality white diamonds are being produced.

With every step forward in the advancement of gem synthesis and treatment techniques, the jeweler and gem enthusiast have required more and better laboratory equipment and training. Scientists immersed in gemology continue to develop new methods and instruments for detection that play a major role in helping to minimize the opportunity for misrepresentation.

Science, gems, and jewelry are inextricably woven together today. And this worries some. Does it mean the romance will fade from buying, owning, and wearing gemstones and jewelry? Hardly. Quite apart from science is the deep human desire for beauty and self-adornment; the love of brilliant colors; the thrill of seeing sparkling white light from a diamond. These are motivations for buying and owning gems. In each of us who loves and appreciates beautiful gemstones is an inner knowledge that every gemstone has a magical charm of its own and is, in its own way, precious. And in each individual gem or piece of jewelry there lies a special aesthetic value and emotional appeal that resists all efforts to be scientifically measured.

In this world of investigative reporters, media probes, and industry scandals, it will be the professional gemologists and gem connoisseurs who labor to know more about the identity of each gemstone, and insure that each is properly and accurately described, who will uphold and maintain the integrity of this exciting field. And, in so doing, they are the ones who will ultimately sustain the magic, excitement, and pleasure found in the jewels we love so much!

Anna M. Miller, GG, ASA
Author of *Gems and Jewelry Appraising*

Acknowledgments

All of the charts that appear here were specifically designed and executed for use in this book; however, in some cases, charts from other publications were used as inspiration and reference. Grateful acknowledgment is given to the following for use of their charts as references, and for photographs and other invaluable contributions:

Gemological Institute of America (GIA)
American Gem Society (AGS)
Accredited Gemologists Association (AGA)
American Society of Appraisers (ASA)
Gemmological Association of Great Britain (GAGB)
American Gem Trade Association (AGTA)
American Gemological Laboratories, Inc. (AGL)
National Jeweler Magazine

Special acknowledgment is also given to:

William Pluckrose and Eric Bruton of the Gemmological Association of Great Britain, for their confidence in our work and special support;

Robert Kammerling, General Manager Technical Development and Dona Dirlam, Head Resource Librarian of G.I.A.; Rodger Bucy, Columbia School of Gemology; Douglas Jaffe, AGL; and Elisha Morgan for special photographic assistance;

Kathryn L. Bonanno, F.G.A.; Kenneth E. Bonanno, F.G.A.; and Karen J. Ford, F.G.A., for their technical gemological contributions;

Steve Liesman and Rosemary Wellner Mills for their editorial assistance;

Monica Wilson for her unrelenting persistence and superb organization, and Seth C. Matlins, whose marketing talent helped make this possible.

PART 1
BEFORE BEGINNING

1 / *Before beginning*

Today, knowing your gems, being absolutely sure about what you are buying and selling, is essential. Major changes in the gem world—new synthetic stones, new treatments to enhance and conceal, new gems, and more stones available in every hue and tone of color—make accurate gem identification more important than ever to both buyers and sellers.

Whether you are the owner of a large retail jewelry chain or small family-run business, someone who enjoys collecting or acquiring gems for personal pleasure, or a serious investor, insufficient knowledge can be costly. It can result in a bad purchase, damage to a reputation, and, equally significant, failure to recognize an opportunity.

Pennsylvania jeweler Sheldon Munn can attest to how costly an incorrect identification might be. One of his best diamond customers came into his store one day with a large sapphire and diamond ring she had purchased for $14,000 at an estate sale (a price only one-fourth what she'd have paid at a retail jewelry store). She expected Munn to verify the ring's genuineness while she still had time to stop payment of her check.

Munn inspected the diamonds and found them to be genuine stones of the finest quality. They were set in an exquisitely worked, handmade platinum setting. The sapphire appeared equally fine, and there was really no reason to suspect that it was anything other than what it seemed.

However, Munn didn't want to make a mistake, and he realized that since his store specialized in diamonds, his knowledge of colored gems wasn't equal to that of diamonds. Fortunately, Munn was

3

enrolled in a course to increase his knowledge of colored gems and had, coincidentally, just been reading about differences in old and new-type synthetics.

After carefully examining the stone with his loupe, he thought he saw an indication that the stone was synthetic. Not sure, he advised his customer to stop the check, explaining that something in the sapphire made him suspicious. Munn recommended that she allow him to take it to the nearest gem-testing lab for a more thorough examination.

His suspicions were justified. The laboratory confirmed that the large, beautiful "sapphire"—surrounded by fine, genuine diamonds—was, in fact, synthetic!

Munn saved his customer from a $14,000 mistake. But, just as important as maintaining his reputation with his customer was the lesson Sheldon Munn learned. He realized that in a case such as this, it would have been very easy to make a mistake. The customer could have walked out the door, content she had acquired a real treasure, carrying Munn's seal of approval. He became even more convinced of the importance of building skill and knowledge of colored gems to match his skill and knowledge of diamonds. Since then, he and others of his staff have become equally proficient with colored gems and diamonds.

Munn's customer didn't find a treasure. But she is not alone in searching for one, hoping to discover something of value that others don't recognize. Each of us yearns to make such a discovery. And we might. There are such treasures still out there, waiting to be found. The key to discovery lies in our ability to recognize a treasure when we see it, and it can happen to you as easily as to anyone else.

Several years ago a former student of my father went into a midwestern pawnshop to kill some time. While there, she discovered a beautiful ring that appeared to contain diamonds and an emerald. The pawnbroker told her the diamonds were unusually fine, which her examination confirmed. The ring was also beautifully designed, with outstanding workmanship. The green stone posed the problem. Was it an emerald or some other less expensive green stone? And, if examination confirmed emerald, was it *natural* or *synthetic*?

She examined the stone carefully with three, simple pocket-size instruments as she learned in my father's class, and concluded that the material was emerald. The only remaining question was whether it was natural or synthetic. The price being asked—$500—suggested that the pawnbroker believed the stone was synthetic.

While viewing the stone with the loupe, however, she thought she saw an inclusion indicative of natural. While she didn't have the necessary equipment to see the inclusion clearly enough to be sure, she decided to buy the ring because she liked it and the price was right, assuming the emerald was synthetic. But she could hardly contain her excitement. She really thought she might have a genuine, natural emerald of very fine quality. As soon as she returned to Washington, the ring was examined at our lab. It contained a fine, genuine natural emerald, with a value of nearly $50,000!

Unfortunately, few have the knowledge to know for sure what they are getting, and many make costly mistakes buying from pawnshops, auctions, fleamarkets, and private estates. But for the knowledgeable, such places can be very profitable.

The key to avoiding costly mistakes and recognizing profitable opportunites is knowing both what to *look for* and what to *look out for*.

In today's gem market one must contend with more gemstone materials than ever before. There are not only the old-type synthetics, which are relatively easy to identify, but new ones spawned by modern, sophisticated technology that are extremely difficult to distinguish from their natural counterparts.

Mother Nature has further compounded the difficulties by creating colored stones that closely resemble one another so look-alikes abound—tanzanite can look like sapphire, tsavorite (a green variety of garnet) can look like emerald, red spinel can look like ruby, and so on.

No matter what color you choose, there are at least two different gems readily available in that color. There are also many new imitations (simulants), and, as more and more venture into the exciting realm of antique jewelry, the oldest forms of imitation and reproduction are resurfacing, sometimes with a modern twist.

What all of this means is that jewelers and gem enthusiasts are more vulnerable. The risk is greater than ever. The need to depend more on your own skill, and less on someone else's, is paramount.

This is why we've written this book.

We recognize that not everyone is inclined to be a professional gemologist, nor are we suggesting it. Yet, many would like to know more about how to identify gems and, until now, there has been very little available to help those who fall into this category. The choice has been either to become a professional gemologist or to remain virtually in the dark.

It doesn't have to be this way. With minimal effort and a nominal investment in several instruments, almost anyone can venture into the world of gemology and begin to experience the thrill and fun of discovery—learning just what a particular stone really is. You can learn to separate real from imitation, one look-alike from another, dyed from natural, and so on. Sometimes just a basic knowledge of how to use a simple instrument is all that is needed to avoid an expensive mistake or recognize a profitable opportunity.

Our experience teaching gem identification has shown us that people from every walk of life can master it—English teachers, auctioneers, homemakers. One doesn't need a scientific or technical aptitude to be competent at most basic gem identification and becoming familiar with the use of certain instruments is not difficult. It only requires patience, persistence, and practice. It can also be great fun and offer personal challenge.

The purpose of this book is to open up the world of gem identification to everyone who has an interest in learning about it, regardless of background or profession. It is meant for those who have little or no scientific background or inclination, for those who have no gemology course available to them in their location, for those who can't stop what they are doing to go to school, and for those who just aren't sure this is anything they really want to spend time and money to learn.

We have tried to make this a practical guide, explaining what instruments you will need to do the job, how to use them, and what to look for, stone by stone. We do not delve into scientific explanations of what you will see. (For those interested in scientific explanations, see our recommended reading list in the Appendix.)

Please *use* the book. We have left blank pages at the end of each chapter so you can make personal notes, especially of your own observations as you practice with each instrument. While years of training and experience are necessary to become qualified as a professional gemologist, with practice and a little hands-on work, you will find it takes surprisingly little time before you will feel more confident about what you are buying and selling.

Before you become *too confident*, however, we hope this book will do one more important thing. In addition to giving you the skill to identify many stones, detect certain treatments, and spot certain fakes, we hope it will help you appreciate the importance of the professional gemologist and gem-testing laboratory. As important as developing your own skill, the need for you to know when your own skill is insufficient—when the help of a professional gemologist or lab should be sought—is equally important. As a general rule, whenever there is doubt, seek the professional. (See Appendix for list).

We also hope this book will be a launching pad for some of you, merely the beginning of the pursuit of gemological knowledge. We would like to encourage you to keep up with changes in the industry by subscribing to gemological journals and attending lectures and workshops whenever possible. One thing that never changes in this fascinating field is that something is always changing.

And finally, we wish to encourage each of you who finds this book interesting and helpful to continue what you have learned here by enrolling in a gemology course. In the Appendix we have provided a list of schools and institutions offering courses in gemology.

In summary, it is our sincere hope that *Gem Identification Made Easy* will make the subject of gem identification fun and interesting, rather than tedious. We hope it will help you:

- Open your eyes to the types of imitations, synthetics, look-alikes, and fakes that can be encountered in today's gem and jewelry world.
- Learn how to tell the difference between them.
- Recognize the limitations of your own skill and when to employ the services of a professional gemologist or lab.
- Become more professional in your business or hobby.

Most of all, we hope it will help each of you become less dependent on what you're *told* . . . and more dependent on *your own gem knowledge*.

Antoinette Leonard Matlins

PART 2
GETTING READY

2 / Setting up the lab

Contrary to what many people believe, it isn't necessary to spend $100,000 (or more) for elaborate gem-testing equipment. An investment of less than $2,000 is sufficient to be a successful gemological detective and accurately identify most gems. Or, for less than $200, one can begin with just three "pocket instruments": the loupe, Chelsea filter, and dichroscope. Used together, these three simple, portable instruments can enable one to properly identify almost 80% of the colored gemstone materials encountered today as well as diamonds and most diamond look-alikes. Once you've mastered these three, you can then add other instruments to help you identify the remaining gemstone material and confirm identification made with the pocket instruments. Some of these other instruments also make identification faster and often easier.

We recommend six instruments for setting up a complete lab: the loupe, Chelsea filter, dichroscope, refractometer, ultraviolet lamp, and microscope. We also recommend several optional pieces of equipment: the spectroscope (for working with fancy-color diamonds it is not optional but essential), the polariscope, and the diamond tester.

Personal preference and practice

Once you are sure the instrument(s) you are thinking of purchasing meet the requirements for gem identification (discussed later in this chapter), the final choice is largely one of personal preference. For example, some find it easier to focus critically with a smaller loupe; some prefer the larger viewing window in the RosGem dichroscope to the size in others.

The most important thing is getting used to the instruments you buy. Practice with them until you feel comfortable. Carry your own instruments with you, whenever possible, because being comfortable with the instrument you are using can affect your proficiency. Some people never leave home without their credit cards—we never leave home without our loupe, dichroscope, and Chelsea filter.

While any one of these instruments alone is usually insufficient to make a conclusive identification, a combination of two or more will usually be enough to tell you what you really have. The key, of course, is knowing how to use them and what to look for.

THE ESSENTIAL INSTRUMENTS

These instruments will be discussed individually in the following chapters, where you will learn in detail how to use them and what they will show. Most are available at major jewelry supply houses (see Appendix). Or you may order directly from Gemstone Press, using the order form provided at the end of this book. Here is a brief overview of each, what they are, how much they cost, their primary use, and types or models we recommend. **Note that prices shown are for reference and comparison, and reflect quotes provided prior to publication. For current prices, check with suppliers.**

Note: Wearing glasses or contact lenses will not impair your ability to identify gems. The only requirement is that you have good vision in at least one eye, with or without the aid of glasses. My father is blind in one eye, and has worn glasses since his early youth, but this didn't stand in the way of his becoming a skilled gemologist. All instruments described here work just as well for the person who wears glasses and require no special techniques. They should not be removed if glasses or contact lenses are normally worn for close work.

10X Triplet-Type Loupe

($30–$90). This is a hand-held magnifier, sometimes called the jeweler's loupe, used essentially to detect chips, cracks, scratches, symmetry in cutting, sharpness of facet edges, and the presence and type of flaws. *Dark-field loupes* ($169–$189) offering dark-field lighting (see page 117) are also becoming an important aid to detection of some treatments and internal characteristics. There are many manufacturers making fine loupes, and we don't feel the brand name is important. However, for gem identification purposes it is essential that the loupe you buy be a *10 power (10X) triplet-type with a black casing* (never purchase a chrome or gold-plated loupe). Such loupes are available from Kassoy, Rubin, GIA, Vigor, A&F, and other suppliers.

A 10X triplet loupe with black housing

Chelsea Filter

($45). The Chelsea filter (sometimes called an emerald filter) is a pocket-sized color filter. Today it is used primarily to spot fakes added to colored stone parcels and mixed in jewelry, and to differentiate emerald from emerald look-alikes, sapphire from sapphire look-alikes, aquamarine from aquamarine look-alikes, and *dyed* green jadeite jade from fine *natural* green jadeite. There are other types of color filters, ranging in price from $20 to $80, some for use with all stones, some only for red, or blue, or green. Some of the most popular include the Walton filter ($80) made in France, the Hanneman Gem Filter set ($49), which includes four filters and the "Gem Filter" by Gepe of Sweden. The new Hodgkinson-Hanneman *Synthetic emerald* filter ($24) is a very important tool—used in conjunction with the Chelsea filter—*to separate natural emerald from most synthetics.*

A Chelsea color filter

Calcite-type Dichroscope

($100). This is a small, pocket-sized tubular instrument used for transparent colored gemstones, to differentiate stones of the same color from one another. It is one of the handiest and most useful instruments, but it will not distinguish natural gems from their synthetic counterparts. Many gemologists consider the new RosGem dichroscope ($99) the best calcite-type, but the GIA, Rayner and other dichroscopes also work well.

Dichroscopes by GIA Gem Instruments and RosGem

Refractometer

($385–$895). This is a small instrument available in either portable or desk models. It enables you to get what is called an R.I. measurement (generally, the higher the R.I., the more brilliant the stone). Since the R.I. differs for every stone, the measurement provided by the refractometer provides the identity of most stones, although it won't distinguish between natural gemstones and their synthetic counterparts. It is used most easily with stones that have at least one flat, polished surface (a "spot" method can be used for cabochons, but this is a little more difficult).

The major shortcoming of most refractometers is that they will not work for stones with a very high R.I., such as diamond, certain diamond imitations, and certain varieties of garnet.

The GIA Duplex II model ($395) is probably the most widely used in the United States, but the new RosGem ($399) is rapidly gaining popularity with its superb precision, monochromatic light source, sturdy construction, and easy portability. One important advantage

The GIA *Duplex II* refractometer with utility lamp

The RosGem refractometer, complete with carrying case, RI liquid, polarizing filter and both monochromatic yellow and white light capability.

of the RosGem is that it doesn't require a special light and operates with a simple inexpensive maglite ($15).The Rayner is also popular, and we like an instrument called the Jemeter ($360), manufactured by Sarasota Instruments. While in our opinion it can't replace conventional refractometers, it *can* be used for those stones such as diamond and CZ, which have a high R.I. and for which other refractometers are ineffective. Its major shortcoming, however, is that it can only be used with faceted stones that have a good, flat polish. Therefore, if you are using it for antique or estate pieces that are worn and lack a good polish, it may not be effective. It may also need periodic recalibration for reliable readings in the "normal" range (below 1.80).

(*Note*: some don't consider the Jemeter to be a refractometer, but a reflectivity meter instead. However, since the reading obtained, unlike reflectivity meters, is given as an R.I. measurement, we consider it a refractometer. Whatever it is called, it can be a very useful instrument to obtain R.I. readings for gem-identification purposes. We use both in our laboratory.)

Ultraviolet (UV) Lamp

($250–$350). This is a relatively small instrument (portable and desktop models are available) used to detect the presence or absence of *fluorescence*—a stone's ability to exhibit color when viewed under ultraviolet light, color not visible in ordinary light. For gem-identification purposes we recommend a hand-held type that provides both long-wave and short-wave light, controlled by individual buttons (so you view the stone under long-wave *or* short-wave, but never under both wavelengths simultaneously). We like Ultra-Violet Products, Inc. models #UVGL-25 ($225) and #UVGL-58 ($215),

Ultraviolet lamps—Ultraviolet Products, Inc., #UVGL-25 and an ultraviolet lamp and viewing cabinet from GIA.

and GIA's Short-wave/Long-wave Ultraviolet Lamp ($240). There are other models, such as those made by Raytech or Spectroline, which are also very good and a little less expensive.

For another $100, GIA makes a very nice, compact viewing cabinet for its lamp, which creates a miniature "darkroom" (necessary to see fluorescence). For $125, a similar cabinet is available for the Ultra-Violet Products' models. Or, just turn off the lights before turning on the UV lamp (if it's daylight, go into a closet and turn off the lights!)

Microscope

($1,600). This is a desk or countertop instrument used primarily for magnification. Many models are also portable. The microscope can be used to observe more clearly the same items observed with the loupe, but its capability for much higher magnification is especially critical in differentiating natural gems from today's synthetics.

For gem identification, you must have a *binocular* microscope that offers both dark-field and bright-field illumination, and a light source at the top of the instrument to *reflect* light from the stone being examined. If you are planning to use the microscope to identify current new-type synthetics, you must have a magnification capability up to 60X. If not, then magnification up to 30X is all you need for other gem identification. Just remember, however, that if you have a gem that appears to be unusually fine, especially "flaw-wise," it could be synthetic. If you lack the proper equipment to see the telltale inclusions, you must verify genuineness with a skilled gemologist or gem-testing laboratory. A "zoom" capability is not necessary in a microscope being used for gem-identification purposes, but it is important if you are planning to use it to determine diamond proportioning and measurements such as the table "spread." The zoom feature will add significantly to the cost of the microscope.

We like the following microscopes:

- RosGem ML 331 ($850–$995) which has all the essential features we recommend for gem identification, with magnification up to 60X; and Model ML 332 ($1,995) which offers a zoom feature to 60X. The price includes a flexible fiber optic light cable. Light and portable. Carrying case optional.

RosGem ML 331

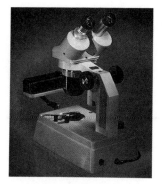

GIA's *Gemscope II*

- GIA "Gemscope Model 2" ($1,200)—has all essential features, with magnification up to 30X. An adapter to increase magnification up to 60X is available ($140). The overhead light source is extra ($165). With zoom ($2,895).
- Rubin & Son's "Rubinscope" #1164 ($950) has all essential features, with magnification to 45X. Overhead light source is extra; "Rubinscope" #1264, same as above, but with "zoom" feature, $1,895.
- Kassoy Microscope model #MIC611 ($895)—has all essential features, with magnification to 30X. By adding eyepieces ($30), magnification can be increased to 45X; model #MIC631 ($1,295) has the basic features with magnification to 30X; model #MIC631Z, same as MIC631, with zoom feature, $1,895.
- Gemmological Instruments Ltd. Microgem SKC ($800)—has all essential features, with magnification to 30X.

Kassoy's *Gemscope*

Gemmological Instruments'
Microgem SKC

By selecting carefully, as you can see, one can buy all the instruments needed for under $2,000. Also, note that most instruments are small enough to take along with you when you travel.

Loupe (pocket size)	$ 50
Chelsea filter (pocket size)	40
Dichroscope (pocket size)	100
Refractometer	400
Ultraviolet Lamp (small portable model with viewing cabinet)	350
Microscope (12 lbs./portable model)	1,000
	$1,940

OPTIONAL INSTRUMENTS

In addition to the six instruments we've just discussed, you may wish to add four optional pieces of equipment. We do not consider them essential for the beginner, but they do have specific uses that can make identification of certain types of stones faster and more definitive. In some cases, they are the only instruments that will tell you what you need to know.

The best way to determine whether to buy them is to read the chapters describing each one and see if they deal with situations you think you'll encounter. And, of course, there is no need to rush out and buy all these instruments at once. You might work with a few for six months and then determine you need additional equipment. For example, if you find you are frequently working with fancy-color diamonds, especially yellow diamonds, you might find that a spectroscope—essential for differentiating *natural* fancy-color diamonds from those that obtained their color by irradiation—is something that could save you a lot of time and help you feel more secure about your conclusions. If you think other instruments might be useful to you, you can always purchase them as your skill—and needs—change.

Spectroscope

($1,600–$4,000). There are two types of spectroscope in common use for gem identification, the prism type and diffraction-grating type. The standard diffraction type is less expensive, but the prism type has two advantages—it admits more light into the instrument, and it is easier to read in the dark blue end of the spectral display. There are also several new diffraction models with fiber optic lighting and digital readouts that eliminate the problems found in standard diffraction models, but they are more expensive. Whether you buy a diffraction type or prism type, we recommend models that come as a unit, complete with light and stand, because we think they allow better control of both the instrument and the light intensity and direction necessary for successful use. Models that can be inserted into a microscope in place of an eyepiece also work well (but not without the microscope). The OPL hand-held model can be very useful in the field.

Wavelength prism spectroscope by Beck

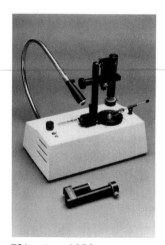

GIA prism 1000

Diffraction-grating spectroscope by GIA Gem Instruments

The spectroscope shows a complete color spectrum, exhibiting vertical black lines or bars at certain points of the spectrum that indicate the specific gemstone identity. Its most important uses, gemologically, are to distinguish natural fancy-color diamonds from diamonds that have obtained their color by irradiation; to separate naturally green jadeite jade from dyed and impregnated jadeite; and to separate natural blue sapphire from most synthetic blue sapphire. Some prefer the spectroscope to other instruments for much broader gemstone identification.

Spectroscopes we like include GIA's Prism 1000 ($2,895, mounted) and Beck's prism spectroscope ($3,800). They are easy to read and very precise. There is a new *video spectroscope* that we've used and find promising. It is available through Hanneman Gemological Instruments for $750, including the monitor, camera, adapter, spectroscope, reference spectra, and fiber optic light. Standard diffraction grating spectroscopes such as the OPL portable model sell for as little as $50, but, as we've mentioned, many are less reliable and more difficult to use than other types.

Polariscope

($200–$330). The polariscope is a desktop instrument used to detect optical properties of gemstones. For gem identification, we think the best polariscopes are the GIA Illuminator Polariscope ($215), the Rayner ($275) and the new portable RosGem polariscope ($60). To get the full benefit from this instrument, we also recommend using an immersion cell ($30), benzyl benzoate ($15), which is essential for amethyst, and rubbing alcohol.

GIA Gem Instruments' *Illuminator*   Rayner Polariscope   RosGem *Portable*
Polariscope   Polariscope

The polariscope is being used increasingly today because of its value in separating synthetic amethyst from genuine. This is the only affordable instrument currently available that can make this separation. Because of the wide circulation of synthetic amethyst, often represented as genuine, this instrument meets an important need. It can also be used for other gem-identification purposes.

Immersion Cell With Diffused Light Unit

($120–$190). Immersing stones in liquid using diffused light facilitates seeing important identifying characteristics. Invaluable with the polariscope, microscope, or untrained eye. Essential to detect diffused sapphire. We like the portable models by RosGem and GIA.

Electronic Diamond Tester

($150–$295). Diamond testers are available in both portable and desktop models. They are very easy to

RosGem Immersion Cell

use and most work simply by pressing a metal point against one of the stone's facets. The tester will then give a signal indicating if the stone is a real diamond or not. They have become very popular because they require no gemological skill and make diamond testing both fast and easy. They are also helpful for small, mounted stones that can be difficult to examine with other instruments. The diamond tester can also be used to assure another party that their stone is, or is not, a diamond. However, most will only tell you that and cannot identify what the stone is.

Popular models include:

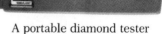

- GIA's Gem Diamond Master (portable)–$250.
- Ceres' Czeck Point (portable)–$169.95.
- Diamond Star (portable)–$95.

A portable diamond tester

- Rayner Diamond Tester (desktop)–$275.

A CHECKLIST OF INCIDENTALS YOU MAY NEED

Before you get started, here is a quick checklist of other useful items.

- *Good light* (see Chapter 3). You will need two types of light—a source for *incandescent* light, such as the light from an ordinary light bulb in a household lamp; and *daylight* light, or light from a lighting unit or fixture that has Daylight-Type fluorescent tubes. We recommend a desk-type lamp that provides both, ideally with a flexible arm attached to the base.
- *Portable penlight or flashlight*. This can come in very handy, especially for colored stones, and can be purchased at many places, including the drugstore. Jewelry supply houses sell them from $4 to $20.
- *A pair of locking tweezers*. We recommend a medium point tweezer with a self-locking feature ($13–$20).
- *Retractable prong tweezers*. These make it easier to hold unmounted stones. Push the end (like a ballpoint pen) to release a 3-prong or 4-prong tweezer to snugly grip the stone you wish to examine. Prongs retract when finished ($8.95–$20).
- *Bottle of rubbing alcohol* ($.50–$1.00).
- *Bottle of nail polish remover* ($1.50).
- *Can of compressed air*. This can be obtained from any photo or jewelry supply house. Any brand will do. "Dust Off-II" has a special formulation for jewelry and costs $32 including the trigger valve; refills are $9; pocket size, $6.50. "No Dust" (available at photo supply houses) costs $20; refills are $4.
- *Liquids*
  Methylene Iodide—a liquid with many uses. $26 for 30 ml bottle.
  Refractive Index Liquid—necessary for most refractometers. $15 (10 g).
  Benzyl Benzoate—a liquid used with the polariscope when examining amethyst. $15 (30 ml).

- A magnifying headpiece such as the OptiVISOR ($25–$40) or VigorVISOR ($20–$30). Available in various powers of magnification. It can be particularly helpful when you need both hands free.

*Opti*VISOR magnifying head-piece (other manufacturers such as Vigor also make a similar product). Particularly useful when you need both hands free.

- *A roll of white toilet tissue* (a coarse, lint-free brand) serves a variety of purposes.

A Word About Specific Gravity Liquids

In this book we limit our discussion to *instruments* we consider important for gem identification. We do not include gem-testing *liquids*. However, using liquids can be an easy and quick aid for determining the identity of many stones and spotting look-alikes.

Of particular importance are "specific gravity" liquids used to determine the specific gravity of gemstone substances. Some don't consider a lab complete without a set of these liquids. We will briefly discuss such liquids, but anyone interested in using liquids should learn more about them and how to use them before you begin. We recommend starting with Richard T. Liddicoat's *Handbook of Gem Identification*, 12th Edition (GIA, Santa Monica, CA), or Robert Webster's *Practical Gemmology*, 6th Edition (N.A.G. Press, London).

What Is Specific Gravity (S.G.)

The specific gravity of a substance is a measurement indicating how heavy (dense) that substance is—it shows the ratio of the weight of the substance compared to the weight of an equal volume of water.

Let's use cubic zirconia (CZ) and diamond to explain specific gravity. The specific gravity of CZ is 5.65. That means it will weigh 5.65 times more than an equal volume of water. By comparison, diamond has a specific gravity of 3.52. That means diamond weighs

3.52 times more than an equal volume of water. CZ has a specific gravity almost 1.6 times more than diamond. In other words, CZ is 1.6 times *heavier* than diamond.

What does this really mean? Let's take an unmounted CZ and an unmounted diamond that appear to be the same size—round, brilliant-cut stones, measuring 6.5 millimeters in diameter. We know that a 6.5 millimeter round diamond will weigh approximately one carat on a diamond scale. If CZ and diamond had the same density (weight), the same specific gravity, then the CZ would also weigh approximately one carat. But when we weigh the CZ, we find out it weighs much more. The scale will show almost 1¾ carats! Even though they look as if they're the same size, the carat weight will be different because the density of cubic zirconia is greater than the density of diamond.

The higher the specific gravity, the heavier the substance; the lower the specific gravity, the lighter the substance. If you compare a CZ that actually does weigh one carat with a diamond that weighs one carat, the CZ will look *smaller* than the diamond since it is a heavier substance. For the same reason, a one-carat ruby (S.G. 4.0, which is higher than diamond) may look smaller than a one-carat diamond; and a one-carat emerald (S.G. 2.72, which is lower than diamond) may look larger than a one-carat diamond.

Since each stone has a different specific gravity, by immersing it in a liquid with a specific gravity close to that of the stone you suspect it to be, one can easily approximate the stone's specific gravity—by observing whether it sinks or floats; if it floats, how buoyant it is in the liquid; or, if it sinks, how quickly or slowly.

Knowing a stone's specific gravity provides an important aid in identification. While liquids are usually not precise enough to give a positive identity if used alone, when used in conjunction with the refractometer or other instruments, they are often all that is needed to confirm identity.

For those interested in using liquids, the following can be very useful:

- *Methylene iodide* (diiodomethane). This is the liquid we consider the most important. We have already recommended it because of its many uses.
- *Benzyl benzoate.* This liquid, and other liquids made by

mixing benzyl benzoate with methylene iodide, are useful for determining an unset stone's density or specific gravity.

- *Tetrabromoethane* (acetylene tetrabromide). This liquid is also used to help determine specific gravity. It is also important in helping to separate jadeite from nephrite jade.

GIA sells a *Specific Gravity Liquid Set* ($150) which contains five of the most useful liquids.

WARNING: THESE LIQUIDS CAN BE HARMFUL IF INHALED, SWALLOWED, OR ALLOWED TO HAVE PROLONGED CONTACT WITH SKIN. EXERCISE CAUTION WHEN WORKING WITH THEM.

The Value of a Good Library

In addition to the instruments and incidentals listed in the preceding pages, we want to stress the importance of having a reliable library for reference and assistance. We have provided a list of books in the Appendix that we think you will find particularly useful. While you may not be able to acquire all the books we recommend at one time, for gem-identification purposes we recommend especially Richard Liddicoat's *Handbook of Gem Identification*, Robert Webster's *Gem Identification* and *Gemologist's Compendium*, and Gubelin/Koivula's *Photoatlas Of Inclusions in Gemstones*; for diamonds, Eric Bruton's *Diamonds*; and for general information about buying gems, our earlier book, *Jewelry & Gems: The Buying Guide*.

In addition to books, you should subscribe to at least one of the journals on gemology listed in the Appendix. It is essential to keep up to date on new developments in treatment and synthesis. As we have pointed out repeatedly, this field is ever-changing. In fact, there could be changes taking place even now, as this book goes to press. Your only protection against change is keeping yourself informed. We especially recommend *Gems & Gemology* and the *Journal of Gemmology*.

3 / Proper lighting for gem identification

As you begin to explore the world of gems, you will undoubtedly encounter some words or terms that will be new and sometimes complicated-sounding. As you will see, most are really not complicated at all. There is one very important area, however, that requires an understanding of very specific terms. Before we begin, it's important to understand them.

One of the most important tools of gem identification is usually taken for granted by beginners—the "light" they use as they work. Gem identification employs one sense above all else—the sense of sight. Even the most expensive instruments will do us little good if they are used with incorrect light because the lighting itself influences what we see. Improper lighting can result in a more difficult or even an incorrect identification.

We want to make sure you understand the need for proper lighting and what it is and will briefly explain the different types of light needed with each instrument. Before starting to use any instrument, check the chapter describing it to learn special lighting instructions.

When it comes to lighting, you must think about three things as you examine stones:

1. **Intensity**—Is the light source bright enough for you to see what you need to see, or is it so weak you have to strain?

2. **Position of light source**—Is the light coming from over the stone, from behind or underneath it, or from the side?

3. **Type of light**—Is the light *incandescent* or *natural daylight?* Or *fluorescent? Monochromatic* or *white* light?

27

INTENSITY OF LIGHT

Intensity describes simply the strength or brightness of light. Intensity can be increased or decreased, for example, simply by taking a lamp shade on or off. Some lamps, and even some penlights, have a feature allowing you to change the intensity.

For gem identification, "normal" light, light that isn't too bright or too weak, is usually sufficient. When working with some instruments, a small utility lamp such as those sold by GIA often comes in handy. A utility lamp makes it easy to direct light where you really need it while working.

Never examine a stone if the light is very weak. We are always amazed when friends ask us, for example, to evaluate a piece of jewelry while dining in a lovely candlelit restaurant. When we tell them there isn't enough light to see, they don't understand. As you will realize when we discuss the loupe and other instruments, examining a stone with insufficient light, or with a very dark background, reduces your ability to see flaws or inclusions that may be present. Working in poor conditions—especially bad lighting—increases chances for making errors.

POSITIONING OF LIGHT

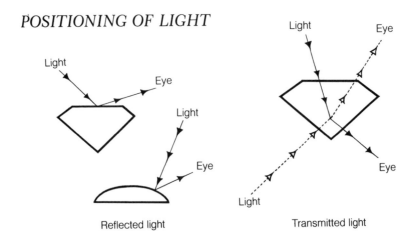

Reflected light   Transmitted light

Knowing the direction from which the light should be coming as you examine a stone is very important. Light can come from overhead, from under the stone, or through any of its sides.

Reflected Light

Reflected light refers to light shining on the surface of the stone. When reflected light is called for, you must have light coming from *overhead* while tilting the stone at a slight angle so that the light will bounce back off the surface rather than continue through the stone. An example of looking at something in reflected light can be easily found at a lake. When you look out at just the right angle, you will often see a spot on a lake that looks very shiny, almost like a mirror. That mirror-like illusion is created by light being *reflected* from the surface. You are looking at a section of the lake with "reflected light."

Using reflected light is especially important when examining colored gems. It can help you spot a "garnet-topped doublet" (an ingenious fake we'll discuss later, often found in antique jewelry), a dangerous crack that breaks the surface of the stone, or, possibly— when you've become very experienced—a glass-filled cavity (a technique used to fill a crack and enhance color in gems such as ruby).

Transmitted Light

If you're examining a stone with transmitted light, this means you are examining it as light travels *through* the stone.

The light can be coming from any direction—overhead, behind, or from the side. The light travels through the stone and illuminates its interior. Sometimes it is helpful to use a flat white business card to reflect light from the card into the stone. This often reduces glare and enables you to see into the stone more clearly.

With the loupe you will use both transmitted and reflected light. The majority of examinations will be done using transmitted light, but reflected light will sometimes help you spot certain inclusions, or notice differences in reflection off certain facets—a definite red flag.

With the dichroscope, you must use transmitted light. A penlight works especially well with this instrument to give transmitted light. A small utility lamp such as the one sold by GIA, on *top* of which you set the stone being examined, also provides transmitted light and eliminates reflected light. Both the penlight and the utility lamp offer the added benefit of stronger light since the stone can be held close to the light source.

You can also examine a stone with the dichroscope using light coming from a ceiling fixture. Just hold the stone and dichroscope up, looking into the light, with the light coming through the back of the stone.

TYPES OF LIGHT

As we discuss the various instruments and how to use them for gem identification, you will repeatedly encounter four terms referring to types of light: incandescent, daylight, fluorescent, and monochromatic.

When we talk about light, what usually comes to mind is "visible" light—the light we can actually see. But few people really understand light, and a full understanding involves some fairly complex scientific principles. We will try to explain only what you need to know, as simply as possible.

First one must understand that there is both *visible* light and *invisible* light. Light travels in waves, and the length of the wave determines whether or not we see it. It also determines what *color* the light will be when we see it.

The longest wavelength we are able to see produces RED; the shortest produces VIOLET. The visible colors, sometimes called the visible spectrum of light, include (starting with the longest wavelengths visible to our naked eye and proceeding to the shortest) red, orange, yellow, green, blue, indigo and violet.

White Light and Monochromatic Light

When *all* the colors of the visible spectrum are blended together, we get *white* light. We use white light with most gem ID instruments.

Sometimes, however, we want to use "monochromatic" light. Monochromatic light is light composed of only *one* of the colors of the spectrum. In monochromatic light, six of the seven colors in the visible spectrum are filtered out, and only one (mono) color (chromatic) remains. A yellow monochromatic light is normally used with refractometers. Many utility lamps such as those sold by GIA provide both white light or yellow monochromatic light. However, if you don't have a yellow monochromatic light, you can make a filter to produce a good substitute by simply covering your light with several pieces of yellow cellophane (such as a candy wrapper).

Incandescent Light

Incandescent light is white light. It has all the colors of the *visible* spectrum blended together. The word "incandescent" means "to grow hot" or "to glow" and is used when referring to light produced by the glowing or heating of an object—candlelight is incandescent light; an ordinary household lamp, which contains an ordinary light bulb (which "glows" from a heated filament inside) gives incandescent light.

Natural Daylight

Both visible and invisible wavelengths are present in natural daylight. As a result, the color we see in gems can sometimes look different in daylight than in incandescent light. For example, alexandrite, a color-change stone, is green/blue-green in natural daylight, but raspberry red in incandescent light. It's no wonder that when it was discovered—outside, in daylight—it was thought to be an emerald. What a shock someone must have had when they looked at the stone again that evening in the glow of a lantern or candlelight!

In many instances, one can use either daylight or incandescent light. However, where we specify "fluorescent" or "daylight-type fluorescent" light, we mean incandescent light should *not* be used. Or, if we specify incandescent, then *fluorescent* light should not be used. For example, we specify using incandescent light when using the Chelsea filter. While natural daylight is also acceptable, fluorescent light is *not*. It will not produce the same effect.

Fluorescent light

Two types of fluorescent light are commonly encountered in homes and offices, both in desk lamps and ceiling fixtures—"cool white" and "daylight" type. Fluorescent lights produce wavelengths that go beyond our visible spectrum to include some degree of "ultraviolet"— a wavelength beyond visible "violet." In daylight-type fluorescent light, there is a greater concentration of ultraviolet rays than in "cool white." Normally, where we specify fluorescent light, we will be specifying daylight type. We should point out here that we use daylight type for gem identification and most color grading. However, for color grading diamonds, using this type of light may result in error (we explain why in the chapter on Ultraviolet Lamps).

For the gem identifier's purpose, you need to recognize that fluorescent light is produced by those long frosted glass tubes mounted in ceilings (sometimes recessed and often behind diffusers, which create the worst possible light for viewing jewelry—all jewelry in these lights looks "deadish").

What you must find out, however, is whether those tubes are producing "cool white" or "daylight" type light. If you don't know, it is written on one end of the tube. If you can't reach the tube, you might be able to tell by the type of light you are seeing—"daylight type" has a much stronger white with a bluish tint, while "cool white" has a faint yellowish tint.

We recommend using a desk-type lamp with "daylight" fluorescent tubes (if the lamp you are using does not have such tubes, simply change them). If you don't have a fluorescent lamp and are going to buy one, we recommend one of the circular models that combine both fluorescent lighting with incandescent lighting (approximately $100). We like the type with a flexible extension arm attached to the base. However, the circular fluorescent tube that normally comes with these lamps is usually "cool white" so you *must replace it with a daylight-type tube that you can obtain from an electrical supply house.*

Invisible Light—Ultraviolet

As we mentioned earlier, there is both visible and invisible light. We have talked about visible light. Now we will take a moment to describe invisible light. For our purposes, the only type of invisible light one needs to know about is "ultraviolet light." Ultraviolet light is invisible because its wavelengths are much shorter than what the human eye can see. On one end of the visible spectrum we have violet, which has the shortest visible wavelength. Ultraviolet goes beyond this— "beyond violet."

One of the most important instruments the gem identifier uses, the ultraviolet lamp, is a special lamp that provides *only* ultraviolet light.

Gemologists use a lamp that supplies two different wavelengths of ultraviolet light—long-wave and short-wave. Some gems will reveal a distinctive color when viewed with long-wave or short-wave ultraviolet light, color that is *not seen* when the stone is viewed in ordinary light. These stones are exhibiting a property we call fluorescence. Fluorescence is easily seen with the proper use of the ultraviolet lamp. Some stones exhibit color only when viewed with short-wave light, some only when viewed with long-wave light, and others will show color under both waves. The colors revealed, and the wavelengths under which they are revealed, provide important clues to the identity of many gems. This property is discussed in greater detail in the chapter on the Ultraviolet Lamp.

Invisible Light—X-ray

X-ray light is a type of invisible light similar to ultraviolet light and can be used to observe many similar phenomena. However, X-ray light is very dangerous and we do not recommend its use for gem identification.

Suggested Lighting for Gem Identification Instruments

	Incandescent	Fluorescent	Transmitted	Reflected	Special Comments
Loupe	Yes	Yes	Yes	Yes	
Chelsea Filter	Yes	No	Yes	Yes	
Dichroscope	Yes	Yes	Yes	No	
Refractometer	Yes	No	Yes	No	Most accurate when used with *monochromatic yellow light,* such as that found in GIA utility lamp, or, by making a filter for your light with several sheets of yellow cellophane.
Ultraviolet Lamp	No	No	No	No	This instrument is used to provide a special type of light. A "darkroom" or darkened viewing cabinet is required for proper use.
Microscope	Yes	Yes	Yes	Yes	
Spectroscope	Light source is usually self-contained.				
Polariscope	Light source is usually self-contained.				
Diamond Tester	Not applicable.				

NOTES

PART 3

UNDERSTANDING THE ESSENTIAL INSTRUMENTS

4 / The loupe

10X triplet type loupe

WHAT IS A LOUPE?

The loupe is the most widely used and most familiar gem-identification instrument. It is the first of the three pocket instruments, which, just as they sound, are small enough to be carried in a pocket.

The loupe is simply a special type of magnifier. Loupes come in various powers of magnification: 6X, 10X, 14X, 20X, and 24X. A 6X loupe, for example, presents an image six times larger than what is being viewed. For gem identification, the loupe must be a Hastings triplet-type in a black housing—not gold or chrome-plated. We recommend 10X power for reasons we explain below.

The triplet-type loupe is essential because it has been made specially to correct two problems other types of magnifiers have—the presence of traces of color (chromatic aberration) normally found at the outer edges of the lens; and visual distortion (spherical aberration), also usually at the outer edges of the lens.

Eliminating the traces of color present at the edges of an uncorrected lens is particularly important when you use the loupe to color grade diamonds. Even the slightest trace of color that may be present in a non-triplet type can cause improper grading of diamond color. The Federal Trade Commission in the United States requires that the observation of diamonds for grading purposes be made only with the Hastings 10X triplet-type magnifier (10X specifically for determining the clarity [flaw] grade—if it isn't visible with 10X magnification, it doesn't exist for clarity grading purposes).

Correction for visual distortion in the triplet-type creates what we call flatness of field. If we were to look at a gem with a magnifier that was not a triplet-type, any flaw seen at an outer edge of the magnifying lens would be distorted, more or less so depending on how close the flaw is to the edge of the viewing lens. This impairs one's ability to see the flaw clearly, and may result in improper identification of the flaw, and, hence, improper identification of the stone.

We recommend a black housing (casing) because it eliminates distracting glare. Gold or chrome-plated loupes are not recommended because they can throw white or yellow color into stones being examined, especially diamonds. Some jewelers use watchmaker-type loupes, which allow freedom of the hands. If you prefer this type, be sure it is a triplet since most are not. We also recommend the new *dark-field* type since dark-field illumination facilitates detection of fillers and certain internal characteristics.

A Word About Magnification— Higher Power Can Make It Harder to See

Most people think that the higher the magnification, the easier it is to see whatever you are looking at, especially inclusions (flaws). However, this is not exactly true. Unless you understand how magnification works and know how to focus properly, using high-power magnification can be *more difficult* and result in major errors.

It's true that when you have an inclusion in view under higher-power magnification, it's easier to see it clearly, and determine what type it is. However, when you're looking for inclusions, the higher the magnification, the more difficult it may be to spot them. This is because the higher the degree of magnification, the shorter the focus—the depth of field is reduced, so you have less latitude in the area that will be in focus at a given point, making it much harder to focus critically. An inexperienced person can easily miss small inclusions with a higher-power loupe. The loupe might be in focus just in front of, or behind, an inclusion—but not at the very point where the inclusion actually is, causing one to miss it altogether!

Here's why. With a 10X loupe you have a one-inch depth of field. This means that anything present in a stone at a distance of one inch from the end of the loupe will be in focus. In addition, with a 10X loupe you also have a little latitude in terms of the area in focus, which means that something present at a distance of only ¾ of an inch, or 1¼ inch, will also be seen. It may not be clear, or in focus, but you will see that something is there and can then move the loupe accordingly to focus it more sharply. This is not the case with higher power magnification. A 20X loupe, for example, has only a ½ inch depth of field, *and no latitude in front of or behind the ½ inch.* Therefore, if there is something just in front of the exact point that is in focus, or just beyond it, you will not see it. There have been cases where gems examined with a 20X loupe have been called flawless, when they clearly were not. With a 10X loupe one would have seen the flaws that were missed with the 20X!

Some unethical jewelers and dealers who understand the difficulty of focusing at higher magnification have developed a very clever ploy to use with customers. They immediately offer a 20X or 24X loupe to use to "take a closer look." They are well aware that the novice will probably see little or nothing at such high-power magnification, but the unsuspecting novice thinks more highly of this dealer for giving them every possible opportunity to really know what they are buying.

We recommend using nothing higher than 10X. If you wish, you may add a 14X or 20X loupe to your store of gem instruments to observe more clearly what you see with the 10X.

The loupe can help determine whether a stone is natural, synthetic, glass, or a doublet (stones that consist of two parts glued or fused together to simulate any gem desired). It can help identify characteristic inclusions, blemishes, cracks, chips, scratches, and bubbles. And, at the very least, the loupe can help determine the workmanship that went into the cutting of the stone, such as symmetry, proportioning, alignment of facet edges, etc.

HOW TO USE THE LOUPE

Before you begin to examine jewelry, practice with the loupe. Learn to see through it clearly. A 10X loupe, while easier to use than a higher powered one, is difficult to focus initially. With a little practice, it will become simple. Practice on any object that is difficult to see—the pores in your skin, the root of a strand of hair, a pinhead. Play with the item being examined. Rotate it slowly, tilt it, move it back and forth while rotating it, look at it from different angles and different directions. Focus holding the loupe at different distances from the object being examined. It won't take long before you are able to focus easily on anything you wish to examine. When you feel comfortable with familiar things, you're ready to begin looking at jewelry.

The first step is to make sure the stone is clean. A thorough cleaning is mandatory before examination. Steam-cleaning is very good for most gems. Another safe method is to stroke the stone gently with a fine-pointed artist's brush dipped in clean isopropyl rubbing alcohol. This method usually removes bits of dust, fingerprints, grease, and often dislodges embedded dirt wedged under prongs. If you are examining a stone under a microscope, you may be surprised to see how many "flaws" wash off when brushed with alcohol.

Holding an unmounted stone with tweezers, or a piece of jewelry by the metal setting, dip it in a small glass of clean alcohol. Stroke it gently with the brush. When you are finished cleaning it, remove it and dry with a clean cloth, paper towel, or toilet tissue. Blow off any remaining lint, which may have been left while drying the piece, with compressed air, such as Dust Off.

Ultrasonic cleaning is recommended only for diamonds. It should never be used for opals, pearls, emeralds, or any gemstone that is heavily flawed. Ultrasonic cleaning can seriously damage these stones.

If no other means is available to clean the stone, breathe on it in a huffing manner to steam it with your breath. Then, wipe it with a clean cloth, such as a handkerchief or shirt. This will at least remove any superficial grease film.

When the stone is clean you are ready to use the loupe. You shouldn't have any problem if you follow these steps.

Key Steps to Using the Loupe

1. Hold the loupe between your thumb and forefinger. Hold the stone or piece of jewelry being examined similarly in the other hand. If examining a loose stone held in a tweezer, hold the tweezer near the tip for greater security.
2. Bring the loupe close to your eye. To prevent movement or shaking, brace the hand that is holding it against the cheek, nose, or any part of your face that is comfortable. The loupe should be as close to the eye as possible (it is not necessary to remove eyeglasses).

3. Now, bring the object being examined *to the loupe*. The hand that is holding the object must also be braced to prevent movement during examination. Hold your hands together so that the fleshy parts just below the thumbs are pushed together and braced by the lower portion of each hand just above the wrists. The wrist must be free to act as a pivotal point when moving the stone to view it from different angles.

4. Find a sturdy, three-point position. With your hands still braced together, and resting against your cheek or nose, place both elbows firmly on a desk, table, or countertop. If nothing else is available, brace your arms against your chest or rib cage. This is the only way to have a really steady hand, and with gems it's very important to have steady hands to insure proper focus.

How to hold a loupe ▶
when examining a stone

◀ Examining a stone with the loupe, using tweezers

5. If you are examining an unmounted stone, hold it so that the fingers touch only the girdle of the stone. Putting your fingers on the table (top of the stone) and/or pavilion (bottom) will leave traces of oil. The careful use of tweezers instead of fingers is recommended.

6. Rotate the stone and slowly tilt it back and forth to view it from different angles. This is important because, as we mentioned earlier, your eye may be clearly focused on one area of the stone, but can be completely out of focus in the area immediately adjacent—causing you to miss a nearby flaw altogether. By slowly turning and tilting the stone, you will be more likely to focus in on all areas.

7. Focus the loupe both on the surface of the stone and into the interior. To focus into the interior, start at the surface and then slowly move the stone closer to the loupe so that you are changing the distance between the loupe and each area within the stone; pause and look carefully; now slowly move it closer to the loupe again and look carefully, etc. Now repeat this, looking through the sides. And so on. If you focus on the surface of the stone only, or from the top of the stone only, you will not see what is in the interior of the stone.

8. If you are looking for inclusions, wiggle a finger up and down behind the gemstone. This will cause a shadowing and brightening effect inside the stone, which will highlight any inclusions and make them more definitive in shape, color, and size. We call this the Bonanno-Wiggly-Finger-Technique and students have found it very helpful for over 40 years.

LIGHTING AND THE LOUPE

Using Transmitted Light

You will want to hold the stone so that the light is being transmitted through it, from behind, traveling toward your eye.

If you can, hold a white business card behind the stone if you are using an overhead light source. This will reflect light into it and reduce glare, enabling you to see into the stone more clearly.

Most examinations will be done using transmitted light, but it is sometimes helpful to view the stone with reflected light (see Chapter 3). Therefore, also practice with the light shining down on top of the stone, viewing it with the loupe while tilting and turning the polished facets so that light is reflected off the top of each facet.

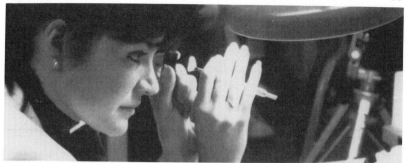

Using loupe with transmitted light, incorporating our *Bonanno-wiggly-finger* technique.

In this way, it is sometimes possible to see scratches or worn edges, certain types of inclusions, or to pick up differences in the "shine" of the upper facets (produced by the light reflection) that would be present in some doublets frequently seen in antique jewelry prior to the production of good synthetics.

It is important to practice using the loupe and focusing it. Practice on things you are already familiar with. Use the wiggly-finger technique. Practice with different light sources—coming from different directions and at different strengths. New *dark-field loupes* (see page 117) are also available today, and are especially useful in detecting certain types of inclusions and the flash-effect in filled diamonds.

WHAT THE LOUPE CAN SHOW YOU

With practice and experience a loupe can tell even the amateur a great deal. It can help determine whether a stone is natural, synthetic, glass, or a doublet; it can help identify characteristic inclusions, blemishes, or cracks; it can reveal important cutting or wear faults. This section will cover what you can see with the loupe generally, and will then discuss in detail diamond and colored gemstone imperfections.

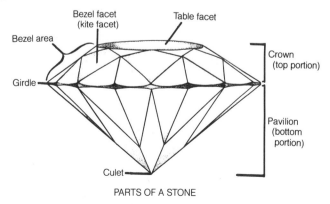

PARTS OF A STONE

Here are some of the first things you'll be able to spot.

• *The workmanship that went into the cutting.* For example, is the symmetry of the stone balanced? Does it have the proper number of facets for its cut? Is the proportioning good? Herein lies an important clue to a stone's genuineness since few cutters put the same time and care into cutting glass as they do into a diamond.

• *Spotting chips, cracks, or scratches on facet edges, facet planes, or table.* While zircon, for example, looks very much like diamond because of its pronounced brilliance and relative hardness, it chips easily. Therefore, careful examination of a zircon will often show chipping, especially around the table edges and the girdle. Glass, which is very soft, will often show scratches. Also, checking around the prongs of a ring setting will often reveal where a setter may have chipped or scratched it while simply working the prongs to hold the stone.

• In stones such as emerald, the loupe can also help you determine whether or not any natural cracks are really serious—how close they are to the surface, how deep they run, and whether or not they make the stone more vulnerable to breakage as a result.

• *Sharpness of the facet edges.* Harder stones will have a sharp edge, or sharper boundaries between adjoining planes or facets. Many imitations are softer and under the loupe the edges between the facets will appear less sharp—they will have a more rounded appearance. With the loupe it is also possible to spot the rounded edges characteristic of molded plastic.

• *Surface texture differences* that help separate real pearls from fake pearls. Because simulated pearls have a painted surface coating, one may see a pebbly veneer when examining a fake pearl with the loupe, rather than the smooth skin that is characteristic of the real pearl (natural or cultured). A simple comparison under the loupe of pearls you know to be real as compared to those that are fake will teach you the difference immediately.

• *Inclusions and blemishes* (also called flaws). Many inclusions and blemishes that cannot be seen with the naked eye can be viewed with the loupe. With minimal experience, you can learn to spot the characteristic bubbles and swirl marks associated with glass. But remember, most inclusions are not easily seen unless you have experience with the loupe. This is the most difficult area of gem identification to master. It requires lots of patience—taking it one step at a time. Try focusing on just one type of inclusion, or types of inclusions found in one particular gem, such as sapphire. It is helpful to seek professional guidance if possible until you feel confident about what you should be seeing. Don't be afraid to keep reference books and pictures of different types of inclusions on hand. For excellent photographs and additional information, we recommend obtaining a copy of *Internal World of Gemstones* by Edward Gubelin, or *Photo-atlas of Inclusions in Gemstones* by Edward Gubelin and John Koivula.

Just learning to focus the loupe so that you are able to spot inclusions that may be present in a stone is an accomplishment that should give you pride. Once you can do this, you should be able to identify what you are seeing simply by referring to the photos provided in this book or in one of those mentioned above.

When examining a colored gem, remember that flawlessness in colored stones is perhaps even rarer than in diamonds. In colored gems, the *type* and *placement* are more important considerations than the presence of flaws in and of themselves. Unlike diamonds, normally they don't significantly reduce the value of the stone. They often provide the necessary key to positive identification, help determine whether or not a stone is natural or synthetic, and possibly indicate the country of origin, such as Burma or Colombia, which may *increase* the value of the stone.

NOTE: *See the color section at the center of the book for photographic illustrations of the inclusions described below.*

DIAMOND IMPERFECTIONS

There are basically two types of flaws observed in diamonds: internal flaws (inclusions) and external flaws (blemishes).

Inclusions (internal flaws)

Pinpoint. This is a small, usually whitish dot (although it can be dark) that is difficult to see with a 10X loupe. There can be a number of pinpoints (a cluster) or a "cloud" of pinpoints (often hazy in appearance and difficult to see).

Dark Spot. A small crystal inclusion or a thin, flat mirror-like or metallic reflective inclusion.

Colorless Crystal. This is often a small crystal of diamond, although it may be another mineral. Sometimes it appears very small, sometimes large enough to substantially lower the flaw grade. A group of colorless crystals can lower the flaw grade considerably.

Cleavage. A cleavage is a crack that has a flat plane which, if struck severely, could cause the diamond to split.

Feather. This is another name for a crack. A feather is not dangerous if it is small and does not break through a facet. Thermoshock, which is exposing a gem to extreme temperature changes, or ultrasonic cleaners, can enlarge it.

Bearding or Girdle Fringes. These are usually the result of hastiness on the part of the cutter while rounding out the diamond. The girdle portion becomes overheated and develops cracks that resemble small whiskers going into the diamond from the girdle edge. Sometimes the bearding amounts to minimal "peach fuzz" and can be removed with slight repolishing. Sometimes the bearding must be removed by faceting the girdle. A lightly bearded stone can still be classified IF, Internally Flawless.

Growth or Grain Lines. These can only be seen when examining the diamond while rotating it. They appear and disappear usually instantaneously. They will appear in a group of two, three, or four pale brown lines. If they cannot be seen from the crown side of the diamond and are small, they will not affect the grade adversely.

Knaat. This is a comet-shaped ridge that can appear anywhere on a diamond's surface, usually on the table. It's actually part of a small diamond crystal that is invisible to the cutter until it suddenly appears during polishing.

Laser Line. Laser treatment is used to make flaws less visible, and thus improve a stone's appearance. For example, a black inclusion can be vaporized with a laser beam and practically disappear. The laser holes can be seen with a 10X loupe. They look like fine, *straight* white threads extending from the facet surface down to the area containing the vaporized inclusion.

Flash effect. This refers to the appearance of an orange or pinkish zone that "flashes" to violet or blue as you tilt or rock the stone while examining it with the loupe, and indicates the presence of a man-made *filler* forced into cracks to conceal them. It can be seen most easily using a dark-field loupe.

External blemishes

Natural. A natural is a remnant of the original diamond skin. It is often left on the girdle in order to cut the largest possible stone from the rough. Naturals usually occur on the girdle and look like rough, unpolished scratch lines. Some exhibit small triangles, called trigons. If the natural is no wider than the normal width of the girdle and does not disrupt the circumference of the stone, some do not consider it a flaw. Naturals are often polished and resemble an extra facet, especially if they occur below the girdle edge.

Nick. This is a small chip, usually on the girdle, and can be caused by wear, especially in diamonds with thin girdles. Sometimes a nick or chip can be seen at a point where two facet edges meet (making a "bruised corner"). If small, the bruised corner can be polished, creating an extra facet. These usually occur on the crown.

Girdle Roughness. This blemish appears as crisscrossed lines, brighter and duller finishing, or minute chipping. It can be corrected by faceting or repolishing the girdle.

Knaat or Twin Lines. These appear as very small raised ridges, often having some type of geometrical outline. They are the result of two diamonds having grown together (twin crystals). They are difficult to see and usually can only be seen if light is reflected off the facets.

Pits or Cavities. These are little holes, usually on the table facet. If deep, they will quickly lower the flaw grade of the stone. Removing the pits involves recutting the whole top of the stone, with a resulting loss in carat weight and a shrinkage in the stone's diameter. Recutting will also affect the symmetry.

Scratch. A scratch is usually a minor defect that can be removed with simple repolishing.

Polishing Lines. Many diamonds exhibit polishing lines. If they appear on the pavilion side and aren't too obvious, they do not lower the value. However, in some small diamonds these scratch lines can be obvious, and are usually the result of a badly maintained polishing wheel.

Abraded or Rough Culet. In a modern-cut stone, the culet is a very small facet, nearly a point. An abraded or rough culet has been chipped or poorly finished and will look larger. This is usually a minor flaw.

If you are planning to repolish a stone to remove an external blemish, remember that it must be removed from its setting and reset after polishing.

INCLUSIONS IN COLORED GEMS

Numerous types of inclusions are found in colored gems. Since certain ones are found in some gems and not in others, they provide an important means of positive gem ID—especially in combination with other test results. Types of flaws to look for include the following:

Feather. A crack that can either be inside the stone or breaking the surface. A large crack that is near the surface, or breaks it, can weaken the stone and make it more vulnerable to damage. One must be particularly careful to check for such cracks when examining emerald, since the oiling of emerald may make cracks more difficult to see. Examining an emerald with the loupe *using reflected light* will reveal cracks that break the surface. Such a crack will appear in reflected light like a little hair or thread on the facet plane and will not disappear after cleaning.

Cracks with a "rusty" look usually indicate a stone is genuine.

Numerous cracks arranged in a web-like or fishnet pattern when seen on the surface of a green stone that appears to be emerald proves the stone is a Lechleitner synthetic.

Needlelike or Fiberlike Inclusions. These look like fine needles or fibers and are sometimes called silk. This type of inclusion can be found in almandine garnet, sapphire, ruby, and aquamarine.

Tube-like Inclusions. These look like long, thin tubes. Sometimes they are filled. They are seen in Sandewana and Zambian emeralds, and synthetic spinel.

Two-Phase Inclusions. This is an inclusion that usually has a "frankfurter" outline with an enclosed bubble—which may or may not move as the "frank" is tilted from end to end. These can be observed in topaz, quartz, genuine and synthetic emeralds, and sometimes tourmaline.

Three-Phase Inclusions. These look like irregularly shaped pea pods, usually pointed at both ends, containing a bubble and a cube-shaped or rhomboid-shaped solid that is adjacent to the bubble. The three-phase inclusion is liquid, solid, and gas. These are found in genuine Colombian emeralds and sometimes in Afghanistan emeralds, and verify the emerald's genuineness and country of origin.

Twinning Planes. These are found in rubies and sapphires and occasionally in some of the feldspar gems, such as moonstone. They have the appearance of parallel cracks that resemble panes of glass lying in parallel planes. In rubies and sapphires, these can often be found to crisscross at 60 and 120 degrees. These types of inclusions can prove the genuineness of a ruby or sapphire, but if too numerous they can both weaken the stone and diminish its brilliance.

Liquid-Filled or Healing Feather. This type of inclusion is found in the corundum family (sapphire and ruby) and is more frequently observed in sapphires than in rubies. It resembles a maze of slightly curved little tubes lying next to one another with each tube separated by a space. The overall appearance often resembles a maze or fingerprint.

Veils. These are small bubblelike inclusions arranged in a layerlike formation that can be flat or curvaceous, broad or narrow, long or short. They may be easily observed in some synthetic emeralds.

Fingerprint. These are small crystal inclusions that are arranged in curved rows in such a way as to resemble a fingerprint. They can be seen in the quartz family (amethyst, citrine, etc.) and in topaz. They closely resemble the liquid-filled healing feathers seen in sapphires.

Dark Ball-like Inclusions. These are found exclusively in Thai rubies. They appear as dark, opaque balls surrounded by an irregularly shaped, wispy, brown cloudlike formation. They are never seen in Burmese stones, which often contain needlelike inclusions not seen in Thai stones. This type of inclusion will confirm beyond doubt the identity of a genuine Thai ruby.

Cleavage Fault. This is a type of break in the stone rather than an actual inclusion. It is observed in topaz, diamond, feldspar, kunzite, hiddenite. It is a plane- or sheet-like type crack and can weaken the stone if it is exposed to extreme temperature change (thermoshock). If struck with a severe blow, the stone may break apart. Also, a cleavage crack may become larger in ultrasonic cleaning.

Curved Striae. These are concentric curved lines that appear in old-type synthetic sapphires and rubies. Sometimes the curvature is very pronounced; sometimes the lines are slightly curved and appear almost straight. They are difficult to see in light-colored stones, such as pale synthetic pink sapphire. They are most easily observed with a microscope, using diffused or weak light.

Swirl Marks. These are found in glass. They are curved, sometimes snake-like, and resemble the swirl marks made when slowly stirring a jar of honey.

Halo or Disc-like Inclusions. Many pastel colored Ceylon (Sri Lanka) sapphires contain flat, disc-like inclusions referred to as halos. These are small fractures that result from the growth of zircon crystals inside the host stone. The small crystal is sometimes visible, or may appear as a small dot at the center of the disc, often extending above it. Halos can also be seen in other gems such as garnet.

Rain. These are dashed lines that resemble rain. They are seen in flux grown synthetic rubies such as the Kashan synthetic.

Bubbles. These inclusions look like little bubbles and occur in various shapes and sizes. Round bubbles usually indicate glass or synthetic, although they can be found in natural amber. In synthetic ruby or sapphire they can be round, profilated (a string of bubbles with a large bubble at the center and progressively smaller bubbles on each side), pear-shaped, or tadpole-shaped. In the last two, the tail always points in the same direction. When numerous bubbles are seen, you are probably seeing air bubbles in glass. However, if you see only a few, higher magnification is required to determine whether what you are seeing is truly a bubble or a *small crystal* that may *look like a bubble when viewed with only 10X magnification.*

If inclusions weaken the stone's durability, affect the color seen, are too easily noticeable or too numerous, they will significantly reduce price. Otherwise, they may not influence price to any great extent. In some cases, if they provide positive identification and proof of origin, they may actually increase the price (as with Burmese rubies or Colombian emeralds). It is also true that flawless colored stones are rare, and so may bring a disproportionately higher price per carat. However, with today's new synthetics we are immediately suspicious of any flawless colored stone and would urge examination by a professional gem lab.

The loupe can be an invaluable aid to today's jeweler. Whether you plan to use it to observe some of the simpler things, such as scratches and chips on a stone, or to begin learning how to spot some of the flaws or inclusions to determine a gem's ID, the extent to which you will feel confident using it depends on the amount of practice you give it.

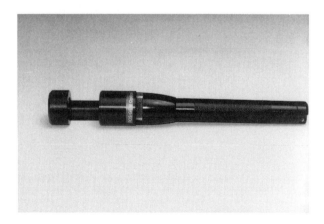

RosGem dark-field 10X loupe simply attaches to standard maglite. Dark-field illumination facilitates detection of the flash-effect in filled diamonds, and other internal characteristics.

5 / *The Chelsea filter*

WHAT IS THE CHELSEA FILTER?

During the past 50 years, a number of optical filters for gem identification have been introduced to the gemologist. The most popular is the Chelsea filter, developed in the early 1930s from a formula worked out by B. W. Anderson and C. J. Payne while teaching at the Chelsea College of Science and Technology in London—hence the name. We like it because it is affordable, widely available, and offers in a single filter what it can take several other types of filter to do.

The Chelsea filter is used for colored gemstone materials, both transparent and opaque. It first came to be called the emerald filter since its original use was to differentiate genuine emeralds from their green look-alikes—green sapphire, tourmaline, peridot, and glass. Emerald would appear pink to red when viewed through the Chelsea filter, while these other stones would not. Unfortunately, in the case of emeralds today, positive identification based on what is seen through the Chelsea filter is no longer an adequate test when used alone. There are genuine emeralds being mined that may not appear red or pink under the filter and synthetics that do. So, while it's still an important aid in the identification of emerald, it must be used in conjunction with the loupe and other instruments.

New uses for the Chelsea filter have renewed its importance. The Chelsea filter proves very helpful in detecting certain dyed and treated stones, and in separating some gems from their common imitations. It offers an effective means for differentiating sapphire-colored synthetic spinel from genuine sapphire, aquamarine-colored synthetic spinel from genuine aquamarine, and natural-colored green jadeite jade from much dyed jadeite. These are all frequently encountered and often confused.

We recently viewed a pair of jadeite earrings that were going to be auctioned by a well-known auction house. The earrings were estimated to fetch $10,000 to $15,000. They looked like exceptionally fine jade, truly "imperial" quality. The first thing we did was pull out a Chelsea filter. And were we surprised! In less than 15 seconds we knew that they were dyed. The earrings were genuine jadeite, but not the magnificent quality they appeared to be. They were inexpensive dyed jade, worth a fraction of the estimate.

The Chelsea filter is really quite a simple instrument. It is a color filter, designed to allow only two wavelengths of light to be transmitted—red and green. Therefore, a stone can only appear red, green, or a mixture of the two when viewed through the filter. The particular optical properties of the stone being viewed determine which color you see.

The Chelsea filter costs about $35 and can be obtained at many of the supply houses listed in the Appendix in the back of the book.

HOW TO USE THE CHELSEA FILTER

The Chelsea filter is the easiest and fastest of all instruments. One simply holds a stone in a good light, looks at it through the filter, and notes what color the stone appears. Normally, the depth of color in the stone being examined determines the depth of color seen when viewed with the filter. For example, a pale green emerald will appear pinkish when viewed through the filter while a deep green emerald will appear red. And so on. When this is not the case, one should be suspicious. The color the stone appears when viewed through the filter—red, green, or some combination of these two—provides an important clue to identity.

As simple as the instrument is, however, many people use it improperly and get incorrect results. Let's take a moment to explain how to use it properly.

1. *Use a strong WHITE light source for viewing the stone.* Incandescent light such as that provided by an ordinary 60- or 100-watt light bulb is excellent. Natural daylight light may also be used. However, *do not use fluorescent light.* Fluorescent light has less of the red wavelength present than white light and will alter what you

see with the filter. For example, when one views a nice, rich green Colombian emerald through the Chelsea filter using proper light, it will look RED. However, if viewed using fluorescent light, in some cases you might not see red at all, or the red may appear much weaker than it should. If you concluded, therefore, that the stone wasn't Colombian, you would be wrong.

2. *Place the stone or jewelry directly UNDER or OVER the light source.* Place the stone or jewelry as close to the light as possible. We prefer using overhead light so that the light passing through the filter has been *reflected* from the object being examined.

3. *Hold the filter as close as possible to the eye.* It is also helpful to close the other eye when using the filter.

4. *Bring your eye/filter to the piece being examined.* The piece being examined must remain close to the light source, so you shouldn't move it away from the light to bring it closer to your eye. Your head must do the moving. Try to get as close as possible to the piece, but preferably no further than 10 inches from it. Protect yourself from the glare of the lamp by keeping the housing from the light source between you and the object being viewed.

You may find that a piece of black cardboard placed behind the gemstone is helpful for observing any coloration seen through the filter. A piece of white cardboard or flat white business card will work even better. Whether you are using a white or black background, be sure it doesn't have a shiny surface.

Examining a stone
with a Chelsea filter

WHAT THE CHELSEA FILTER WILL SHOW

As we mentioned, the Chelsea filter was originally designed for the examination of emeralds and emerald look-alikes. Colombian and Siberian emeralds appeared red when examined with the filter while other green gems did not, and, therefore, could not have been emeralds. However, today this no longer holds true because emeralds mined in places other than Colombia and Siberia often do not appear red, and most synthetic emeralds do. We have also come to learn that gemstones such as the rare chrome tourmaline, which obtains its green body color naturally from the presence of chromium, will exhibit a reddish color through the Chelsea filter.

The most important uses for the filter today include: detecting certain types of dyed-green jadeite; separating fine blue sapphire from blue synthetic spinel; separating aquamarine from aqua-colored synthetic spinel; and separating pink sapphire from pink tourmaline. It is also a very useful tool to detect the mixing of fakes in with parcels of natural stones, in beads and in jewelry containing many stones.

Dyed Versus Natural Color Green Jadeite

Let's take a look at green jadeite as an example of how useful the Chelsea filter can be. The Chelsea filter is invaluable for detecting certain types of *color-enhanced* jadeite, poor quality jadeite that has been dyed to get its rich, deep green color.

Fine green jadeite jade derives its color naturally from chromium, as does chrome tourmaline and Colombian emerald. Normally when chromium is present, it causes whatever gem is being examined to appear *red* when viewed through the Chelsea filter. This is why Colombian emerald and chrome tourmaline always appear red with the filter.

Curiously enough, this is not the case with green jadeite. In fact, with green jadeite we see just the opposite of what we would expect—natural color green jadeite does *not* appear red when viewed with the Chelsea filter. It remains inert (appears the same color with or without the filter). Certain types of *dyed* jadeite, however, will show a reddish coloration (ranging from a weak orange-brown to a pale pink, to red). This coloration is easily seen when the specimen is held against a black cardboard background. *With jadeite, whenever the stone appears REDDISH through the Chelsea filter, you have positive proof it has been treated.* This certainly is simple enough. The presence of red indicates the color has been enhanced, that it is not natural. For those who love jade, the Chelsea filter is invaluable just for its ability to detect such stones, and many a costly mistake has been prevented with it.

But beware. The converse is not true. There are also treated stones which, like natural green jadeite, remain inert. You must be careful not to draw an erroneous conclusion. If the jadeite is inert when viewed with the Chelsea filter, other tests are necessary before you can be sure whether or not the color is natural. The spectroscope can be very useful in making a positive determination here (see Chapter 10). Just remember, *the presence of red is conclusive* evidence of color alteration, but *the absence of red is inconclusive.*

Aquamarine Versus Synthetic Spinel

Now let's look at aquamarine. Today synthetic aquamarine-colored spinel is often misrepresented as genuine aquamarine. The Chelsea filter can tell you immediately if you have synthetic spinel. Synthetic spinel gets its color from the element cobalt, as does much blue glass. When cobalt is present, one will see red with the filter. If the color is light blue, you will see a pinkish color; if dark blue, you will see red. Aquamarine on the other hand will never show pink or red. It appears greenish through the filter. As you can see, while light blue synthetic spinel can easily pass for aquamarine to the naked eye, it is quickly detected with the filter since the synthetic spinel will show a pink tint and genuine aquamarine will show a greenish tint.

Pink Sapphire Versus Pink Tourmaline

Pink tourmaline is a very popular stone today that can be mistaken for pink sapphire. However, once again, the Chelsea filter can be of great assistance. Pink tourmaline will retain its pink color when viewed with the filter, while pink sapphire, the more expensive of the two gems, will appear a strong red.

REACTIONS OF POPULAR GEMS TO THE CHELSEA FILTER

It is very helpful to take the Chelsea filter and use it to look at stones whose identity you already know, making a note of what you see. It takes practice and, as you will see, several stones of the same color may also react similarly under the Chelsea filter. However, by narrowing the possibilities, and then viewing them also with the loupe and the dichroscope, one can positively identify approximately 85 percent of the colored gemstone materials encountered today.

A brief tabulation of reactions of gems when viewed through the filter follows.

Green Stones

Emerald. Most Colombian and Siberian emeralds, as well as most synthetics, exhibit a good red. The depth of the green will determine the depth of the red when viewed under the filter. However, Chatham, Linde, and Regency synthetic emeralds possess such a strong red that it is usually an immediate giveaway, and should make one instantly suspicious.

Indian and African Emerald. Indian emeralds and most African emeralds do not exhibit any red or pink. Some from Zambia and Zimbabwe, however, do occasionally show a pinkish color.

Afghan Emerald. These usually exhibit a weak red.

Brazilian Emerald. These will exhibit a brownish-red.

Emerald-Colored Soudé-type Doublets. This is an imitation gem fabricated from two pieces of material (often colorless synthetic spinel) that have been cemented together with emerald-green colored glue. It is inert when viewed with the filter (continues to look green). This type of doublet can readily be detected by submerging it in methylene iodide and examining it through the girdle while tilting it back and forth in the liquid. The methylene iodide will enable you to see that the top and bottom are colorless, and will reveal the plane of colored glue.

Demantoid Garnet. Fine green demantoid garnet will appear reddish with the filter.

Diopside. Although sold as "chrome" diopside, does *not* appear reddish. Inert.

Tsavorite Garnet. Will appear reddish.

Green Zircon. Most will appear reddish.

Green Dyed Chalcedony. This will appear reddish if the stain used for dyeing was a chromium compound.

Dyed Green Jadeite. Sometimes dyed jadeite will exhibit a reddish or pinkish tint (occasionally appearing orangish or brownish). When it does, you have conclusive proof of color alteration. However, the absence of a reddish coloration does *not* prove that the color is natural. If jadeite is inert (shows no color change) when viewed with the filter, other tests are necessary to determine whether or not its color is natural.

Green Glass. Is usually inert; may appear reddish if it gets its coloring from chromium enhancement.

Green Tourmaline. Most green tourmaline is inert. However, the rare chrome tourmaline will show red.

Green Fluorite. This will exhibit red. *Note:* Not only will green fluorite exhibit red, as does Colombian emerald, but it may also contain three-phase inclusions, which are also seen in Colombian emeralds. A three-phase inclusion is one that encompasses all three states of matter—gas, solid, and liquid. It typically consists of a liquid pocket, inside of which will be a bubble (gas) and a tiny, often rectangular crystal (solid). In cases where three-phase inclusions are observed with the loupe and red is exhibited with the Chelsea filter, other tests are necessary to positively identify the stones.

Alexandrite. Will show a strong red in natural daylight and a stronger red in incandescent light.

Greenish Aquamarine. Will appear green.

Hiddenite (Spodumene). Varieties from North Carolina appear reddish; other varieties appear green.

Peridot. Will appear green.

Green Sapphire. Will appear green.

Green Tanzanite. Although often sold as "chrome" tanzanite, will be inert.

Synthetic Green Sapphire. Will appear red.

Synthetic Green Spinel. Will usually appear green but can appear red.

Synthetic Green YAG (diamond simulant). Will show strong to moderate red.

Red and Pink Stones

Garnet. Red varieties will be inert.

Glass. Inert.

Doublets Inert.

Ruby. Both natural and synthetic ruby will exhibit a strong red, redder than it will appear without the filter.

Spinel. Both natural and synthetic spinel will exhibit red, but a weaker red than ruby.

Pink sapphire. Will appear red, but not as strong as ruby.

Tourmaline. Inert.

Blue Stones

Spinel. This usually shows no color change but can exhibit a weak red.

Synthetic Spinel. Will exhibit strong red due to the presence of cobalt, which acts as a coloring agent; light blue synthetic spinel may appear orangish.

Aquamarine. Will appear green.

Blue Topaz. Most will appear green; "electric" blue may appear brownish-pink.

Blue Tourmaline. Will appear dark, sometimes almost black.

Blue Zircon. Will appear greenish.

Sapphire. Will appear very dark green, almost blackish.

Blue Glass. May appear strong red if the blue coloration results from the use of cobalt. Otherwise, inert or, if light-colored, sometimes greenish.

Blue Tanzanite. Usually appears reddish, but can also be inert.

It is very helpful to take the Chelsea filter and use it to look at stones whose identity you already know, making a note of what you see. It takes practice and, as you can see, several stones of the same color may also react similarly under the Chelsea filter. However, by narrowing the possibilities, and then viewing them also with the loupe and the dichroscope, one can positively identify approximately 85 percent of the colored gemstone materials encountered today.

NOTES

_____

_____

_____

_____

_____

_____

_____

_____

_____

_____

_____

_____

_____

6 / The dichroscope

A dichroscope

WHAT IS A DICHROSCOPE?

The dichroscope is the third pocket instrument. As we mentioned earlier, armed with only these three—the loupe, Chelsea filter, and dichroscope—a competent gemologist can positively identify approximately 85 percent of all colored gemstones. While it takes years to develop professional-level skill, knowing how to use these three instruments will start you on your way.

Like the Chelsea filter, the dichroscope is very easy to use. It is used *only* for transparent colored stones and not for colored opaque stones, or amber and opal.

The dichroscope provides one of the easiest and fastest ways for differentiating transparent stones of the same color from one another. The jeweler who knows how to use this instrument can easily distinguish, for example, a ruby from a red garnet or a red spinel (one of the popular "new" stones seen with increasing frequency); a blue sapphire from fine tanzanite or blue spinel; an amethyst from purple glass; or an emerald from many of its imitations or look-alikes.

The dichroscope we recommend is a *calcite-type* (not a polarizing type). It is a small tubular-shaped instrument that is approximately 2 inches long and ½ inch in diameter. In most models, the tube has a small round opening at one end, and a rectangular opening on the other (in these models, look through the *round* opening). Some models have two round openings, one slightly larger. Look into the dichroscope without any stone or piece of jewelry. Just hold the instrument up to the light, and look through it. Do you see two small rectangular windows at the opposite end? If not, look through the other end. The important thing is to be sure that when you look through the opening, you are looking through the end that allows you to see a pair of rectangular windows at the opposite end.

 Two rectangular windows seen when looking through dichroscope into light

When colored stones are viewed with the dichroscope, some will show the same color in both rectangular windows while other stones will show two colors, or two different tones or shades of the same color. For example, you might see blue in one window and yellow in the other. Or, you might see pink in one window, and red in the other. In either case, the colors you see would be considered "two" colors, even though pink is really a lighter shade of the color red. If you were to see orangy-red in one window and violet-red in the other, this would also be considered seeing two colors, even though they are really different shades of the same color.

One can successfully use the dichroscope without understanding why only one color is seen with some stones and more than one with others. You simply need to know how to use the instrument properly, and what to look for, stone by stone. However, we think it is interesting to understand why, so we will take a moment to explain it in very simple terms.

When a ray of light enters a colored gemstone, depending on the particular properties of that stone, it will either continue travelling through as a *single* ray, or divide into *two rays*. Stones through which it continues as a single ray are said to be "single refracting"; stones through which it splits and travels as two rays are "double refracting." If you look at an object through a strongly double refracting stone such as calcite, you will actually see two images. Try it. Write your name on a piece of paper and then read it through a piece of calcite—you'll see double.

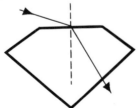

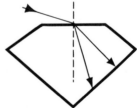

Single refraction: A ray of light enters the material and continues traveling through it as a *single* ray

Double refraction: A ray of light enters the material and *splits* into *two rays,* each traveling at a different angle and speed.

Single refracting stones are those that will always show *the same color* in both rectangular windows of the dichroscope. Only a few gemstone materials are single refracting—diamond, garnet, spinel, glass, colored YAG, colored CZ, and plastic. Therefore, if you have a stone that only exhibits one color, identity can be fairly quick, since there are so few possibilities.

Most gems are double refracting and will show *two colors* (we call them dichroic), one color in one rectangular window of the dichroscope, and a different color in the second window. When a ray of light enters the stone and splits into two rays (as it does with all double-refracting stones), each of the two rays will travel through the stone *at a different angle and speed.* The angle and speed at which light travels determine the color we see. So, if we could separate the rays and see each one individually, we would see a different color for each. This is what the dichroscope does. It separates each of the two rays so we can see both colors.

Stones that show three colors (called trichroic) are also double refracting. But when light enters from certain directions we get one pair of rays (travelling at certain angles and speeds), and when it enters from another direction, we get a *different* pair. In the second pair, one of the two rays will travel at an angle and speed different from either of the two rays in the first pair. Thus the third color. We get two colors (one in each rectangular window) in certain directions, and two colors from another direction, but not the same two colors. One of the colors in the second pair will be different from the colors seen in the first pair.

Same color seen in both rectangular boxes of dichroscope in single-refracting stones.

Different colors, or shades of same color, seen with dichroscope in double-refracting stones.

The specific color or shades of color seen through the dichroscope present a very important clue to the identity of a stone. Let's take two red stones that are approximately the same color red—ruby and red spinel—and view them through the dichroscope. We would be able to identify the ruby immediately because two distinctly different shades of color would appear, one in each of the two small rectangular windows: a strong orange-red would show up in one, and a strong purple-red in the other. However, the red spinel would exhibit the same color in both windows—there would be no difference in tone or shade of red, but exactly the same red. (*Note*: the dichroscope can separate stones that look like one another in color—ruby from glass, sapphire from spinel, and so on—but cannot separate *natural* from *synthetic*. Additional tests are required for that.)

HOW TO USE THE DICHROSCOPE

Although the dichroscope is simple to use, it is important to make sure you have proper light and that you rotate the dichroscope as we will describe below. You must also remember to view the stone from five different directions. Keeping these points in mind, proceed as follows.

1. Hold the dichroscope between your thumb and forefinger, gently resting it against the stone being examined.

Using the dichroscope. Notice that the dichroscope is held very close to the stone and the eye. Holding the tube between the thumb and the forefinger allows easy rotation of the dichroscope as you view the stone. The light is being *transmitted* through the stone.

2. Place the eye as close as possible to the end of the dichroscope. Be sure you are looking through the end that allows you to see a pair of rectangular windows at the opposite end.

3. View the stone with strong light that is *transmitted through the stone*. A small high-intensity utility lamp is a good source for transmitted light (these lamps offer the added benefit of stronger light since the stone can be held close to the light source). A strong penlight also provides good light to use with the dichroscope. Or, use light coming from a ceiling fixture (hold the stone and dichroscope up, looking into the light, with the light coming through the back of the stone).

4. To view the stone with the dichroscope, hold the dichroscope as close as possible to the stone, even touching it (be sure a strong light is coming through the stone, from behind it).

5. Look into the dichroscope. While looking through it, slowly rotate the *dichroscope* (not the stone) at least 180 degrees. Does a second color appear in either of the windows as you rotate it? For example, while looking at ruby you may see the same color in both windows as you begin, possibly an orange-red color. Then, as you turn the dichroscope, you will see a second color appear. You will still see the orange-red color you've seen all along in one window, but in the second window the color may change to violet-red. If there is no apparent change of color in one of the windows, continue rotating the dichroscope until you have turned it a full 360 degrees. If you still don't see a second color, change the direction through which you are viewing the stone.

6. Following exactly the same procedure described above, ex-amine the stone from another direction. You must examine the stone from *five* different directions to be sure that there is, or is not, a second (and sometimes a third) color. The five directions are: top to bottom; side to side; front to back; on a diagonal to one of those directions; on a diagonal to the other direction.

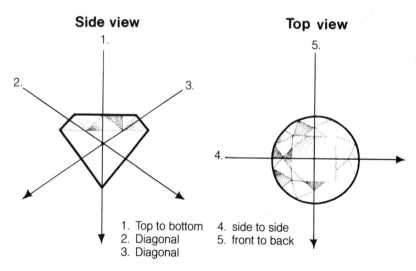

Side view

1.

2.

3.

1. Top to bottom 4. side to side
2. Diagonal 5. front to back
3. Diagonal

Top view

5.

4.

Examine the stone from five directions: top-to-bottom, side-to-side, front-to-back, and from two different diagonals.

Using the ruby again as an example, if we viewed it from only one direction, even though we rotate the dichroscope, we might only see a single color in the two boxes. If we stopped here, we could draw a false conclusion that a genuine ruby were a garnet or spinel. If we do not detect more than one color in the first direction, we must repeat the examination from a second direction, and again from a third direction, and so on, until we have examined it from all five directions.

REMEMBER: AS YOU VIEW THE STONE IN EACH DIRECTION, YOU MUST ROTATE THE DICHROSCOPE.

7. Note the color seen in each window, in each direction. You may see only one color; or two colors (in which case you are observing *dichroism*); or, in some stones, three colors (*trichroism*).

In the case of trichroic stones, you will see one pair of colors in the rectangular windows when viewed from one direction, and a second pair when viewed from a different direction. One color will be the same in both pairs.

Andalusite provides a good example of trichroism. When it is viewed with the dichroscope in one direction, you may see yellow in one window and green in the other. Then, when viewing it from another direction, you might see the same yellow you saw in the first pair of colors and, in addition, a reddish-brown in the other window.

The specific colors seen in the rectangular windows, as well as the number of colors seen (two or three), can help you make a positive identification of most colored stones. But remember, you must observe the stone from at least five different directions. A second color will often fail to show up when viewed from only one direction. And, of course, a third color, which would indicate a trichroic stone, might be present. If you think a stone might be one that exhibits trichroism, you must not stop after seeing a second color, but continue through all five directions until you have, or have not, detected the third. This can be especially important in gem identification since far fewer stones are trichroic and, therefore, the test would give positive ID on the spot.

While the dichroscope is an easy instrument to master, we recommend having someone who is already familiar with it assist you the first time. This will help insure that you are holding it properly and have the proper lighting. It shouldn't take more than 15 minutes to get the hang of it.

WHAT THE DICHROSCOPE WILL SHOW

Once you feel comfortable handling the dichroscope, you are ready to start viewing stones. If only one color is observed with the dichroscope, it usually indicates that you have a "non-dichroic" material (non = no; di = two; chroic = color). You can see from the following list that there are only a few gemstones in this category. If you see two colors, you have a "dichroic" (di = two; chroic = color) material; if you pick up a third color, a "trichroic" (tri = three; chroic = color) material.

In the following pages we have provided lists showing, both by color and by gemstone family, the colors you should see when looking at the popular gemstones with the dichroscope. Such tables are also provided in standard gemology textbooks (see "Tables on Pleochroism").

Once you note the colors you see with the dichroscope, check the chart to see which stone(s) would show those colors. If there is only one, you can now make a positive identification. If there is more than one, you may need to use the Chelsea filter and/or loupe.

REMEMBER: The dichroscope can separate stones that look like one another in color—ruby from glass, sapphire from spinel, and so on—but cannot separate *natural* from *synthetic*. Additional tests are required for that.

LEARN TO USE THE THREE POCKET INSTRUMENTS TOGETHER

Sometimes a gemstone that should show dichroism doesn't. Two stones that demonstrate how checking for dichroism alone may be inconclusive for gem ID are peridot and green zircon. These exceptions offer excellent examples of how useful the loupe, Chelsea filter, and dichroscope can be in assuring accurate gem ID *when used together*.

Peridot and green zircon can resemble each other. There is also green glass that can look like both of them. The dichroic colors of green zircon will differentiate it from peridot and glass (and vice versa) when you can detect them, but sometimes they are too weak to detect. And sometimes green zircon just doesn't exhibit dichroism.

Here's where using another one of our three pocket instruments can be useful.

If you examine a green zircon with a Chelsea filter you will see a reddish coloration, which you will not see with peridot (peridot remains green when viewed with the filter). However, it could still be green glass.

Now your loupe will come to the rescue. First, the loupe may reveal "doubling." This is an optical effect that makes you think you are "seeing double." To observe doubling, look through the stone (check from several different directions). If the edges of the back facets appear double, as if you have double vision, you are seeing "doubling" (sometimes the facet edge, instead of looking like a single line, will resemble a narrow set of railroad tracks).

Zircon will exhibit doubling (peridot will also show doubling of the back facets, but we eliminated it with the Chelsea filter—since it showed reddish, it can't be peridot. Peridot would have remained green). Glass is still a possibility. However, glass will not show any doubling. Zircon does. So, by checking with the loupe to see if we can observe doubling, we can determine the identity of the stone. If we see doubling, we now know we have zircon; if we see no doubling, we have glass.

If you are not sure whether or not you see doubling, the loupe will still aid you. It will tell you from the presence and type of inclusions whether it is glass or zircon. Now we will know for sure that we have zircon.

Next let's take a look at peridot. If you are able to detect trichroic colors in peridot, you will have no question as to its identity. But, like green zircon, sometimes it fails to show trichroism. The loupe, however, would immediately reveal a very strong doubling (double image of the back facet edges), an immediate giveaway for peridot. If, however, you had any question that it might be green zircon (which, as we've just discussed, may also show doubling, although it would not be nearly as strong), the Chelsea filter would give you the immediate answer because it would show green for peridot and reddish for zircon.

Practice using these three pocket instruments together. Within a surprisingly short period of time, you'll become much more confident, and begin to enjoy the rewards of accurate gem ID.

COLORS EXHIBITED BY POPULAR DICHROIC AND TRICHROIC GEMS—BY GEM COLOR

	2-Dichroic 3-Trichroic	S-Strong D-Distinct W-Weak	

Note: Light-colored stones exhibit weak dichroism—hard to detect

Gemstone	Dichroic or Trichroic	Intensity of Color	Colors Seen
PURPLE OR VIOLET GEMS			
CHRYSOBERYL			
Alexandrite	3	S in deep colors	In natural light: emerald-green/ yellowish/reddish In artificial light: emerald-green/ reddish-yellow/red
Synthetic Alexandrite (corundum-type)	2	S in deep colors	In natural light: brownish-green/ mauve In artificial light: brownish-yellow/ mauve
CORUNDUM			
Violet Sapphire	2	S	yellowish-red/violet; or pale gray/green
QUARTZ			
Amethyst	2	D to W	purple/reddish-purple; or purple/blue
SPODUMENE			
Kunzite (lavender)	3	S	colorless/pink/violet
TOURMALINE			
Purple/Violet	2	S	purple/light purple
BLUE GEMS			
BENITOITE	2	S	colorless/indigo-blue (or greenish-blue)
BERYL			
Aquamarine	2	S to W	Blue variety: blue/colorless Blue-green variety: pale blue-green/pale yellow-green to colorless
CORUNDUM			
Blue Sapphire	2	S	greenish-blue/deep blue
IOLITE (Dichroite)	3	S	pale blue/pale straw-yellow/dark violet-blue

TOPAZ			
Blue	3	S to D	colorless/pale blue/pale pink (Note: pink usually is imperceptible.)
TOURMALINE			
Indicolite (blue)	2	S	light blue/dark blue
Blue-Green	2	S	light blue-green/dark blue-green
ZIRCON			
blue	2	D	colorless/blue
ZOISITE (Tanzanite)	3	S	blue/purple/green [Note: Sometimes only two colors will be visible—purple and green.]

GREEN GEMS

ANDALUSITE (green)	3	S	brownish-green/olive-green/ flesh-red
BERYL Emerald	2	S to W	yellowish-green/bluish-green
CHRYSOBERYL Alexandrite	3	S in deep colors	In natural light: emerald-green/ yellowish/ reddish In artificial light: emerald-green/ reddish-yellow/ red
Synthetic Alexandrite (Corundum-type)	2	S in deep colors	In natural light: brownish-green/ mauve In artificial light: brownish-yellow/ mauve
CORUNDUM Green Sapphire	2	S	yellowish-green/green
PERIDOT	3	D to W	yellow-green/ green/ yellowish [Note: It often is difficult to detect two colors; the third usually is imperceptible.]
SPODUMENE Hiddenite (green)	3	S	bluish-green/ grass-green/ yellowish-green or colorless
TOURMALINE Green	2	S	pale green/ strong green; or brownish-green/ dark green [Note: If you see *red*, through Chelsea filter, it's Chrome Tourmaline.]
Zircon	2	W	brownish-green/green (or colorless)

YELLOW GEMS

BERYL Heliodor (yellow)	2	S to W	pale yellow-green/ pale bluish-green
CHRYSOBERYL Yellow	3	S in deep colors	colorless/ pale yellow/ lemon-yellow

CORUNDUM Yellow sapphire	2	D to W	very weak yellowish tints
QUARTZ Citrine	2	D to W	yellow/paler yellow (or colorless)
SPODUMENE Yellow	3	S	yellow/pale yellow/deep yellow
TOPAZ Yellow	3	S to D	honey-yellow/straw-yellow/ pinkish-yellow [Note: In topaz, a third color seldom is seen.]
TOURMALINE Yellow	2	D	light yellow/dark yellow
ZIRCON Yellow	2	W	brownish-yellow/yellow

BROWN OR ORANGE GEMS

CORUNDUM Sapphire	2	S	yellowish-brown to orange/ colorless
QUARTZ Smoky	2	D to W	brownish/reddish-brown [clear differentiation]
TOPAZ Brown/Orange	3	D	colorless/yellow-brown/brown
TOURMALINE Brown/Orange	2	S	yellow-brown/deep brown; or brownish-green/ dark green
ZIRCON Brown	2	W	yellow-brown/reddish brown

RED/PINK GEMS

BERYL Morganite	2	S to W	pale rose/bluish rose
CHRYSOBERYL Alexandrite	3	S in deep colors	In natural light: emerald-green/yellowish/ reddish In artificial light: emerald-green/ reddish-yellow/ red
Synthetic Alexandrite (Corundum-type)	2	S in deep colors	In natural light: brownish-green/ mauve In artificial light: brownish-yellow/mauve
CORUNDUM			
Ruby	2	S	orangish-red/purple-red
Pink Sapphire	2	S to W	Two slightly different shades of pink; often difficult, if not impossible, to detect in pale stones.
QUARTZ Rose	2	D to W	pink/pale pink [clear differentiation]
TOPAZ Pink	3	S to D	colorless/very pale pink/pink
TOURMALINE Rubellite (Red)	2	S	pink/dark red (or magenta)
Zircon Red	2	W	clove-brown/reddish-brown

Gems That Show No Dichroism

Garnet
Spinel
Colored Diamond
Colored Diamond Simulants
Glass
Plastic

[*Note: If dichroism* **is** *observed, it cannot be any of the above.*]

Popular Gems' Usual Dichroic or Trichroic Colors By Gem Family

2-Dichroic
3-Trichroic

S-Strong
D-Distinct
W-Weak

Note: Light-colored stones exhibit weak dichroism—hard to detect

Gemstone	Dichroic or Trichroic	Intensity of Color	Colors Seen
ANDALUSITE (green)	3	S	brownish-green/olive-green/ flesh-red
BENITOITE	2	S	colorless/indigo-blue (or greenish-blue)
BERYL			
Emerald	2	S to W	yellowish-green/bluish-green
Aquamarine	2	S to W	Blue variety; blue/colorless Blue-green variety; pale blue-green/pale yellow-green (or colorless)
Morganite (pink)	2	S to W	pale rose/bluish-rose
Heliodor (yellow)	2	S to W	pale yellow-green/pale bluish-green
CHRYSOBERYL			
Yellow	3	S in deep colors	colorless/pale yellow/lemon-yellow

Alexandrite	3	S in deep colors	In natural light: emerald-green/ yellowish/reddish In artificial light: emerald-green/ reddish-yellow/red
Synthetic Alexandrite (Corundum-type)	2	S in deep colors	In natural light: brownish-green/ mauve In artificial light: brownish-yellow/mauve
CORUNDUM			
Ruby	2	S	orangish-red/purple-red
Blue Sapphire	2	S	greenish-blue/deep-blue
Green Sapphire	2	S	yellowish-green/green
Orange/Brown Sapphire	2	S	yellowish-brown to orange/colorless
Pink Sapphire	2	S	two slightly different shades of pink; often difficult, if not impossible, to detect in pale stones
Violet Sapphire	2	S	yellowish-red/violet; or pale gray/green
Yellow Sapphire	2	D to W	very weak yellowish tints
IOLITE (Dichroite)	3	S	pale blue/pale straw-yellow/dark violet-blue
PERIDOT	3	D to W	yellow-green/green/yellowish [Note: it often is difficult to detect two colors; the third usually is imperceptible.]
QUARTZ			
Amethyst	2	D to W	purple/reddish-purple; or purple/blue
Citrine	2	D to W	yellow/paler yellow (or colorless)
Rose	2	D to W	pink/pale pink [clear differentiation]
Smoky	2	D to W	brownish/reddish-brown [clear differentiation]
SPODUMENE			
Kunzite (lavender)	3	S	colorless/pink/violet
Hiddenite (green)	3	S	bluish-green/grass-green/ yellowish-green (or colorless)
Yellow	3	S	yellow/pale yellow/deep yellow
TOPAZ			
Blue	3	S to D	colorless/pale blue/pale pink [Note: pink usually is imperceptible]
Brown/Orange	3	D	colorless/yellow-brown/brown
Pink	3	S to D	colorless/very pale pink/pink

Yellow	3	S to D	honey-yellow/straw-yellow/ pinkish-yellow [Note: in topaz, a third color seldom is seen.]
TOURMALINE			
Blue-Green	2	S	light blue-green/dark blue-green
Brown/Orange	2	S	yellow-brown/deep brown (or brown-black or greenish-brown)
Green	2	S	pale green/strong green; or brownish-green/dark green [Note: If *red* through chelsea filter, it's Chrome Tourmaine.]
Indicolite (blue)	2	S	light blue/dark blue
Purple/Violet	2	S	purple/light purple
Rubellite (red)	2	S	pink/dark red (or magenta)
ZIRCON			
Blue	2	D	colorless/blue
Brown	2	W	yellow-brown/reddish-brown
Green	2	W	brownish-green/green (or colorless)
Red	2	W	clove-brown/reddish-brown
Yellow	2	W	brownish-yellow/;yellow
ZOISITE (Tanzanite)	3	S	blue/purple/green [Note: Sometimes only two colors will be visible—purple and green.]

NOTES

7 / The ultraviolet lamp

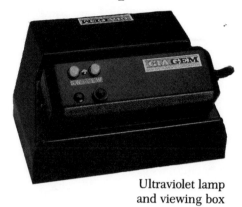

Ultraviolet lamp
and viewing box

WHAT IS AN ULTRAVIOLET LAMP?

An ultraviolet lamp is a small lamp, very simple to use. It can be an invaluable aid in gem identification, and also for detecting some types of treatment.

The ultraviolet lamp, also called a UV lamp, produces a special type of light (actually radiation) called *ultraviolet*. These lamps are used to reveal the presence or absence of *fluorescence* in gems. Fluorescence refers to the stone's ability to exhibit color when viewed under ultraviolet radiation—color that is not visible in ordinary light. Some fluorescent gems continue to glow even *after* the UV light is turned off. These gems are exhibiting a property called *phosphorescence*.

The ultraviolet lamp serves many purposes for the gem identifier. By viewing gems with an ultraviolet lamp in a blackened environment, we are able to see different reactions depending on the gem and, in some cases, determine whether or not it's been treated. Long-wave ultraviolet light has proven especially useful for testing emeralds and indicating whether or not they've been oiled. It is also very useful for separating synthetic white spinel from diamond, and in helping to distinguish between natural blue sapphire, heated blue sapphire, and the older Verneuil synthetic blue sapphire. Testing for fluorescence in diamonds is also critical when color grading them, as we discuss later, to insure proper grading.

There are several types of ultraviolet lamp, but for gemological purposes you must have a lamp that independently produces both *long-wave* and *short-wave* ultraviolet radiation. Several manufacturers produce ultraviolet lamps. We recommend hand-held models such as #UVGL-25 by Ultra-Violet Products, Inc., GIA Gem Instruments' long-wave/short-wave ultra-violet lamp, Spectroline's #ENF240, or Raytech's #LC-6. These models also provide separate control buttons so you can use short-wave when needed or, simply by pushing another button, long-wave (but never both wavelengths simultaneously). Some lamps provide only short-wave; others only long-wave. Be sure the model you select provides both (see Chapter 2).

In addition to the lamp, we recommend a "black box"—a viewing box or cabinet specially designed for hand-held lamps. This will allow you to view the stone or jewelry in a darkened environment, which helps eliminate normal light and enables you to observe the presence of fluorescence and, possibly, phosphorescence more easily. You can easily make a basic black box by painting a cardboard box with flat black paint and cutting out a small viewing window at the top and an opening to accommodate the lamp. Some equipment supply houses and ultraviolet light manufacturers sell viewing cabinets. If you wish to purchase one, we recommend those with protective eyepieces. They range in price from about $100 to $150.

UNDERSTANDING ULTRAVIOLET LIGHT AND FLUORESCENCE

Ultraviolet light and fluorescence are not really difficult to understand. In fact, fluorescence is one of nature's most interesting mysteries to observe. You simply need to know that there is *visible* light and *invisible* light all around us. Light travels in waves, and the length of those waves determines whether they are visible or invisible, and what color we actually see. Some light waves are too short to be visible to humans; some are too long to be visible. The colors we see, such as red, blue, or green, have wavelengths that occur in a range visible to the human eye. Ultraviolet has wavelengths that go beyond what we are able to see, and so they are invisible to us.

The ultraviolet lamp emits ultraviolet light rays. These rays are too short to be visible to the human eye. However, when they strike certain gems, properties within those gems *change the length of the invisible wavelengths into longer wavelengths so that they become visible.* When this happens, colors appear that were not visible before viewing with the ultraviolet lamp. When a gem material produces colors when viewed with the ultraviolet lamp, colors not seen without it, we say it *fluoresces* or it has *fluorescence.* The ultraviolet lamp enables us to know whether or not a stone fluoresces and, if so, the color of the fluorescence.

Some stones also *phosphoresce.* This means that they will continue to glow for a period of time after turning *off* the lamp. The phosphorescence (the continued glow) may be weak or strong. It may last only a split second or it may last for several hours.

FLUORESCENCE AND GEM IDENTIFICATION

The ultraviolet lamp enables us to observe fluorescence. Under its ultraviolet rays, fluorescent substances glow with color that can't be seen in normal light. Even stones that appear drab brown, black, or gray in normal light may exhibit a brilliantly glowing blue, red, or green under ultraviolet light—where invisible ultraviolet rays have been converted to visible wavelengths. If your local museum has a fluorescent gem or mineral display, make a trip to see it. It can be quite a treat!

The precise color seen under ultraviolet light will be determined by the properties of the substance being viewed. Certain stones will glow one color, while others will glow a different color; some fluoresce under long-wave, others under short-wave, and some under both long- and short-wave.

The information provided by the ultraviolet lamp can be an important clue in gem identification. It will immediately show you whether or not the stone fluoresces or phosphoresces and, if so, whether the reaction is produced under long-wave, short-wave, or both (this is why you must have an ultraviolet lamp that produces both long- and short-wave light). While it is seldom a conclusive test, it can be a fast and easy way to confirm your diagnosis when used in conjunction with other tests.

HOW TO USE THE ULTRAVIOLET LAMP

Before beginning our discussion, we want to stress that SHORT-WAVE ULTRAVIOLET CAN BE DANGEROUS IF USED CARE-LESSLY.

Caution must be exercised when using short-wave ultraviolet.

- *Never look into any ultraviolet light.* Keep it turned *away from your eyes* at all times. Short-wave ultraviolet light can cause serious eye injury. You may wish to use a pair of special goggles that can be obtained from equipment suppliers listed in the Appendix, or wear eyeglasses with glass lenses (short-wave radiation will not go through glass).
- *Avoid continuous exposure to skin.* Don't expose your skin to its rays for longer than necessary. Short-wave rays can cause serious skin burns after only minutes of exposure.
- *Do not turn on the lamp until everything is in proper position.* This will help avoid unnecessary exposure.

1. *Clean both the stone being examined and the mounting in which it may be set.* Substances such as skin oils, lint, or dirt under a prong may fluoresce and distort your conclusions.

2. *Put the stone or piece of jewelry being examined in a nonreflective darkened environment.* It's important to examine the piece in as dark an environment as possible. Use a special viewing cabinet designed for ultraviolet examination, or black box such as we've described earlier in the chapter. Place what you are examining on a flat black background (a piece of black construction paper will do in a pinch). If you don't have a proper viewing box, go into a room without windows (such as a closet) and view the piece in the dark. Just remember to keep the lamp turned away from your eyes.

3. *Hold the lamp directly over the item being examined, WITHOUT TURNING IT ON.* Direct the light down onto the item, *holding the lamp as close to it as possible.*

4. *NOW turn the lamp on.* First depress the long-wave button. Press only one button at a time.

View the stone under long-wave. Note whether or not the stone fluoresces and, if so, what color, and the intensity. If it doesn't fluoresce, note that it is inert (which means it shows no change).

View the stone under short-wave. Repeat the step above, depressing the short-wave button. Again, note whether or not there is any fluorescence, and, if so, its color and intensity.

5. *View the stone from several different directions.* Remember to keep the stone as close as possible to the lamp. Be sure not to mistake the purplish glow from the lamp itself (being reflected from the stone's facets) for weak fluorescence. The stone must glow from within.

6. *Turn off the lamp.* Note whether or not the stone continues to glow. If it does, it's exhibiting phosphorescence. Note the color and duration.

7. *Remove the item from the viewing area.*

Remember: *While using the ultraviolet lamp, always keep it turned away from your eyes and never look into it.*

What the Ultraviolet Lamp Will Show

As we've already mentioned, the ultraviolet lamp will reveal the presence of fluorescence in gems and thus aid in gem ID. Below we have provided charts that show the colors gemstones may exhibit under long- and short-wave UV-light, and how ultraviolet examination can help separate look-alikes. There is also a list of phosphorescent gemstones. However, note that not all stones fluoresce. Furthermore, it is important to be aware that in some gem families, stones that are found in certain places may fluoresce while stones from other places will not. Also, if there are traces of iron in a gemstone (such as we find in rubies from Thailand), fluorescence may be very weak or not exhibited at all.

Before you begin to use the charts, however, we'd like to make a few general comments.

Testing Emeralds. Long-wave ultraviolet examination has proven especially useful in testing emeralds. Natural emeralds, whether Colombian, Zambian, Pakistani, Brazilian, or Afghan, very seldom fluoresce under long-wave light (in other words, they seldom show any color change). However, synthetic emeralds often do. Those produced by hydrothermal and flux-melt techniques fluoresce very strongly—they turn intense red under long-wave UV light. Also, the new Linde-type synthetic emerald being produced by Regency fluoresces a very strong red. The Chatham and Gilson synthetics also fluoresce strongly (although some of the older Gilson synthetics did not)—the Chatham turns an intense red, and the Gilson turns orange-red or olive-brown.

Ultraviolet examination of emeralds is also important for another reason. Many natural emeralds are soaked in oil. While oiling may improve the color and overall appearance of the stone, and even strengthen it in some respects, the procedure actually conceals cracks that would otherwise be visible. In emeralds that have been oiled, ultraviolet examination will reveal what the oiling process has concealed.

When examined under the ultraviolet lamp, the *oil* that has been used usually *fluoresces*, thereby revealing the presence of the cracks. Here, since the ultraviolet lamp enables you to see them, it can assist you in determining whether or not the cracks present make the stone unusually vulnerable to breakage—by revealing whether or not there are too many; whether or not any are abnormally large; whether or not they penetrate the stone too deeply; and whether or not they are positioned in a part of the stone, which might be more susceptible to an accidental blow that might result in a break (such as a corner or under the table facet).

Testing Blue Sapphire. The ultraviolet lamp also has an important use today in distinguishing the older Verneuil-type synthetic blue sapphire from natural blue sapphire, and some natural-color blue sapphire from sapphire that has been heated to enhance its color.

The Verneuil-type synthetic blue sapphire appears frequently in old jewelry made after 1910. Such sapphires used to be easy to spot because they always contained certain telltale signs, concentric curved lines called curved striae. Today this is no longer the case. These telltale signs *can be removed by treatment*, and one might mistake the synthetic for natural. When viewed under short-wave ultraviolet light, however, the synthetic will show a blue-white fluorescence. Natural blue sapphire will not.

The ultraviolet lamp is also useful to help spot some sapphires that have been heated to improve their color. Not only will Verneuil-type synthetic sapphires show a blue-white fluorescence, but so will some heated blue sapphires. If you see blue-white fluorescence, you should be immediately suspicious. You either have a Verneuil-type synthetic that has had the curved striae removed, or you have a genuine sapphire, but one that has been heated to enhance color. In this case, the synthetic can easily be distinguished from the heated genuine by the presence of disc-like inclusions, which occur only in natural sapphire.

A Few Additional Comments

Separating synthetic white spinel from diamond. Another important use of the ultraviolet lamp is to separate synthetic white spinel from diamond. Spinel is often seen in older jewelry in place of diamonds. Even today, small melee-size (usually under $15/100$ths carat) stones used in jewelry sometimes turn out to be synthetic white spinel rather than diamond. The ultraviolet light, however, can help you spot these imposters. When viewed under short-wave ultraviolet light, synthetic white spinels will exhibit a strong milky white fluorescence, whereas *genuine diamonds never fluoresce white.*

Diamonds should always be examined for fluorescence prior to color grading to insure accuracy. Testing for fluorescence not only helps separate diamond from its imposters, but it is very important in the color grading of diamonds. Some diamonds fluoresce and others do not. Of those we have personally examined, about 50 percent have shown fluorescence. Usually, if a diamond fluoresces, it will show blue, yellow, or chartreuse (a pale yellowish-green color).

If a diamond fluoresces, one can make a mistake when color grading the stone if a fluorescent light is being used. And fluorescent light is everywhere today—in most offices, many jewelry stores, even the sun. A fluorescent light source emits ultraviolet rays just as the ultraviolet lamp does, but to a less intense degree. Therefore, if you are using a fluorescent light to color grade a diamond that fluoresces blue, the stone will exhibit some degree of blue. The presence of this blue can cause the diamond to appear whiter than it actually is (when seen under normal light). If the diamond has not been checked for fluorescence, this can result in the stone being given a better color grade than it deserves.

In the same way, if a diamond fluoresces yellow, the stone will exhibit more yellow in the body color when viewed in fluorescent lighting, and appear to be less white than its true body color, causing you to give it a lower color grade than it deserves. We might mention here that, in our opinion, diamonds that fluoresce blue, while having no greater value than those that do not, offer a little extra to the purchaser. Whatever the actual body color of the stone, when worn outside in daylight where it will be exposed to the ultraviolet rays of the sun, or indoors where there is fluorescent light, the color may appear better than it actually is. Grandmother's "blue-white" diamond was probably a stone that exhibited a blue fluorescence!

Detecting Polymer-impregnated Jade. Much jade today is bleached and then coated or filled with some type of polymer such as wax or opticon. When exposed to long-wave ultraviolet radiation, the presence of a bluish-white to yellowish-green fluorescence indicates that it *has* been treated in this way.

Other Uses for the Ultraviolet Lamp

The ultraviolet lamp is also helpful in distinguishing the following stones from one another: pink topaz, pink sapphire, and pink tourmaline; lapis and dyed jasper ("Swiss lapis"); reddish-brown amber and plastic look-alikes; blue zircon and aquamarine; natural black pearls and dyed black pearls; and natural black opal from sugar-treated black opal.

And, finally, fluorescence—or its absence—is important to note when doing appraisals. When appraising jewelry, particularly jewelry set with diamonds, indicating whether any of the diamonds fluoresce, where they are located in the piece, and what color they show, can be of particular value in cases involving stolen property or in instances where there is any question of stone switching.

Examination of stones or jewelry by ultraviolet lamp may be one of the quickest and simplest tests available today.

Even when inconclusive alone, in combination with other instruments such as the loupe, dichroscope, or Chelsea filter, this test may be all you need for a positive ID. Properly used, the ultraviolet lamp can be a real friend to the gem enthusiast.

Fluorescent Gemstone Chart

Gemstone	Short-Wave	Long-Wave
Alexandrite**	red	red
Alexandrite-type synthetic corundum (sapphire)	red; orange (usually)	reddish
Amber	white, yellow, orange	same as short-wave
Amethyst, natural	usually inert; deep blue	same as short-wave
Amethyst, synthetic	inert	inert
Aquamarine	inert	inert
Benitoite**	strong blue	inert
Cubic Zirconia (colorless)	strong orange or yellow (new material may be inert)	same as short-wave but weaker
Chrysoberyl		
Chartreuse tint	yellow-green	inert
Alexandrite**	red	red
Yellow, dull green and brown varieties	inert	inert
Diamond	weak colors; usually inert	weak to strong blue, orange, chartreuse, yellow or inert

(Diamonds can fluoresce all colors except violet. General fluorescence is weak to strong blue; yellow also is fairly common.)

Gemstone	Short-Wave	Long-Wave
GGG diamond simulant (colorless)	moderate to strong, orange, chartreuse, or inert	same as short-wave but weaker
Emerald		
Natural	usually inert or reddish	same as short-wave
Synthetic	usually weak red	usually strong red
Gilson-type synthetic	weak red or inert	strong red or inert
Jade		
Natural lavender	weak brownish-red	same as short-wave
Dyed lavender	weak brownish-orange to brownish-red	strong to very strong orange
Kunzite**	weak orange-pink	strong orange-pink
Moonstone**	strong to weak reddish	greenish to yellow
Opal**	white, green, yellow	blue, white

(Opal often exhibits phosphorescence also)

Gemstone	Short-Wave	Long-Wave
Pearl		
Cultured white**	weak whitish	strong bluish-white (Some old cultured may show "tannish" as in the natural pearls)
Natural white	usually inert	strong to weak white or tan
Natural black	inert	red or brownish
Cultured, dyed black	inert	inert to greenish
Cultured, natural black	inert to weak white	inert
Peridot	inert	sometimes reddish
Ruby		
Natural	strong red	very strong red

(some dark stones, such as some Thai rubies, may be weak to inert)

Gemstone	Short-Wave	Long-Wave
Synthetic	strong red	stronger red than short-wave

Synthetic Ramora	chalky yellow or weak bluish "bloom"	
Sapphire		
Natural blue	usually inert	inert
Ceylon-blue** (the light blue variety seen in older jewelry)	weak orange or reddish	usually moderate to strong red to yellow-orange
Ceylon-yellow**	orange-yellow	strong orange
Blue, heat-treated	milky bluish-white	inert
Blue, synthetic	usually deep green	usually inert
Orange, synthetic	red	red
Pink, natural	strong red	strong red
Spinel		
Natural red	moderate to strong red	strong red
Natural mauve	yellow	yellow-green
Synthetic white**	strong white	inert
Tourmaline		
Deep red	medium bluish/lavender	inert
Yellow (Tanzanian)**	pale yellow	orange
YAG (diamond simulant)	weak red to inert	inert
Zircon		
Colorless	yellow to orange or inert	weak to strong yellow, mustard yellow or inert
Blue	yellow to orange or inert	weak to strong yellow, mustard yellow or inert

**Gemstone always fluoresces

Use of Ultraviolet Examination for Separating "Look-Alikes"

Gemstone	Long-wave	Short-wave	Comments
Diamond vs. Cubic Zirconia	orange weaker orange	*weaker orange* orange	Some diamonds show orange fluorescence under long-wave light and a *weaker* orange under short-wave. Cubic zirconia (CZ) OFTEN shows orange fluorescence, but IN REVERSE ORDER. This reversal is a sure test for diamond versus CZ.
Natural Ruby vs.	red	red	Thai stones are inert to weak red.
Synthetic Ruby vs.	very strong red	very strong red	Much stronger than natural. Kashan weaker than Verneuil type synthetic, but stronger than natural.
Red Spinel vs.	weaker red than ruby	weaker red than ruby	NO DICHROISM
Red Garnets vs.	inert	inert	NO DICHROISM
Red Glass	usually inert	usually inert	NO DICHROISM

Natural Blue Sapphire vs.	inert to moderate red	inert to mod. red; some show whitish to light green glow.	Inclusions will identify.
Syn. Blue Sapphire vs.	usually inert	pale bluish-white to yellowish-green	Heated natural blue sapphires may also fluoresce pale bluish-white. Types of inclusions will distinguish.
Syn. Blue Spinel vs.	usually inert	occasionally bluish-white	NO DICHROISM. Strong red with Chelsea filter (not seen in sapphire).
Benitoite	inert	*strong* blue	DICHROISM—blue and colorless
Natural Emerald vs.	inert/weak red	inert	May show yellow-green fluorescence in cracks/inclusions *from the oil* used in the oiling process.
Syn. Chatham vs.	red	red	Inclusions differ from natural.
Syn. Gilson vs.	inert, orange-red or olive-brown	inert or weak orange	Inclusions similar to Chatham but cleaner.
Syn. Linde (Regency)	very strong red	weaker red	Inclusions differ from natural/other syn.
Black Opal vs.	bluish-white	bluish-white	
Sugar-treated "Black Opal"	usually inert	usually inert	Examination with loupe will reveal fine pinpoints on polished surfaces.
Nat. Black Pearl vs.	light red or brownish	inert	Velvety appearance under long-wave
Dyed Black Pearl vs.	inert	inert	
Dyed Black Cultured	inert or greenish	inert	
Pink Sapphire vs.	Strong orange-red	weak orange-red	
Pink Topaz vs.	light orange-red or whitish-green	same as long-wave	
Pink Tourmaline	inert	inert	
Blue Zircon vs.	mustard-yellow or inert	inert or weaker mustard-yellow	Dichroism in both is the same. However, zircon shows strong *doubling* of black facets.
Aquamarine	inert	inert	
Citrine Quartz vs.	inert	inert	
Yellow Topaz vs.	weak orangy-yellow to orange	inert	

NOTES

8 / The refractometer

WHAT IS A REFRACTOMETER?

The refractometer is considered by some to be the most important of all gem-testing instruments. It is a fairly small, portable instrument, almost rectangular in shape, approximately 6 inches long by 3 inches high by 1 1/2 inches wide. It measures the angle at which light rays bend (refract) as they travel through a substance, and provides a numerical reading from a scale you see when you look through the eyepiece. The cost of a good refractometer runs from $385 to $895 (see Chapter 2).

When we discussed the dichroscope (Chapter 6) you learned that as light rays strike a transparent stone, the speed at which they travel is altered, causing the rays to bend (refract) as they travel through it. In some stones the ray travels through as a single ray (single refracting substance); in others the light ray splits into two rays (double refracting). Whether or not a stone is single or double refracting depends on its particular physical characteristics. As you will remember, certain gems show single refraction (such as diamond, spinel, garnet) and others exhibit double refraction (such as emerald, zircon, sapphire).

The refractometer also can be used to determine whether or not a stone is single or double refracting (you will get only one reading on its scale if it is single refracting, and two readings if it is double refracting). But the refractometer does much more. It is of particular importance because it is one of the few instruments that can give you information for *opaque* stones (stones you cannot see through, such as lapis) as well as transparent or translucent stones.

The primary use of the refractometer is to measure the angle at which light travelling through the stone is bent or refracted. This measurement is called the Refractive Index (R.I.). Since the Refractive Index usually differs from gem species to gem species, this provides an invaluable clue for accurate gem ID.

Finally, the refractometer will give you another important piece of information. For stones that are doubly refracting, simply by computing the difference between the two R.I. readings you obtain from the refractometer, you will be able to compute the strength of the stone's double refraction. This is called birefringence. Birefringence also differs from gem to gem, and so it, too, offers an important gem identification aid.

Many types of refractometers are used for numerous industrial purposes. Some are very sophisticated and expensive, but for gem identification adequate refractometers are available for under $400 (see chapter 2). The GIA Duplex II is popular, and the new RosGem is getting outstanding reviews. The Jemeter, by Sarasota Instruments, is also getting good reviews for use with gemstones that have very high Refractive Index readings. Rayner, Topcan, and Eickhorst also make fine refractometers.

Use a utility lamp such as that pictured here with the *Duplex II* refractometer, or a light such as the GIA *Fiberlight*

The GIA Duplex II refractometer with utility lamp

As with most of the gem-identification instruments you are learning to use, the refractometer is both fast and easy to handle. Once you understand how to use it, the refractometer *alone* can often supply enough information for positive identification of many stones.

HOW TO USE THE REFRACTOMETER

Before you begin, the first step is to have a proper light source. You will need both a white light source (such as a halogen lamp) and a monochromatic yellow light source that filters out all colors of the spectrum except yellow (see Chapter 3). If you don't already have one, you may find it useful to invest in a utility lamp such as the one made by GIA that furnishes both white and monochromatic yellow light, depending upon which you need.

Now we are ready to begin. As we mentioned earlier, the information obtained with the refractometer results from its ability to measure the degree of bending or refraction that takes place when a light ray strikes a stone. When the stone is properly examined with the refractometer, you can observe a "shadow edge" or green line (depending on the type of light used with the refractometer) imposed on a scale that you see through the eye piece. But the key to seeing this line and obtaining the correct reading (its Refractive Index reading, R.I.) is proper use of the instrument.

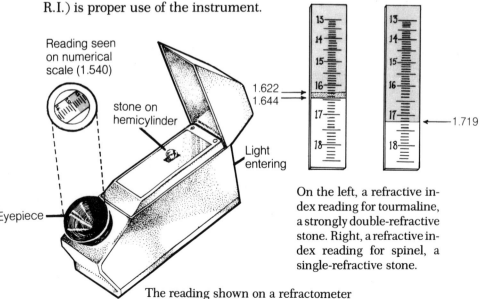

Reading seen on numerical scale (1.540)

stone on hemicylinder

1.622
1.644

Light entering

Eyepiece

1.719

On the left, a refractive index reading for tourmaline, a strongly double-refractive stone. Right, a refractive index reading for spinel, a single-refractive stone.

The reading shown on a refractometer

The refractometer has a scale that shows the R.I. of a stone. The scale can show R.I.s as low as 1.35 or as high as 1.80. The R.I. of most gems falls well within this range, so the reading provided by the refractometer will tell you what most gems are.

An important advantage of the refractometer for gem identification is that it can provide an R.I. reading on any stone that has a good polish. It makes no difference whether the stone has a flat or curved surface, or whether it's transparent, translucent, or opaque. Therefore, it can even be used for stones such as jade, opal, and lapis. The only requirement is that the stone have a good polish. The better the stone's polish, the clearer the reading you will get with the refractometer. However, if the stone has a poor polish, as you may find when examining softer stones such as malachite or rhodochrosite, it may be very difficult—if not impossible—to get the R.I. reading.

The major weakness of most refractometers is that they *cannot give readings for stones that have an R.I. higher than 1.80.* The instrument simply doesn't have the capability to provide such high readings. This means they are ineffective for stones such as diamond, diamond look-alikes such as zircon, and certain varieties of garnet, to name a few. The Jemeter, however, does not have this problem and has an advantage over traditional refractometers because it is effective for stones with R.I.s higher than 1.80.

For purposes of convenience, we will be using a GIA Duplex II refractometer. If you have a different type, there may be minor differences, but the basic procedures still apply.

The technique you will use with the refractometer differs slightly depending on the stone's surface and degree of polish. We will first describe the technique for examining stones with flat surfaces and a good polish (stones such as faceted sapphires or rubies).

Familiarize yourself with the refractometer. As you look at the instrument, you will notice it has a lift-up cover on top. Lift it and you'll see a flat working surface about 2½ inches long by 1½ inches wide. A small rectangular-shaped piece of glass is set into the center of this working surface. This piece of glass is called the hemicylinder. It's important to exercise care taking the stone on and off the hemicylinder because the glass is soft and can scratch easily if you're careless. If badly scratched, it can prevent your getting a reading on the refractometer.

Next, look at the front of the refractometer and notice the opening.

This is where light enters the instrument. Be sure to position your light *in front of this opening*. Also, be sure your light source provides both white and monochromatic yellow light.

Check the eyepiece. Notice that it has a polarizing filter that rotates. We will explain how this is used later in the chapter.

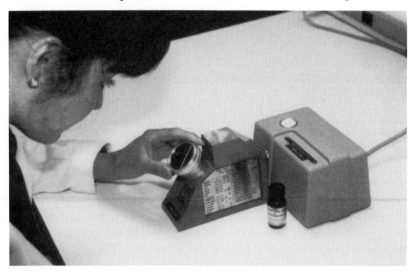

Using the refractometer—Notice the light is positioned in front of the slit at the end of the instrument, and the gemologist is rotating the polaroid filter.

Determining the R.I. of a Stone with a Flat Surface

1. *Carefully place a small drop of refractive index liquid on the hemicylinder.* Included with your refractometer is a small bottle of refractive index liquid supplied by the manufacturer (if not, contact the manufacturer or instrument supplier). Place a small drop of this liquid at the center of the hemicylinder. This liquid eliminates air between the stone and glass so that optical contact is established between the two surfaces. Such contact is necessary to obtain a reading from the instrument. Refractive index liquid refills can be obtained for about $14.50 a bottle from the manufacturer or supplier.

2. *Place the stone on the hemicylinder.* Find the largest facet with the best polish (usually the table facet). Make sure it's clean (rub it on a chamois, soft cloth, or piece of paper to remove dust and dirt). Carefully place the stone on the glass so that this facet is making

contact with the drop of liquid you've just placed there. Some find it easier to place the drop of liquid on the metal surface beside the hemicylinder, dip the facet in the liquid, then gently place or slide it onto the glass. If the stone is set in jewelry, be sure the prongs aren't in the way of the facet making contact with the liquid *and* the glass. The prongs should rest *below* the facet surface to insure optical contact between liquid and stone.

3. *Place a white light in front of the refractometer.* At the front of the refractometer you will see an opening through which light enters the instrument. Place a white light in front of this opening (the utility lamp we recommended earlier works well here).

4. *Look through the eyepiece.* Look into the instrument, keeping your head about 6 inches from the eyepiece. Move your head back and forth slowly until you see a shaded or shadowy area that does *not* move. Notice that at the end of this shaded area is a green line. It may be necessary to move the stone forward or backward gently to see it. (*If you must move the stone, use your fingers. Never use tweezers because they can scratch the hemicylinder glass.*) The shaded area will extend from a low numerical reading at the top of the scale to a higher numerical reading further down. The numerical reading you see at the green line is the approximate refractive index of the stone. Take the reading to the nearest thousandth (0.000) and write it down.

5. *Repeat the procedure using a monochromatic yellow light.* When using monochromatic yellow light, you will not see a *green* line. You get the refractive index from the reading at the *base of the shaded area*. The monochromatic light sharpens the base of the shaded area so it is easier to read. Again, note the R.I. to the nearest thousandth (0.000).

6. *Slowly rotate the polarizing filter.* The refractometer has a polarizing filter that fits over the eyepiece. Slowly turn this filter 180 degrees and note if the shaded edge moves. If not, turn the *stone* 45 degrees and rotate the filter again. Note whether or not the shaded edge moves. Move the stone another 45 degrees, and repeat the process. Continue with two more rotations of the stone (until you have rotated the stone a full 180 degrees), turning the polarizing filter each time.

If the shaded edge does not move, you have a SINGLE REFRACTING stone. Note the R.I. reading on the scale, check the

R.I. Table For Single Refracting Stones at the end of this chapter, and you will probably know the identity of the stone.

One word of caution. If you are looking at a transparent, faceted stone with an R.I. that falls between 1.45 and 1.65 it is probably glass. There are many different types of glass, each with a different R.I., but seldom lower than 1.45 or higher than 1.65. Amber is the only transparent gemstone material that falls within this R.I. range (1.54). Chalcedony also has a R.I. of 1.54, but is translucent or opaque rather than transparent.

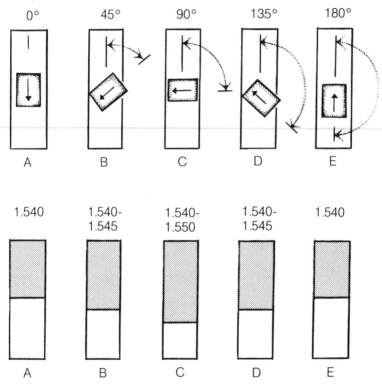

Observing the R.I. as you rotate the stone

If the shadow edge DOES move, you have a DOUBLE REFRACTING stone. Rotate the *filter* 180 degrees and write down the number you see on the scale at the shadow edge. Rotate the *stone* 45 degrees and turn the filter again, noting the number you see on the scale. Keep repeating this process until you have turned the stone

180 degrees (halfway around) in small increments, rotating the filter each time and noting the R.I. readings you see. Now, write down the highest and lowest reading you were able to obtain.

For example, in the first viewing the readings may have been 1.644 and 1.624; in another viewing the readings may have been 1.643 and 1.624. The highest reading of the four would be 1.644; the lowest of the four would be 1.624. Therefore, the R.I.s for the stone would be 1.644 and 1.624. Using the *highest* and *lowest* readings, check the Refractive Index Table in the Appendix for corresponding readings to determine what stone you have—in this case you'll find that the stone is tourmaline.

Caution: If the reading is 1.80, use other tests to verify identity. If you use a standard refractometer to try to identify a stone that has an R.I. of 1.80 or higher, you will not be able to get a reliable reading. As we mentioned earlier, standard refractometers are only useful for stones with R.I.s lower than 1.80 (the Jemeter is an exception and can give reliable readings for stones with much higher R.I.s). If the stone you are examining has an R.I. of 1.80 or more, the shadow edge will go right into the 1.80 portion of the scale, but this is not the stone's R.I. Instead you are actually reading the CONTACT LIQUID. The liquid itself has an R.I. of 1.80. Do not confuse this reading with that of the stone. Since there are few stones with R.I.s over 1.80, other tests can usually determine identity easily and quickly.

Determining Birefringence

Birefringence indicates the strength of a stone's double refraction. The higher the birefringence, the stronger the double refraction. The stronger the double refraction, the easier it will be to see doubling of the back facet edges with the loupe (see Chapter 4).

Once you know you have a double refracting stone and have determined its two R.I.s from the highest and lowest readings, it is very easy to determine the birefringence. Simply subtract the lowest R.I. reading from the highest R.I. reading and you have it. When using the loupe to examine any stone that has a birefringence over 0.020, you will easily see doubling of the back facet edges (as if you're "seeing double"). Checking the stone's birefringence offers a good way to double-check a stone's identity. A Birefringence Table is provided in the Appendix.

Troubleshooting

If you are unable to see a shaded zone on the refractometer and cannot obtain a refractive index reading, it means one of the following:

- a. The stone is not making contact with the drop of liquid.
- b. The facet is badly scratched or inadequately polished.
- c. The facet is not flat.
- d. The facet is not making contact because the prong protrudes beyond the facet's surface.
- e. The stone is tarnished and fails to give a reading. Emeralds that have soaked too long in jewelry cleaner often become tarnished, old amethyst can tarnish, and old glass can tarnish.
- f. The stone being viewed has a very high refractive index—such as diamond, zircon, CZ, YAG, GGG, synthetic rutile, and some garnet varieties—and the refractometer cannot read it. As we mentioned earlier, most refractometers can't provide readings on stones that have an R.I. higher than 1.80.

Determining the R.I. on a Curved Surface: The Distant-Vision or Spot Method

The refractometer works best with stones that have a large, highly polished, flat surface, but it can also be used for very small or badly scratched stones, and stones with curved surfaces (cabochons). Using the refractometer for such stones, however, requires a technique called the *distant-vision* or *spot method.*

1. *Use white light.* Place a strong white light source in front of the refractometer opening. White light is preferred because it has more brilliance that enables you to see more easily what you're looking for.

2. *Place a very small drop of liquid on the glass hemicylinder.* It is very important to use as small a drop of liquid as you can, preferably the size of a pinhead. The smaller the better when using this method. Note, however, that the very small drop of liquid will evaporate after only several minutes. If you are still examining the stone, be sure you still have contact liquid between it and the hemicylinder. If there is no liquid, you will be unable to get a numerical reading.

3. *Place the stone carefully on the liquid.* Most stones that require the spot method are oval or round. If oval, be sure to place it so that the length of the oval runs parallel to the length of the hemicylinder.

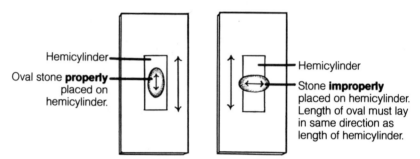

Proper placement of oval cabochon on hemicylinder

With very small stones set in jewelry it may be difficult to make contact with the drop of liquid. Once you do establish contact, it may be necessary to use a piece of Tacky-wax, chewing gum, or other sticky substance to secure it so that the stone can't move and lose contact with the liquid.

4. *Stand up.* While standing, move your head up and down slowly—and to the right and left—until you see an oval or football-shaped image on the refractometer scale. Now move your head up and down slowly until the football image is half light/half dark. Read the *midpoint* between the light and dark areas of the football—where the light portion meets the dark portion. Take the reading on the refractometer scale at that point.

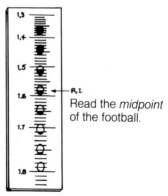

Taking a *spot reading*

The spot method gives only a single reading (even for double refracting stones), but one that is close to the R.I. of the stone. You should practice this several times on different stones (whose identity you already know) to get better experience. Jade can be fun to practice with — jadeite, for example, will probably read 1.65 and nephrite probably 1.62. Just be sure to take the reading at the spot that is half light/half dark, as in the diagram.

Troubleshooting

If you are unable to obtain a refractive index reading using this method, it means one of the following:

a. The stone is not making contact with the drop of liquid. Be sure the liquid has not evaporated.

b. The surface is badly scratched or inadequately polished. Check it with the loupe because sometimes a cabochon surface appears shiny when it really has numerous, tiny scratches that prevent getting an R.I. reading.

c. The stone is tarnished (dulled from exposure to air, body fluids, chemicals) and fails to give a reading. Emeralds left too long in jewelry cleaner often tarnish. Old amethyst and old glass can also tarnish.

d. The stone being viewed has a very high refractive index—such as diamond, zircon, CZ, YAG, GGG, synthetic rutile, and some garnet varieties—so your refractometer cannot read it. As we mentioned earlier, most refractometers can't provide readings on stones that have an R.I. higher than 1.80. Note that with the spot method, you may still see a football-shaped shadow, but you will not observe a light-dark division giving you the necessary midpoint reading.

All you need now is a little practice, a little confidence, and you'll be ready to start using your refractometer on a daily basis.

CARING FOR YOUR REFRACTOMETER

When removing stones or placing them on the hemicylinder glass, exercise care. Remember, the hemicylinder scratches very easily.

If the contact liquid evaporates and hardens into little crystals on the hemicylinder, moisten the crystals by adding another drop of liquid and then wipe the glass gently. Don't try to wipe them off while dry because the crystals are abrasive and will scratch the glass hemicylinder.

If the stone you are examining becomes stuck to the hemicylinder, add another drop of liquid to the area to soften the hardened crystals. Then, gently remove the stone.

To help protect the hemicylinder, cover it with a thin layer of vaseline when you store it for any length of time. This will prevent tarnishing, which can affect the refractometer's reliability. When you wish to use it again, the vaseline can be easily and quickly wiped off with a little nail-polish remover.

Gently clean both the hemicylinder and the stone after using the refractometer, making sure to remove all traces of the liquid.

If the hemicylinder glass becomes too scratched or pitted, replace it or get it repolished ($65.00).

Check the calibration of the refractometer occasionally. To do this, simply take a stone you know, such as amethyst or citrine, and obtain a reading with the refractometer. If it gives you the correct reading, it is accurate. If not, it will need to be recalibrated (follow the manufacturer's instructions).

Always be sure to gently remove any excess liquid from the hemicylinder before putting your refractometer away. If it has a cover, use it.

WHAT THE REFRACTOMETER WILL SHOW

As we've already explained, the refractometer will give you numerical readings of a stone's Refractive Index (R.I.), which is simply a measurement of the extent to which a light ray is bent (refracted) when it strikes its surface. Most gemstones are doubly refracting, and it is easy to obtain the two R.I. readings and then refer to the Refractive Index Table in the Appendix to determine the identity of a stone from those numerical readings. The singly refracting stones are not so numerous, however, and we would like to make some special comments on them.

It's important for you to understand that while a singly refracting stone will show only one reading on the refractometer scale, that reading may not be the same for all members of a particular gem family. Some singly refracting gem families that have more than one variety, such as garnet, may have different R.I. readings, depending on the variety. For example, pyrope garnet (a red variety of garnet) may have an R.I. reading of 1.746 while rhodolite garnet (another reddish variety of garnet) a reading of 1.76, and almandine (a purplish red variety of garnet) a reading of 1.79. Also, almandine can have a reading higher than 1.80 and not be readable on the refractometer. However, when examining a particular singly refracting stone, no matter what variety, it will give only *one* R.I. reading.

Gemstones and other substances you might encounter that are singly refracting include spinel, opal, amber, glass, plastics, ivory, jet, and garnet. Diamonds, CZ, YAG, and GGG are also singly refracting, but their refractive indices are too high (over 1.80) to be read on the refractometer unless you are using a special type such as the Jemeter.

One can really have fun with the refractometer but, as we've recommended, try to spend some time with someone who already knows how to use it. A few minutes with someone knowledgeable can provide the assurance you may need to be sure you're doing it right and seeing what you're supposed to be seeing. Once you master the refractometer, it's an instrument you will probably use every day.

REFRACTIVE INDEX OF POPULAR SINGLE REFRACTING GEMSTONE MATERIALS

(See appendix for list of doubly refracting gems)

Gemstone	Approx. R.I.	Notations
Opal (genuine and synthetic)	1.44–1.46	In synthetic, colors are inside boundaries and lizard-skin-like markings are seen.
Sodalite	1.48	Looks like lapis lazuli, but the R.I. for lapis is 1.50.
Obsidian (natural glass)	1.48–1.51	May be transparent to opaque, black, gray or reddish. Color can be solid or streaked.
Amber	1.54	Smoke from touching with hot needle produces a smell like burning cedar while plastic imitations produce disinfectant-like odor.
Plastics - many types: Casein Polystyrene Bakelite	1.49–1.66 1.55–1.56 1.59 1.61–1.66	All are soft and can be cut with a knife. Also warm to touch. Since they are soft, will show wear after minimal use.

Gemstone	Approx. R.I.	Notations
Glass	1.50–1.65	Any transparent faceted stone having an R.I. within this range will be glass. Amber is an exception, but is seldom faceted and can be scratched with a knife. Note: Some glass can have an R.I. as low as 1.48 and, in rare cases, as high as 1.78.
Jet	1.64–1.68	A fossilized wood that has turned to coal. Used extensively in Victorian and mourning jewelry. Resembles black onyx, but much lighter.
Spinel genuine, blues/reds genuine, some blues and other colors Synthetic	1.715–1.735 1.74–1.80 1.72–1.74	The R.I. is usually close to 1.72. Colorless spinel is very rare, so if it appears to be, it is probably synthetic. If so, it will glow a strong milky-white under short-wave ultraviolet examination. (see Chapter 7). Also, strong ADR seen with polariscope proves synthetic (see Chapter 11).

Gemstone	Approx. R.I.	Notations
Garnet	1.73–1.89	
Pyrope	1.74–1.75	
Rhodolite	1.75–1.77	
Grossularite		
Hessonite	1.742–1.748	"Cinnamon stone" is hessonite garnet.
Tsavorite	1.742–1.744	"Tsavorite" is an expensive emerald-green type.
Hydrogrossularite	1.73	Resembles jade and often sold as Transvaal jade. It is not jade.
Almandite	1.76–1.83	Medium to dark purple-red. Most common variety. Can be found in four- and six-rayed star type. Needle-like inclusions often can be seen with the loupe.
Spessartite	1.790–1.82	Red, orange, brownish-orange and yellow type. Now comes from Brazil. Lively gem.
Andradite (Demantoid)	1.86–1.89	This green variety is called demantoid and is expensive. The refractometer may not provide an R.I. reading because its R.I. is too high to be measured on most

Continued

		refractometers.* It can be identified by the horse-tail inclusions that usually can be seen with the loupe. It is also very lively.
Garnet-Topped False Doublets	1.77±	These are encountered in much older jewelry and were used before synthetics became available. They are constructed from a piece of garnet, usually almandite, fused to a piece of colored glass. Depending upon the color of the glass, one could "create" any gem—ruby, sapphire, emerald, etc. When examined with the refractometer, you will get the R.I. of the garnet rather than the R.I. of the stone being simulated.
Diamond	2.417	Most refractometers* cannot provide readings for these gems because the R.I. is too high. Don't mistake a reading of 1.80 for that of the stone; it is the R.I. reading of the *liquid* used with the instrument.
Cubic Zirconia	2.15	See "diamond" notation.

* *The Jemeter refractometer can provide R.I. readings for such stones— stones with very high R.I.s.*

NOTES

A Foil-backed "Pink" Topaz Necklace

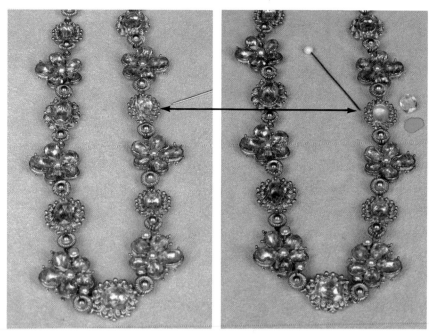

Foil-backed pink topaz necklace

Notice the pink foil that has been removed and the *colorless* topaz alongside

Notice the back of the necklace is *closed* — the gold completely conceals the backs of the stones themselves. Also, notice the gold on the back of the left-hand stone is smooth and unbroken while the gold on the back of the other stone has a "V"-shaped crack. The crack allows air to enter, which oxidizes the foil and causes it to change color.

Notice the stone on the left is a distinctly different shade of color than other stones in the necklace. This has resulted from oxidation.

PHOTOS: E. MORGAN

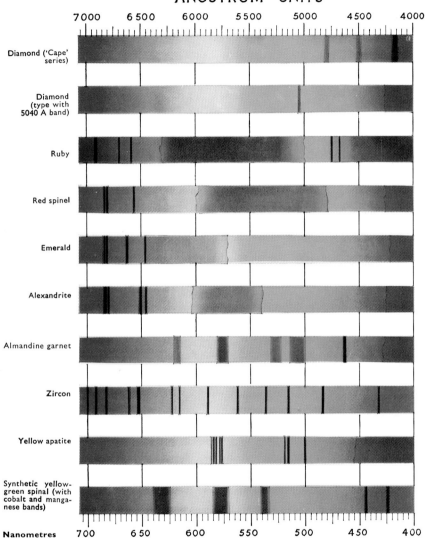

Absorption spectra of gemstones.

Note that the scales are shown linear, as with a diffraction grating spectroscope.

ANGSTROM UNITS

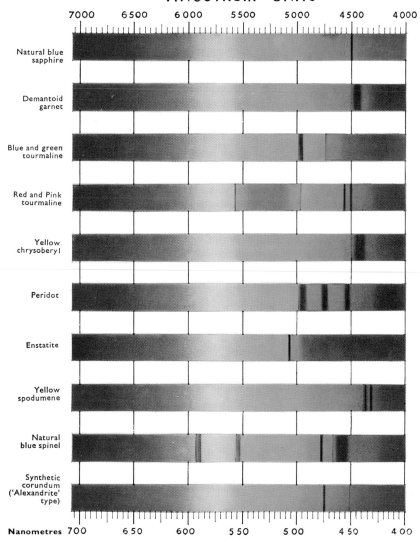

Absorption spectra of gemstones.

The scales here are linear, not condensed towards the red end as with a prism type spectroscope.

Reproduced from "Gemmologists' Compendium" by Robert Webster FGA
(N.A.G. Press Ltd, England).

Some Diamond Inclusions and Blemishes Seen with the Loupe
INCLUSIONS

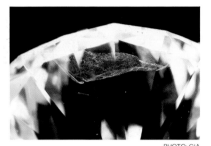

PHOTO: GIA

A Cloud-like inclusion in diamond

PHOTO: GIA

Black crystal inclusions in diamond

PHOTO: GIA

"Reflector" inclusions, showing same inclusions reflected many times

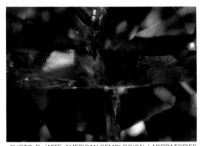

PHOTO: D. JAFFE, AMERICAN GEMOLOGICAL LABORATORIES

A feather

PHOTO: GIA

Cleavage

PHOTO: GIA

Bearded girdle or girdle fringe

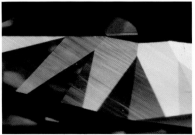

PHOTO: B. KANE, GIA

Graining

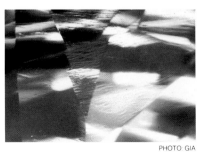

PHOTO: GIA

Surface graining

Diamond Inclusions continued

Laser drill holes

A knaat in table facet

Inclusions before laser drilling

Inclusions after laser drilling

BLEMISHES

Natural on the girdle

Nick or chip on girdle

Twinning

Scratch on table facet

Some Inclusions Seen in Colored Gems With the Loupe

PHOTO: R. BUCY, COLUMBIA SCHOOL OF GEMOLOGY
"Silk" in Corundum

PHOTO: GIA
Needle-like inclusions in almandite garnet

PHOTO: R. BUCY, COLUMBIA SCHOOL OF GEMOLOGY
Growth tubes in aquamarine

PHOTO: R. BUCY, COLUMBIA SCHOOL OF GEMOLOGY
Needle-like inclusions of rutile in quartz

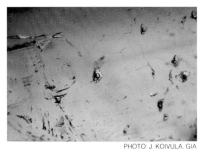
PHOTO: J. KOIVULA, GIA
Two-phase inclusions (liquid & gas) in tourmaline

PHOTO: J. KOIVULA, GIA
Three-phase inclusions in beryl

PHOTO: GIA
Liquid-filled or healing feather in sapphire

PHOTO: GIA
Fingerprint inclusion in almandite garnet

Inclusions in Colored Gems continued

PHOTO: R. BUCY, COLUMBIA SCHOOL OF GEMOLOGY

Ball-like inclusions seen in Thai ruby

PHOTO: R. BUCY, COLUMBIA SCHOOL OF GEMOLOGY

Curved striae in synthetic sapphire

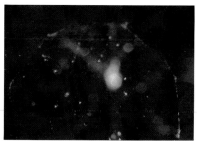

PHOTO: R. BUCY, COLUMBIA SCHOOL OF GEMOLOGY

Bubbles in synthetic ruby

PHOTO: GIA

Swirl lines in glass

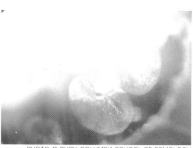

PHOTO: R. BUCY, COLUMBIA SCHOOL OF GEMOLOGY

Halo inclusion seen in peridot, resembling a lilypad

PHOTO: AMERICAN GEMOLOGICAL LABORATORIES

Disc-like inclusion in sapphire

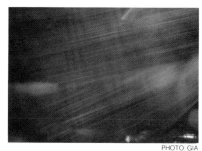

PHOTO: GIA

"Rain" seen in Kashan synthetic ruby

PHOTO: R. BUCY, COLUMBIA SCHOOL OF GEMOLOGY

Profilated bubbles in synthetic ruby

Some Inclusions Seen Under the Microscope

PHOTO: J. KOIVULA, GIA

Gas bubbles in man-made glass

PHOTO: GIA

Bubble with tail in YAG

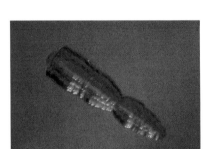

PHOTO: J. KOIVULA, GIA

Bubble in flame-fusion synthetic ruby
(50X)

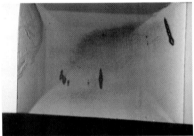

PHOTO: R. BUCY, COLUMBIA SCHOOL OF GEMOLOGY

Profilated bubbles in synthetic ruby

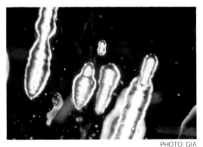

PHOTO: GIA

Semi-profilated gas bubbles in synthetic
spinel

PHOTO: GIA

Color zoning in amethyst

PHOTO: R. BUCY, COLUMBIA SCHOOL OF GEMOLOGY

Zoning in sapphire

PHOTO: R. BUCY, COLUMBIA SCHOOL OF GEMOLOGY

Two-phase inclusion in beryl

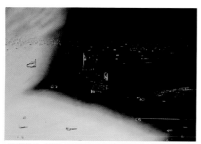

PHOTO: D. JAFFE, AMERICAN GEMOLOGICAL LABORATORIES

Two-phase inclusions in emerald

PHOTO: J. KOIVULA, GIA

Fingerprint inclusion in chrysoberyl (60X)

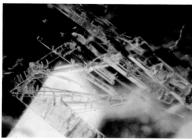

PHOTO: J. KOIVULA, GIA

Lilypad-shaped halos with negative crystal
at center, in peridot (45X)

PHOTO: GIA

Healing-feather or liquid-filled inclusion
in sapphire

PHOTO: J. KOIVULA, GIA

Lath-like crystals of actinolite in emerald

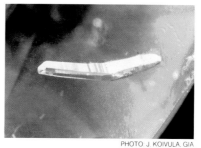

PHOTO: J. KOIVULA, GIA

Rare negative crystal in sapphire.

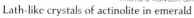

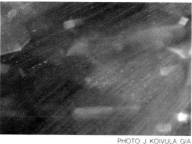

PHOTO: J. KOIVULA, GIA

"Rain" seen in Kashan synthetic ruby
(40X)

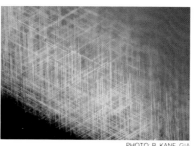

PHOTO: B. KANE, GIA

"Silk" in natural sapphire. Notice needles
intersecting at 60 degrees

Solid crystal inclusion of pyrite in emerald

Curved striae in synthetic sapphire

Nail-head inclusions in Linde synthetic
emerald

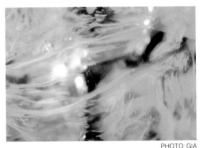

Veils seen in flux-grown synthetic
emerald

Three-phase inclusions in natural
Colombian emerald

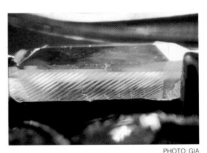

"Venetian blind" inclusion. Seen in green,
yellow and brown zircon

Red garnet crystal in diamond

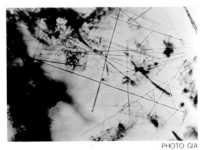

Tremolite needles in emerald from
Sandewana

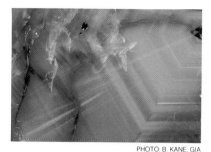

PHOTO: B. KANE, GIA

Zoning in sapphire

PHOTO: J. KOIVULA, GIA

Flux-grown inclusion, occasionally seen in pink sapphire

PHOTO: R. BUCY, COLUMBIA SCHOOL OF GEMOLOGY

Inclusions of byssolite in demantoid (andradite) garnet. Typical "horse-tail" inclusion

PHOTO: GIA

Snakes in amethyst

PHOTO: R. BUCY, COLUMBIA SCHOOL OF GEMOLOGY

"Zebra stripes" in amethyst caused by micro-twinning

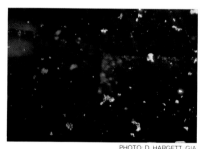

PHOTO: D. HARGETT, GIA

Fine crumbs, like breadcrumbs, in synthetic amethyst (45X)

PHOTO: J. KOIVULA, GIA

Mica in emerald

PHOTO: J. KOIVULA, GIA

Crazing seen on surface in Lechleitner synthetic emerald-coated beryl

PHOTO: B. KANE, GIA

White, wispy veils in flux-grown
Chatham synthetic sapphire

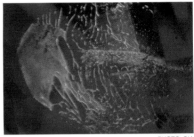

PHOTO: GIA

Flux fingerprint in Chatham synthetic
ruby (50X)

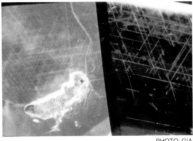

PHOTO: GIA

Needle-like inclusions in two natural rubies

PHOTO: GIA

Flux fingerprint in synthetic emerald

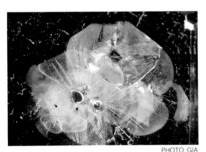

PHOTO: GIA

Halos in natural Thai ruby

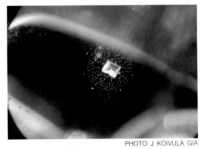

PHOTO: J. KOIVULA, GIA

One large and many tiny octahedra in
spinel

NOTES

9 / The microscope

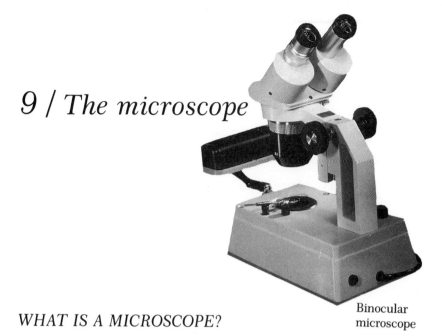

Binocular microscope

WHAT IS A MICROSCOPE?

The microscope has always been an important instrument for gem identification, but today it is indispensable because of its value in detecting new treatments and new-type synthetics.

The microscope, like the loupe, is a magnifier. The 10X loupe that we discussed in Chapter 4 is a low-powered magnifier, and the microscope is a high-powered magnifier that enables you to view things not visible with low magnification, and to see more clearly whatever is observed with the loupe. It is essential for distinguishing new-type synthetics from their natural counterparts, and for detecting various types of treatment. With slight modification, the microscope can also be adapted for use as a dichroscope, polariscope, refractometer, and spectroscope.

When we discuss microscopes, however, we are not referring to just any type. Those used by doctors, for example, are useless for the gemologist. For gem identification, one needs a binocular, stereoscopic microscope that offers a magnification range from 10X to at least 30X. This microscope has two eyepieces as opposed to a monocular microscope with only one. Monocular microscopes will give you a reversed image that can be very confusing when looking at gemstones. The stereoscopic binocular microscope does not reverse the image. Furthermore, it is constructed in a manner that creates a three-dimensional effect when you view the stone.

113

A good basic microscope for the gem identifier will cost between $850 to $1,800, depending on the features you select (see Chapter 2). It must provide both dark-field and bright-field illumination. A reflected-light source is also mandatory. If you plan to use it to examine the latest synthetics, you must have a magnification capability up to at least 60X. If you are working with diamond proportioning and measurements, a continuously variable zoom feature is also desirable, but is costlier ($1,995 and up) and is not essential if identification is the only goal.

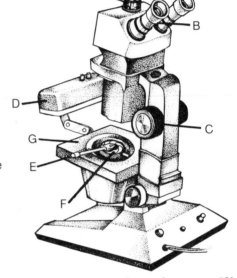

Parts of the microscope

A. Zoom Power
B. Eyepieces
C. Focusing Knob
D. Overhead Lightsource
E. Stone Holder
F. Iris Diaphragm
G. Stage

In addition to the microscope, we recommend purchasing a 2X adapter that fits onto the microscope lens to increase magnification twofold. With an adapter, a 30X microscope will magnify to 60X. We also recommend purchasing a stoneholder (tweezers) attachment if one is not included with the microscope (most models include them). The stoneholder will enable you to hold whatever is being examined more easily and steadily; it also improves your ability to carefully zero in on each area of the stone. As we discussed in Chapter 4, the higher the magnification, the more difficult it is to focus. Holding the item steady and examining it carefully in every area are essential to avoid missing something accidentally, especially when using very high magnification.

Mastering the microscope requires more time and practice that most other instruments. It takes time to become confident that you are using it properly, that the lighting is correct, that you are focusing it properly, and that you are seeing what you should be seeing. If possible, it is helpful to find a gemologist to work with for a few hours when you start out. But however long it takes, don't give up. Mastery will come, and it will pay off.

The microscope can open the door to some thrilling experiences— identifying a synthetic that by all other tests appears natural; determining that a stone has been treated; knowing absolutely what the origin of a fine gem may be (such as Burma ruby or Colombian emerald) by its own special telltale signs. All it takes is understanding how to use it, what to look for, a little guided practice, and patience.

Before we begin, we recommend obtaining a copy of *Internal World of Gemstones* by Edward Gubelin or *Photoatlas of Inclusions in Gemstones* by Gubelin and John Koivula. These books provide superb photographs that are very helpful in learning to recognize different types of telltale inclusions.

HOW TO USE THE MICROSCOPE

The first step in using the microscope is learning to adjust it to your eyes. Just follow these steps.

Focusing the Microscope

1. Tilt the microscope at its base so that when you look through it (from a sitting position) you feel comfortable and have no strain on your back.

2. Adjust the eyepieces so they comfortably accommodate the distance between your eyes. Binocular microscopes allow you to do this by pushing the eyepieces apart or pulling them together. Adjust them until you are comfortable looking through both eyepieces with both eyes.

3. Adjust the focus:

a. Move the tip of the stoneholder attachment to the center of the opening through which the base light shines. Turn the knob that controls the magnification power to a high setting. Now close the left eye and, using the right eye only, look through the right eyepiece and focus on the tip of the stoneholder by carefully turning the focusing knob. Focus very, very slowly until the tip is clear and sharp.

b. Without touching the focusing knob, close the right eye and use the left eye only. Looking through the left eyepiece, focus on the stoneholder by moving the top of the *eyepiece* itself, not the focusing knob. (The top of the left eyepiece is adjustable, the top of the right eyepiece is not.) Focus on the stoneholder sharply, as you did with the right eyepiece.

c. Now, with both eyes open, look through the microscope at the tip of the stoneholder, which should be in sharp focus. Close one eye and look at the tip again with the open eye. Repeat using the other eye. Whichever eye is open, the tip should be in sharp focus. If not, repeat steps (a) and (b).

Examining Gems with the Microscope

Once you are comfortable focusing the microscope you are ready to examine a stone or piece of jewelry with it. Proceed in the following manner.

1. *Be sure the stone is clean.* Use a small brush (such as an artist's brush) dipped in rubbing alcohol (isopropyl) to carefully remove dirt and dust. Wipe the stone with a lint-free cloth. Use compressed air (see Chapter 2) to remove any remaining dust. This will eliminate the possibility of confusing dust with something in or on the stone.

Caution: If you have an ultrasonic cleaner, *never* use it for opals, pearls, aventurine, sunstone, malachite, tanzanite, and most emeralds. It can damage these stones and any stone that has cleavage cracks, numerous inclusions, or fractures.

2. *Examine the stone using dark-field illumination.*

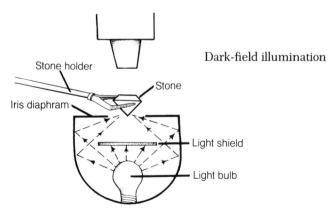

Dark-field illumination is the type most often used for gem identification. To use dark-field illumination, cover the light bulb with the flat, non-reflective black shield provided under the iris diaphragm (the lever to adjust the shield is normally on top of the microscope stage, near the stoneholder). This blocks direct light from going through the stone (bright-field). Place the stone in the stoneholder and position it just above the iris diaphragm so that light is simultaneously entering the stone *through its sides* (lateral lighting). You must be sure not to position the stone too high above the light source or you will not get lateral lighting. With dark-field illumination, the lateral lighting combined with the blackened background from the light shield causes inclusions to stand out more clearly and makes them easier to see and identify.

3. *Examine the stone under low power magnification.* Using dark-field illumination as explained above, begin to examine the stone, looking through both eyepieces with both eyes open. Start with low power magnification (7X–10X) because lower power gives a wider area of observation—the size of the area that will be in focus at a given point—making it easier to spot inclusions. Carefully examine each area of the stone, turning the focusing knob slowly and focusing into the stone at different depths. Turn the stone to a different position and examine it again so that you view different portions of it, from different angles.

4. *Gradually increase the magnification.* Try to remember the position of anything you have seen under lower magnification so you can find it to view more carefully under higher magnification. Something you have seen under lower magnification may seem to disappear at higher magnification. This happens because the field of observation becomes smaller as magnification is increased. Since the area actually in view becomes smaller as the power at which you examine an object goes up, the object seen at lower magnification may no longer be inside the area in view. By slowly and carefully moving the stone you will be able to find it again.

Look for inclusions not visible under lower power. Be sure to turn the stone to examine it from different directions and angles following each increase in magnification.

Higher magnification enables you to spot internal characteristics and inclusions not visible at lower magnification. It also enables you to examine more clearly what you see under lower magnification.

This is particularly important for inclusions that look like bubbles at low power. Bubbles usually indicate glass. An inclusion that appears bubble-like at 10X, however, may turn out to be something else—such as a rounded crystal—when viewed under higher magnification. Higher power examination of bubble-like inclusions may prevent the embarrassment of identifying as glass something that isn't!

  5. *Examine with bright-field illumination.*

Bright-field illumination

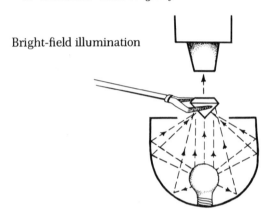

Bright-field illumination is accomplished by placing the stone over the light source so that it is illuminated from behind. The shield used to create dark-field illumination is not used here. Bright-field illumination highlights certain types of inclusions, particularly in emerald. It is also useful to observe twin planes, and to examine more carefully fractures or cleavage lines seen with dark-field. Again, remember to turn the stone, and view it from every angle.

  6. *Examine with diffused bright-field illumination.*

Diffused bright-field illumination

Diffuser plate such as that sold by GIA (or tissue — don't leave tissue over light too long or it may burn).

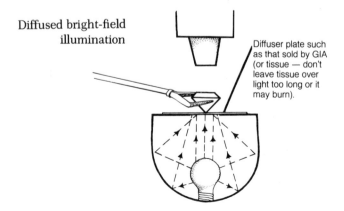

In this method the light enters the stone from behind as in bright-field, but it has been *diffused.* To diffuse the light, simply place a white facial tissue or a thin sheet of white paper over the light-source opening. Diffused light will permit easier observation of weak curved striae and weak color-zoning or banding difficult to see in pale colored stones.

7. *Examine with vertical (overhead) illumination.*

Overhead (vertical) illumination—Light shines directly on top of stone (from overhead light attached to microscope, fiberoptic or other strong light).

This method calls for shining the light directly on top of the stone so that light might reflect off inclusions within the stone. This method may enable you to see fine, needlelike inclusions such as those found in Burmese rubies and sapphires because these inclusions will reflect the light back to you. With sapphire it can also help you see reflections that will reveal halos or flat platinum crystals (shaped like triangles or little hexagons) indicating synthetic, and disc-like inclusions indicating heat-treating. For black opal, it may reveal the telltale flat, disc-like air bubbles often difficult to detect by any other method, proving the stone is a *doublet* and not genuine black opal.

8. *Examine with horizontal illumination.*

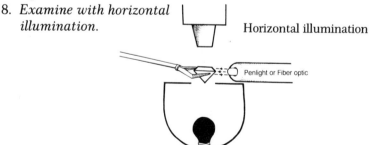

Horizontal illumination

Penlight or Fiber optic

This method calls for using a narrow beam of light (a fiber-optic light source or penlight), directed through the stone *from the side* while the stone is being viewed through the microscope from the top. Pinpoint crystals and tiny bubbles are more easily seen this way because they stand out more brightly.

9. *Examine with pinpoint illumination.*

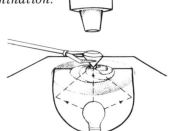

Pinpoint illumination—
Note that the iris dia-
phragm is almost fully
closed.

This method calls for light coming from directly behind the stone, *through a narrowed opening* obtained by closing the iris diaphragm to the desired degree. It is especially useful for observing curved striae more easily.

Now all it takes is practice. Experiment with stones you already have. Try looking at the same stone using different types of lighting techniques. Try to become familiar with certain types of inclusions such as those we will discuss now.

WHAT THE MICROSCOPE WILL SHOW

The real excitement of gem identification begins with competent use of the microscope. The microscope gives you a significant edge by enabling you to identify many of the new-type synthetics that, using all other tests, might otherwise appear to be natural. It can often tell you whether the color of a fine gem is natural or enhanced, whether cracks have been filled, and, in many cases, the probable origin of a gem.

We recently had an interesting experience that shows how valuable the microscope can be. At the Tucson Gem Show, one of the most important gatherings of colored-stone sellers in the country, a dealer was selling precious topaz at a very attractive price. Like other gem buyers, we are always looking for good value. We always become suspicious, however, when the price seems *too* good. We assumed the stones had been treated to enhance the color but the dealer assured us the color was natural. When we pressed further and asked how he could sell such fine color, natural topaz at such an attractive price, he said he obtained rough material at the mines and cut it himself.

We weren't convinced. He agreed to accompany us to examine one of his stones under the microscope. Using immersion (examining the stone while it's submerged in a special liquid) the microscope told us immediately that the color was not natural. We knew it had been treated because we saw something never present in a natural-color stone—a bright pink halo-like border encircling it. The dealer admitted to bombarding the material (with radiation) in an attempt to create "pink" topaz. He failed to create pink but did create a more beautiful color. Unfortunately, such color is not permanent.

It isn't always so easy to detect treatment. We are still unable to tell in some cases. We don't yet know how to separate naturally blue topaz, for example, from topaz that has been irradiated to make it blue (in the case of blue topaz, the resulting color appears to be permanent). But great progress has been made in revealing various types of gem treatment, synthesis, and simulation, and every day we make important new discoveries.

In most cases, inclusions offer the key. The microscope's importance for gem-identification purposes lies in its ability to provide more precise information about the inclusions present in a gem material.

What Is an Inclusion?

The term inclusion applies to any foreign body enclosed within a gemstone. An inclusion can be a gas, liquid, or solid enclosed within the stone. In gemstones, the term also applies to cleavage cracks, fractures, growth lines, color zoning, and crystals (of the same composition as the host gemstone, or some altogether different substance).

Inclusions provide valuable information because no gem material—whether made by humans or by nature—is entirely free of inclusions. They may not be visible to the unaided eye, or under 10X magnification, or even under 30X. It may be necessary to use 60X magnification to find them, but inclusions are always present.

Some inclusions are quite beautiful and make a stone more interesting, as in a specimen of ordinary quartz that can become quite *extra*ordinary when it is contains lovely thin, golden, needlelike crystals of the mineral rutile (rutilated quartz). Some inclusions are so large and ugly they destroy both the beauty and value of a stone that might otherwise have been a gem. Some are so small they don't detract from the stone's beauty or value at all, and, in fact, may add to it by proving country of origin or whether or not color is natural.

The key is knowing what types of inclusions to look for, what they look like and where they should or should not appear. We'll begin by describing the different types of inclusions found in gemstones.

NOTE: *See the color section at the center of this book for photographic illustrations of the inclusions described here.*

Types of Inclusions Found in Gems

Bubbles. These inclusions look like little bubbles of various shapes and sizes. Nice round bubbles usually indicate a synthetic or glass, though they can be found in natural amber. In synthetic ruby or sapphire, they can be round, profilated (a string of bubbles with a large bubble at the center and progressively smaller bubbles on each side), pear-shaped, or tadpole-shaped. In the last two, the tail always points in the same direction.

Clouds. Groups of fine bubbles or cavities.

Color Zoning. A term referring to uneven distribution of color. Inclusions often appear as whitish or colorless parallel planes. Zoning is frequently observed in ruby, sapphire, amethyst and citrine.

Dark Ball. Dark, opaque ball-shaped inclusion surrounded by an irregularly shaped, wispy, brown cloudlike formation. These are found exclusively in Thai rubies and are never seen in Burmese rubies.

Dendritic. Rootlike or treelike inclusions such as those seen in moss-agate.

Feather. Another term for an internal crack.

Fiberlike or Needlelike. Inclusions of long, thin crystals that resemble needles or thin fibers. Often long thin crystals of rutile, as in rutilated quartz, or tourmaline, as in tourmalinated quartz. Can be seen in garnet, sapphire, and ruby.

Fingerprint. Small crystal inclusions arranged in curved rows in such a way as to resemble a fingerprint or maze. Seen in quartz and topaz. They closely resemble the healing-feathers seen in sapphires.

Halo or Disc-like. A halo is an inclusion resembling small, flat disc-like wings with a small zircon crystal in the center. They are stress cracks caused by radioactivity or strain associated with the growth of the zircon crystals. The zircon crystal often appears as a small dark dot at the center of the disc. Another type of disc-like inclusion, usually difficult for the novice to distinguish from a halo, provides an indication of *heating*. Unlike most halos, it is mirrorlike and exhibits *multiple breaks around the border* of the "halo." Note: it takes great skill to tell by inclusions whether or not a gem is enhanced. A gem-testing lab specializing in enhancement (such as A.G.L. or G.I.A.—see Appendix) should be used.

Healing-Feather (Liquid Filled). An inclusion consisting of a maze-like arrangement of tubes. Often seen in sapphire.

Laser-Hole. A microscopic hole created by a laser beam penetrating into a diamond to reduce the visibility of flaws and thus improve appearance. A visible black flaw, for example, can be vaporized and practically disappear. The laser path can be seen, however, as a fine straight line resembling a white thread, going from the outer surface of the stone into the center. There will be a small, dot-like break at the surface of a facet where the laser beam entered.

Lath-like. Long, thin, flat (like a lath) crystals.

Negative Crystal. A cavity with a distinctive crystal shape. These are interesting because what you see is really just an outline (since it is not solid). However, the outline will always show the same shape as that of the crystal-form of the host material. If you are examining a piece of quartz with a negative-crystal inclusion, for example, the negative-crystal will have a hexagonal outline because the shape of a quartz crystal is hexagonal. Often seen in quartz and topaz.

Profilated Bubbles. A string of round bubbles in a straight row with the largest in the center, getting progressively smaller toward each end of the row. Often seen in synthetic corundum and synthetic spinel.

Rain. A type of inclusion that looks like dashed lines resembling falling rain. They are seen in flux grown synthetic rubies, such as the Kashan synthetic.

Sheaves. An inclusion of the mineral cacoxenite, found in amethyst. It gets its name because it looks like the top half of a sheaf of wheat, coming to a point at the bottom.

Silk. Thin intersecting needlelike crystals that exhibit a sheen similar to that of silk fabric when examined with reflected light. Often seen in ruby and sapphire.

Solid. A solid crystal or mineral fragment present in the host.

Striae. Curved concentric lines seen in old Verneuil synthetic ruby and sapphire.

Swirl Marks. Found in glass, these are curved lines and curlicues, swirling through the stone, usually in a darker color than the host substance. Can also be called striae, but unlike that described above, these will not be *concentric.*

Three-Phase. Cavities that contain liquid, a gas bubble, and a solid (usually a crystal). They may look like irregularly shaped pea pods, usually pointed at both ends. Within the pod (which is liquid filled) there is a bubble (gas) and, adjacent to the bubble, a cube or rhomboid-shaped crystal (solid). All matter is in either a gas, liquid, or solid state, but this type of inclusion contains all three states, hence its name. In emerald, the presence of a three-phase inclusion containing a cube or rhomboid-shaped solid proves the stone is natural and not synthetic.

Twinning. Resembles parallel lines, but are actually planes, like panes of glass lying in parallel planes. Often found in rubies and sapphires, and occasionally in some feldspar gems like moonstone. When present, twinning can prove genuineness for ruby or sapphire but, if too numerous, may weaken a stone and reduce its brilliance.

Two-Phase. Inclusions that usually have a "frankfurter" outline with an enclosed bubble that may (or may not) actually move as the "frank" is tilted from end to end. These are seen in topaz, quartz, synthetic emerald, and some tourmaline.

Veils. Small bubblelike inclusions arranged in layer formations that can be wispy, flat or curvaceous, broad or narrow, long or short. These may be easily observed in some synthetic emeralds.

Venetian-Blinds. An inclusion occurring in green, yellow, and brown zircon. We call these "venetian blind" inclusions because they look like venetian blinds that are slightly closed, slightly turned down.

Find photos of these inclusions in the center color insert and try to become familiar with what they look like. See if you can spot some in stones from your own inventory. Have fun.

SOME POPULAR GEMS UNDER THE MICROSCOPE

We have put together the following guidelines to assist you, stone by stone. In addition, refer to pages 47–53. Many commonly encountered inclusions seen when examining popular gems under the microscope are included, but there are too many inclusions to try to cover them all. You must also remember that new discoveries may make information here obsolete. It is important to keep up to date by reading gemological journals and trade publications. Persistent practice is also essential for learning to recognize particular inclusions and avoid confusing those that are similar. Where possible, we encourage you to try to locate a skilled gemologist to assist you at the beginning. And don't hesitate to keep books handy for reference.

Diamond

Colorless Diamond Crystal. A small diamond crystal that has grown within the host diamond. It can look like a dot or bubble with a loupe, but by using the microscope you can see clearly it is a crystal with an octahedral shape (like two pyramids placed base-to-base).

Zircon Crystal. A crystal of zircon that has grown inside the host diamond, "frankfurter" shaped with a more-or-less square cross-section.

Garnet Crystal. Transparent red crystals, well-formed or distorted, inside the diamond.

Diopside Crystal. Dull opaque (not transparent) green or transparent emerald-green crystals of diopside are sometimes observed inside a diamond.

Small Black Spot. Often erroneously referred to as "carbon spots," black inclusions are usually the black mineral called magnetite, or sometimes hematite or chromite. Black carbon inclusions are usually wispy and veil-like and are very rare.

Chrome Spinel Crystals. Deep, cherry-red, opaque crystals that are probably crystals of chrome spinel. Sometimes they may appear black in larger pieces and may be confused with magnetite.

Cleavage. This is a crack or break that has a flat plane and usually starts at the girdle. It is straight, not jagged. It may be very small or quite noticeable. If it is very pronounced and the stone is placed in an ultrasonic cleaner, the cleavage may become larger.

Feather. Another name for a crack. Differs from cleavage because it does not occur on a plane, but is jagged in appearance (sometimes resembling a feather). If pronounced, it can weaken the stone. An ultrasonic cleaner can make it worse.

Laser Beam Line. Stones with visible inclusions may be lasered— struck with laser beams to make the inclusions less visible. Under magnification you can spot the laser path. You will see a fine straight line (like a thread) penetrating the stone, beginning at the surface of a facet as a small dot-like break.

Emerald

Three-phase Inclusion. Seen in Colombian and Afghan emeralds. In Colombian stones, they resemble a Chinese snow-pea or a pointed pea pod; in Afghan stones, they resemble a finger. A three-phase inclusion that contains a square- or rectangular-shaped solid is positive proof that the emerald is natural and not synthetic.

Iron Pyrite. Emeralds from Chivor (Colombia) and some from Zambian (Africa) often contain beautifully formed crystals of iron pyrite. Iron pyrite, also known as "fool's gold," is easily recognizable by its brassy, metallic luster. It is often cubic in shape.

Mica. Small, thin, flat, hexagonally shaped black mica platelets are often seen in emeralds from Pakistan, Transvaal, Zambia and Tanzania. They are usually black. *Note*: mica can also be seen in another green gem, peridot.

Tremolite. Fiberlike tubes, sometimes slightly curved, and often jumbled like a randomly tossed box of soda-pop straws, often seen in small (under one carat) fine, deep green emeralds from Sandawana.

Rectangular Cavity with Bubble. Two-phase inclusion that is a more-or-less rectangular shaped cavity with a bubble at one end, often seen in emerald. It can be L-shaped, with the bubble at the base of the "L."

Lath-like. Long, thin, flat inclusions of the mineral actinolite. This inclusion is often seen in Siberian emerald.

Synthetic Emerald

Crazing. This is crack-like webbing resembling a fish net. It is seen on the surface of Lechleitner synthetic emerald coated beryl.

Nail-head. Regency synthetic emeralds (formerly Linde) will exhibit thin rodlike crystals, all pointing in the same direction. Some have an enlargement at the end of the crystal resembling the head of a nail, hence this name. (These emeralds will exhibit a very strong red fluorescence when viewed under the ultraviolet lamp.)

Wispy Veils. Wispy, undulating ribbonlike veils are a common inclusion seen in Chatham synthetic emerald, and are also often seen in Gilson synthetic emerald.

Ruby

Silk. These are intersecting needlelike crystals that intersect each other, often at 60 degree and 120 degree angles. When examined with reflected light, they exhibit a sheen similar to the sheen of silk fabric, hence the name. Sometimes they can be seen with the loupe, but often the microscope is required. It is important to examine the stone with reflected light to see these needles clearly. When viewed this way, they can exhibit many colors. Silk is often seen in Burma ruby, occasionally in rubies from Kenya, but never in Thai rubies or synthetics. The presence of silk proves genuineness.

Ball-like. These are inclusions of pyrrhotite crystals. These crystals are ball-like in appearance and are surrounded by a yellowish-brown cloudlike veil. They are typical of Thai stones and are never seen in Burma stones. Some Thai stones have more than one ball.

Halo. These inclusions look like discs or haloes encircling a dark spot. They are actually tension cracks radiating from a zircon crystal, which is the dark spot in the center. The tension that produces these cracks results in one of two ways: either the zircon has expanded from heat and the expansion creates stress that creates cracks; or the zircon was radioactive and the radiation being produced creates stress, which creates cracks. *Important*: Don't confuse with disc-like inclusions seen in gems that have been heated to enhance color. *Haloes will always have a dark spot at the center.* Disc-like inclusions seen in heat-treated gems won't.

Twinning Planes. These are more common in Thai rubies than Burmese. They are never present in synthetics so their presence proves genuineness. They may resemble fiberlike or needlelike inclusions when seen from certain directions, but they are actually planes—if you tilt the stone slightly and can observe planes going through the stone from one side to the other, you are observing twinning planes.

Healing-Feather (also called Liquid Feather). These inclusions are frequently seen in rubies from Cambodia and Sri Lanka (Ceylon). They resemble numerous slim, elongated tubes. Some are longer, some shorter, but all tend to point in the same direction and lie in a plane. The plane can be twisted and/or wavy.

Bubblelike Webbing. This type of inclusion is seen in natural and synthetic. If the bubbles are filled, the stone is synthetic; if hollow (open or unfilled), the stone is natural. You must use high-power magnification (at least 45X to 60X power) to tell whether or not the bubbles (holes) are filled.

Synthetic Ruby

Profilated Bubbles. Bubbles or clouds of small bubbles, sometimes stacked in a row with a larger bubble at the center and progressively smaller bubbles on each end. These will only be seen in old-type synthetics (Verneuil).

Curved Striae. Concentric curved lines (sometimes the curve is so slight they can appear almost straight) seen in old-type synthetic ruby and sapphire. Positive proof of synthetic material when clearly observed.

Bubblelike webbing. (See above).

Rain. These are dashed lines that resemble rain. They are seen in flux grown synthetic rubies, such as the Kashan.

Blue Sapphire

Sapphires have all the inclusions described above for ruby *except* ball-like inclusions.

Pastel-colored Ceylon Sapphire

These stones are usually highly included and will exhibit haloes, healing feathers, inclusions containing inclusions, and so on.

OTHER POPULAR GEMS UNDER THE MICROSCOPE

Aquamarine

Rods. Very thin visible parallel tubes that seem to enclose a fine light-brown powder. These are often seen in aquamarine. There can be many or few, but too many will affect the stone's beauty and value.

Ghost Lines. Parallel lines that are visible one moment and disappear the next. If you examine your stones carefully, you'll find ghost lines present in over 90 percent of all aquamarines. When examining aquamarines, turn the stone very slowly and focus very carefully. When you see one or more parallel lines that seem to disappear simply by tilting the stone a speck, you are viewing ghost lines. They may be in only one section of the stone, or several.

Garnet

Almandine

Rutile Needle Inclusions. Any purple-red garnet with long, thin needlelike inclusions of rutile will be almandine. The needles can be randomly oriented or crisscross at 90 degrees or at 70 and 110 degrees. Those that produce numerous needles intersecting at 90 degrees can produce a four-rayed star; those intersecting at 70 and 110 degrees, a six-rayed star.

Haloes. Seen in almandine garnets from Sri Lanka.

Tsavorite

Lath-like Inclusions. This lovely green variety of garnet may contain long, thin, flat (lath-like) crystals of the mineral actinolite.

Demantoid

Horse-tails. Rare green demantoid garnet (much more expensive than tsavorite) contains fine fiberlike inclusions of the mineral byssolite. These inclusions are often tufted and resemble a horse's tail. They can be swirled or randomly located.

Quartz

All varieties. Negative crystals, needlelike (crystals of rutile, tourmaline), lath-like (long, thin, flat crystals of actinolite).

Amethyst

Snakes. Fine, long, thin, ruby-red snake-shaped crystals (hematite or goethite). Often seen in genuine amethyst.

Multiple Twinning. Also called "zebra stripes" (Gubelin), these look like the teeth on a wood saw. They are usually stacked in fairly parallel rows.

Color Zoning. Color is seen in parallel planes or layers.

Sheaves. An inclusion of the mineral cacoxenite. It gets its name because it looks like the top half of a sheaf of wheat, coming to a point at the bottom.

Fingerprint. Numerous small crystal inclusions arranged in a pattern that resembles a fingerprint or maze.

Synthetic Amethyst

Fine Crumbs. Very small whitish crumblike inclusions. When present in a fine-colored amethyst that shows no other inclusions they indicate synthetic material.

Citrine

Color Zoning. Similar to zoning seen in amethyst.

Praseolite (greenish quartz)

Twinning. Zigzag, parallel lines showing multiple twinning is often visible on a polished facet.

Rose

Needlelike. Small needles of rutile are seen under high magnification in 95 percent of all rose quartz. The cloudiness associated with most rose quartz results from the presence of these rutile needles.

Spinel

Octahedra. Spinels often exhibit small octahedral crystal inclusions (of the mineral hercynite). An octahedron resembles two pyramids with their bases placed together. If present, they prove the spinel is genuine. Sometimes, if very small, they can look like small dots. Examination with the microscope at higher magnification will reveal whether or not they are really octahedra.

Frankfurters. Some hazy blue spinels may contain crystal inclusions that resemble a frankfurter.

Zircon Crystals. Often seen in blue and lavender spinel.

Topaz. Same as in quartz.

Tourmaline

Cracks. Tourmaline exhibits an odd-shaped, mirrorlike crack typical only of tourmaline. It is flat and broad with jagged points at the ends. Once you see them, you'll always be able to recognize them.

Zircon

Venetian Blinds. An effect that resembles a partly closed venetian blind is often seen in green, yellow, and brown zircons.

AN IMPORTANT TIP: Any gemstone showing a rust-colored crack is genuine (as in some rubies). Attempts at introducing a "rusty" look into synthetic stones haven't been successful.

NOTES

PART 4

OPTIONAL INSTRUMENTS

10 / *The spectroscope*

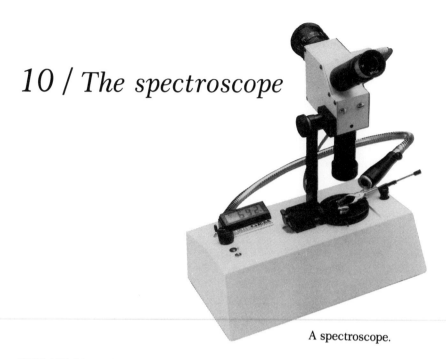

A spectroscope.

WHAT IS A SPECTROSCOPE

The spectroscope is a relatively small instrument that analyzes light passing through a stone. It has never really been appreciated until recently. For whatever reasons, many gemologists have ignored it, preferring other instruments. However, the rapid growth in the fancy-color diamond market is changing attitudes about its value. We believe it is indispensable, one of the most interesting instruments to use, and one that should be added sooner or later to complete your gem-identification laboratory.

For those experienced in using it, a spectroscope provides one of the quickest ways for identifying mounted or unset stones, including rough material (material that has not been cut and polished). It is especially useful with stones for which the refractometer (see Chapter 8) is ineffective—unpolished stones or stones with a very poor polish, stones with a very high Refractive Index, any stone mounted in such a way that it is impossible to place it on a refractometer, and cabochons that may be difficult to read on a refractometer. *It is the only instrument widely available for separating natural-color diamonds from those that have obtained their color by irradiation or*

135

heating. It is also particularly useful for distinguishing natural-color green jadeite jade from dyed, some varieties of natural sapphire (especially blue) from synthetics and look-alikes, and natural alexandrite from synthetic color-change corundum and synthetic color-change spinel.

Two types of spectroscope are in common use: the "prism type" and the "diffraction-grating type." For gem identification, either type is acceptable. The standard diffraction type is less expensive, but the prism type has two advantages: it admits more light into the instrument; and it's easier to read in the dark blue end of the spectrum. However, there are several new diffraction models—with fiber optic lighting and digital readout—that have essentially overcome these limitions. While somewhat more expensive, they're becoming increasingly popular.

We do not recommend most portable or hand-held types because they are usually more difficult to read and some models cannot provide readings in the dark blue portion of the spectrum. Many models also limit your ability to adjust the light entering the instrument.

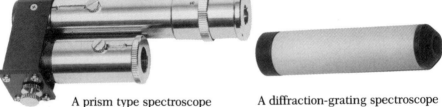

A prism type spectroscope   A diffraction-grating spectroscope

In this chapter we'll explain how to use the standard prism type spectroscope unit, equipped with a good light source and stand. While the actual operation may differ slightly between this type and the diffraction or digital types, the basic principles will still apply and you should be able to easily adjust the technique described here to your instrument.

The prism spectroscope resembles two connected tubes, one next to the other—a taller "tube" which is the spectroscope proper, and a shorter tube that contains an illuminated scale. It has an adjustable slit at the end, through which light passes. Simply stated, this instrument divides white light into the spectral colors and analyzes it as it passes through a gem substance. It is really an easy instrument to use, and can be very interesting from a visual point of view. If you like rainbows, you'll love it!

As we discussed in the chapter on lighting, when all the colors of the visible spectrum are present (red, orange, yellow, green, blue, indigo, and violet) we get white light. To understand the spectroscope, all you need to realize is that *when white light travels through a gem material, one or more of the wavelengths that produce color are ABSORBED by the gem.*

This is not something we see with the naked eye, but if we could watch as light travels through a stone, if we could observe all the colors making up the white light as it enters, we would see that certain colors simply disappear as the light passes through it. This phenomenon—called selective absorption—provides a very useful clue to gem identity.

What the spectroscope actually does is enable us to see this phenomenon in many gems—to know what color has been absorbed—by producing a vertical black line or bar in the space where the spectral color that disappeared should be. By seeing what has disappeared, what is missing from the full spectrum, we get a distinct spectral picture for that gem. This picture is its "characteristic absorption spectrum"—the pattern of color seen, and the placement of the black bars, that is *characteristic* for a particular gem.

Since no two gem materials absorb the same wavelengths (color) in the same way, we can identify characteristic spectra for many gems. Unfortunately, not all gems exhibit a clear, distinct pattern, but when they do, these characteristic absorption spectra provide a quick, positive identification of the substance being examined, and, in some cases, tell whether or not the color is natural.

USING THE SPECTROSCOPE

First, before using the spectroscope to examine a gem, take a look though the eyepiece. Place a strong light in front of the instrument, shining up through the slit at the end. If you are using a diffraction type, be sure to use as strong a light as possible (fiber optic is recommended). As you look through the eyepiece you will see the full visible spectrum—a rainbow of seven colors—proceeding in a horizontal line from red on one end to violet on the other. If you are using

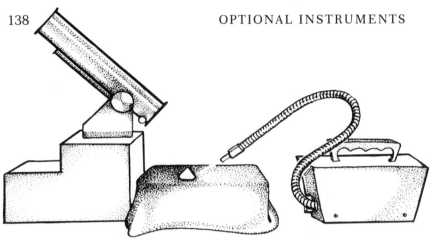

Setting up to examine a stone with the spectroscope. Notice the stone is sitting on black cloth. A strong light is positioned so that the light rays are reflected from the stone into the spectroscope slit. A fiber optic light is ideal, but a strong light such as that used here is usually effective.

a diffraction type, the spectral colors will be equally spaced. If you're using a prism type, the blue/violet end will look a little "spread-out" relative to the other colors, and the red/orange end will look a little compressed. That is, the orange and red colors seem crowded together, and the violet and indigo colors look spread apart. *Note:* In the new digital spectroscopes, the spectrum is viewed vertically rather than horizontally.

When you examine a stone with the spectroscope, you will continue to see the spectrum, but with a noticeable difference—a vertical black bar will appear at one or more places within the spectrum (some gems can have 10 or more lines!). Sometimes the bar is a very broad bar with hazy edges; sometimes it is a very narrow line and hard to see. *These black lines or bars occur wherever color has been absorbed by the gem material.* In other words, you are seeing black because the color that should be present at those same points has been absorbed by the gem.

You will also see a series of numbers along the top of the spectral display. These numbers go from 400 to 700 (in the older models the numbers go from 4000 to 7000). The sequence of numbers begins with 400 at the violet end of the spectrum and progresses through the spectrum to 700 at the red end. By noting where the black bars appear, at what numerical reading, you can easily check a chart and often identify a gemstone immediately.

Let's take a look at demantoid garnet (a variety of green garnet) as an example of how fast and easy the spectroscope can be to use. The refractometer can't be used for this gem because of its very high RI. But it's easy to identify with the spectroscope. When you look through the eyepiece you will see a lovely, colorful rainbowlike spectrum— and something more. In most demantoid you will observe a very strong bar in the violet end of the spectrum (see absorption spectra at end of chapter) at about 440 (4400). This is because the gem has absorbed some of the violet wavelength as the white light travelled through the stone, so we no longer see it. We see a black bar in place of the missing wavelength. If the demantoid is a rich, deep green, you will also note in the extreme red portion, at about 700, two very distinct black bars, very close together like railroad tracks (we call this a doublet). Again, as the white light travelled through the stone, some of the red wavelengths were absorbed, so we see black bars in place of where the red should be. When this pattern is present, the gem can only be demantoid garnet. It is the only green gem exhibiting this particular spectral (absorption) pattern.

Now let's examine blue sapphire. As you look through the eyepiece at the spectral display, you will see, in addition to the colors of the rainbow, a vertical black bar at the 450 (4500) mark, in the violet end of the spectrum. The deeper the color of the sapphire (or any gem), the more distinct the bar. Sometimes it is very easy to see, sometimes a little difficult, but if the stone is a rich blue sapphire, THERE WILL ALWAYS BE A BLACK BAR AT 450 (see absorption spectra). If the stone is another gem, such as blue spinel or tanzanite, you will not see it.

The spectroscope can also be helpful in distinguishing natural blue sapphire from synthetic. In most synthetic blue sapphire you will not see any bar at 450. So, if the color is a nice rich blue, and other tests suggest sapphire, you will know that the stone is synthetic if there is no line at 450. In some synthetics, you may see a *faint* blue line at 450. But if the material is a rich, *deep* blue, genuine sapphire it will exhibit a *distinct* line. A faint line in a rich blue stone should immediately suggest synthetic.

In the past, the spectroscope could immediately provide positive identification of genuine blue sapphire. Unfortunately, this is no longer true. Today there is an exception. One synthetic blue sapphire cannot be detected with the spectroscope—the Chatham synthetic. This synthetic exhibits almost the same absorption spectra as natural blue sapphire. While there are not many in circulation, you must be aware of them. If you have a very fine sapphire, and believe it to be genuine, to be absolutely sure you must examine it carefully with the microscope (which will reveal triangular or hexagonal platelets of platinum in the *synthetic*), or send it to a professional gem-testing lab.

HOW TO USE THE SPECTROSCOPE

1. *Be sure to use a good, strong light.* Having proper light is the key to successful use of this instrument. The stone must be intensely illuminated. Most spectroscope units contain their own light source. If you are using one that does not, it is important to have a very strong light that can be positioned to provide both transmitted and reflected light. A fiber optic light, or the intense light produced by a movie or slide projector can do the job.

2. *Be sure that only light that has been transmitted through the gem being examined, or reflected from it, enters the slit on the spectroscope.* Try to position the light and the spectroscope so that the slit in the spectroscope is as close as possible to the stone being examined, and the light is being transmitted or reflected directly into the slit. Try to prevent extraneous light from entering the slit.

3. *Use the spectroscope in a darkened room.* When examining a gem with the spectroscope, it is helpful to do it in a darkened room both to reduce extraneous light and so the eyes adjust more easily to what they are seeing in the spectroscope.

4. *Use transmitted light when examining transparent or translucent stones.* When using the spectroscope for transparent stones (stones you can see through clearly) or translucent stones (stones you can see through, but not clearly, as in "frosted glass"), simply place the stone in front of the spectroscope, *between* the spectroscope and the light source. This way, the light will travel from behind the stone, *through it*, up into the spectroscope.

5. *Use reflected light to examine opaque stones.* With an opaque stone (one you cannot see through, such as turquoise), position the stone in front of the spectroscope, with the light positioned *above* it so that it hits the surface of the stone and the rays bounce off the surface into the spectroscope opening.

6. *With very dark stones, use a fiber optic illuminator or the pinpoint setting on a utility lamp.* A very strong light beam is required for dark stones to make sure they are adequately illuminated. If you have difficulty transmitting sufficient light, try using reflected light instead of transmitted.

7. *Adjust the slit at the base of the spectroscope, through which the light travels.* If the black bar or line is difficult to see, try adjusting the slit opening. Sometimes, by opening or closing it slightly, making it wider or narrower, the black bar can be more easily observed. (We do not recommend models without an adjustable slit.) Bars in the violet/blue end of the spectrum can be particularly difficult to see. Here the prism type instrument offers an advantage because the space given to the violet/blue end of the spectrum is spread out so the bars can be more easily seen.

8. *Make sure the instrument is steady.* The spectrocope must be steady or you will not be successful using it. This is another reason we do not recommend hand-held models. Use a stand to hold the spectroscope.

9. *Examine the stone from more than one direction.* If you cannot detect any distinct absorption bars, if you can pick up no distinct pattern, try examining the stone from several different directions. Sometimes you will be able to produce the pattern from one direction, but not from another.

10. *Avoid overheating the stone with prolonged exposure to the light.* The intense light required for proper illumination may cause the stone to get hot. Overheating can both damage a stone and reduce the spectroscope's effectiveness. Characteristic lines are especially difficult to detect in a treated diamond that has become overly hot from the intense lamp necessary to illuminate it. When heated, some stones lose their absorption spectra totally; others can lose it partially. Don't keep the stone being examined in the heat of the light for longer than necessary. Prior to examining, we recommend spraying the stone with a can of compressed air while holding the can upside down—this will produce the cooling agent, freon. It may give the stone a whitish appearance momentarily, but this will quickly evaporate. It will not hurt the stone or your reading. *Caution*: to cool a stone that is already hot, allow it to cool somewhat prior to spraying (to prevent possible damage from thermoshock).

WHAT THE SPECTROSCOPE WILL SHOW YOU

As we discussed earlier in the chapter, the spectroscope will show you the "characteristic spectra" of many gems—a characteristic pattern created by vertical black lines or bars occurring in a particular portion of the color spectrum where color has been absorbed by the gem. Charts have been produced showing these patterns, the "absorption spectra" for different gem materials. Simply by using these charts, and comparing them to what you are seeing with the spectroscope, you can determine the identity of many stones. However, remember that it does not always separate natural from synthetic, and you must always keep up to date on the production of new synthetic material that may react differently with the spectroscope than previous synthetics.

Absorption Patterns Are Not Exact Reproductions

The spectra you will find here (and in other books) are not exact reproductions of what you will see. There is always some degree of variation. Don't expect them to match perfectly. If the pattern is close, that's usually enough.

More important, note that the pattern of the absorption spectra seen with a prism type spectroscope will look different from that seen with a diffraction type.

Prism Type. As we've mentioned, in the spectrum produced by the prism type spectroscope you will notice that the colors seen at the violet/blue end are spread out over a wider space than the other colors, while those at the red end are crowded together into a narrower space. The spreading of the colors at the violet/blue end provides an advantage because normally it is more difficult to see the bars in the violet/indigo portion. Spreading out the colors here makes them easier to see.

Diffraction type. In the spectrum produced by the diffraction type spectroscope, you will notice that the colors are equally spaced.

Since the spacing of the spectral colors is different, the pattern produced by the black bars seen with a prism spectroscope may look very different from what is seen with the diffraction type. However, the numerical display will correspond even if the pattern looks different visually.

A FEW OF THE MOST IMPORTANT ABSORPTION SPECTRA TO KNOW

The spectroscope is especially important today for the following gems.

Alexandrite

Both natural and synthetic alexandrite show a pronounced doublet (two bars close together) in the red portion of the spectrum. The first is at about 680 (6800); the second at about 678 (6780). They may also exhibit a weak doublet at around 640 and 650. Neither synthetic color-change spinel nor synthetic color-change corundum, two gems often misrepresented as alexandrite, will exhibit this pattern or show the doublet in the red portion of the spectrum.

Fancy-color Diamond

It will be extremely difficult to see the lines in diamonds unless they are kept cool. Spray the stone with an upside-down can of compressed air to coat it with freon prior to examination. If you live near an ice cream store, see if you can get a piece of dry ice on which to place the diamond (remember to use gloves when handling dry ice). Try opening the slit to its widest position to see the lines more easily.

In general, treated diamonds will exhibit more lines than natural. Also, if the red/orange portion of the spectrum is more or less blocked-out and appears blackish or grayish, suspect treatment.

Yellow. In the case of an intense, bright yellow diamond, the presence of a distinct line in the dark violet area of the spectrum at about 415 usually indicates treatment. A line at 415 is characteristic of off-color yellowish diamonds (cape stones). A colorless diamond will have no bar or line at this point. However, stones with an off-white, yellowish color will have a line at this point. The more pronounced the line, the more off-white or yellowish the diamond. Natural-color bright fancy yellow diamonds do not exhibit this line. The presence of a *faint* line at 415 in an *intense* "fancy" yellow is immediately

indicative of an off-white diamond that has been irradiated to enhance the yellow.

Brown. Exhibits a weak line at 498, a stronger line at 504, and a
weak line at 533.

Green. May exhibit a strong 504 and very faint 498.

Some Characteristic Lines in Artificial Colored Diamonds

Brown—592, 504, 498, 465, 451, 435, 423, 415
Green—741, 504, 498, 465, 451, 435, 423, 415
Yellow—592, 504, 498 (will appear stronger than the line at 504),
478, 465, 451, 435, 423, 415.
Pink (with orange fluorscence)—A strong line at 480 and a bright
(not black) fluorescent line at 570.
IMPORTANT NOTE: The presence of a line at 592 is positive proof
of treatment. When absent, search for lines at *both* 498 and 504, with
the line at 498 being the stronger of the two. While lines at 498 and
504 may be present in natural stones, when they are both present in
a stone, with the 498 line stronger, they provide positive proof of
treatment.

Blue Sapphire

All natural blue sapphire will show a black bar in the violet/blue end
of the spectrum, at 450 (4500). It may be difficult to see, especially
in very pale blue Ceylon stones. The deeper the color, the more
distinct the line will be. A *faint* line in a *deep blue* sapphire indicates
synthetic. Most synthetic blue sapphire will not show the 450 line,
nor will blue spinel, tanzanite, and glass. *The exception*: a new
synthetic blue sapphire made today by Chatham will exhibit essentially the same spectrum as natural blue sapphire. When you see the
line at 450, other tests must be conducted to be sure it is genuine and
not one of the Chatham synthetics.

Demantoid Garnet

As we discussed earlier, since the Refractive Index of demantoid
garnet is so high, the refractometer cannot be used to identify the
stone. Therefore, the spectroscope is especially useful for this gem.

Rich, deep green stones show a doublet at the extreme red end, at about 700; sometimes they also exhibit two weak bars in the orange/ red area at about 625 and 645. Ordinary yellow green stones exhibit a very strong band in the violet, at about 440.

Natural Green Jadeite

Rich green jadeite always exhibits an unusual pattern in the red/ orange portion of the spectrum. You will see a triplet—three bars— with each bar stronger than the one adjacent to it. The strongest bar will be at about 685; the next bar is weaker and appears at about 660; the third bar is the weakest and appears at about 630 (the 630 bar may be too weak to see).

Very fine green jadeite may exhibit bars that resemble three steps leading into each other, with each step a distinctively deeper shade of color (the most deeply shaded step beginning at the farthest end of the visible red and continuing to about 685, the next step beginning at about 685 and continuing to 660, and the most lightly shaded step beginning at 660 and continuing to 630). This pattern is never exhibited by dyed green jadeite, or other materials dyed to look like it.

Note: When the Chelsea filter suggests jadeite might be naturally green, be sure to use the spectroscope for positive proof.

ABSORPTION SPECTRA FOR POPULAR GEMS

In the color insert section at the center of this book we have provided absorption spectra to assist you in recognizing characteristic spectra for several popular gems. Note that these patterns are seen using a DIFFRACTION spectroscope rather than prism. The *Handbook of Gem Identification* (Richard T. Liddicoat) provides excellent photographs of spectra seen using the prism type. Since many of our readers may already have Liddicoat's book, and more people are choosing diffraction types today than previously, we decided to provide diffraction type for comparison.

If you are using a prism spectroscope, these spectra will still be useful to you, as long as you recognize that the pattern of the bars and colors may have a different appearance than what you are actually seeing with your instrument. If you are using the prism type, rely on the numerical scale rather than the visual pattern.

In addition to Liddicoat's book, characteristic spectra for the prism type may also be found in *Gems* by Robert Webster and for characteristic diamond spectra we recommend *Diamonds* by Eric Bruton (see Appendix).

With practice, you can become very quick at recognizing the most familiar absorption spectra. But beginners should not rely entirely on the spectroscope unless the pattern is so distinct there is no doubt. Don't expect too much at first. Practice on stones with distinct patterns and build your skill slowly.

NOTES

11 / *The polariscope*

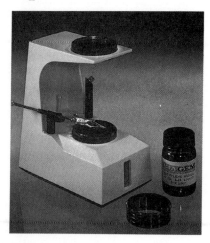

A Polariscope and
immersion cell

WHAT IS THE POLARISCOPE?

The polariscope is another instrument being employed increasingly by those interested in gem identification today, primarily because of its use in separating genuine from synthetic amethyst. The polariscope is a simple instrument, consisting of two round polarizing filters, one directly above the other, with a good light shining up from the bottom.

The upper filter can be rotated. It is usually about three inches above the lower piece, which is stationary.

HOW TO USE THE POLARISCOPE

We will discuss how to use the polariscope step by step, depending on your purpose for using it. First we'll see how to use it to determine whether a gem is single or double refracting (see Chapter 6). Next we'll discuss how to use it to separate natural from synthetic amethyst. In addition, we will mention how to use it to separate jade and chalcedony from glass or other single-refracting gems that might try to imitate it.

147

Using the Polariscope To Determine Whether a Gem Is Single- or Double-Refracting.

Until we learned of its use with amethyst, the primary purpose of the polariscope was to separate single- and double-refracting gems. To use it for this purpose is easy.

1. *Find the dark position.* First, before putting the stone in the polariscope, look through the top filter and turn it slowly. As you turn the filter, the light will become brighter and darker. In a complete rotation, it will go "bright" twice and "dark" twice. Turn the filter until you find the darkest position (this is called "crossed polars" or "crossed polarization"). Now stop.

2. *Place the stone in the polariscope between the two filters.* Place the stone in the polariscope between the two filters. We find it helpful to put the piece being examined in a small immersion cell or beaker filled with rubbing alcohol or water.

3. *Rotate the stone.* Rotate the stone laterally, approximately ¼ turn. Does it go brighter? Turn the stone another ¼ turn. Does it now go darker? If the stone is double-refracting, it will go bright, then dark again, then bright again, and dark again as you rotate the stone a full 360 degrees. In a full rotation, it will go bright twice, and dark twice. A stone that is single-refracting will remain dark continuously.

REMEMBER: After placing the stone in the polariscope, *turn the stone*, not the top filter.

AN IMPORTANT EXCEPTION: Now that you've learned how easy it is to use the polariscope, we must explain that there is an exception to the rule. We have just said that a single-refracting gem will stay dark continuously. This is true most of the time, but not in single-refracting gems that exhibit what is called "anomalous double refraction" (ADR), which means *false* double refraction.

How To Check for Anomalous Double Refraction. False double refraction is exhibited by all synthetic spinel and many garnets. If the stone you are examining appears to be one of these you must check for ADR. If you aren't sure, you must use other tests to be sure.

In Garnet. Garnet will behave in one of three ways as you rotate the stone:

1. It may behave as a normal single-refracting gem and remain dark during a full 360 degree rotation. In this case, you know the gem is single-refracting.
2. It may show *wiggly dark lines* going across the stone at random as you rotate it. This is a sure indication of ADR, of *false* double refraction. You know when you see these lines that the stone is single-refracting.

Anomalous double refraction in synthetic spinel— looks wiggly, cross-hatched

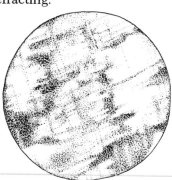

3. It may show typical bright-dark, bright-dark behavior just as in a normal double-refracting gem. In such cases, you must use other tests to be sure.

In Synthetic Spinel. With synthetic spinel you will always see wiggly black lines going across the stone at random as you rotate it. This is definite proof that the stone is not double-refracting, but single-refracting.

Using the Polariscope To Separate Natural Amethyst from Synthetic

Using the polariscope for amethyst requires a slightly different technique.

1. *Find the optic axis.* One must first find the optic axis of the stone being examined. You don't need to understand what the optic axis is, but you do need to know how to find it.

Again, before placing the stone in the polariscope, rotate the top filter until you find the darkest position and stop.

Place a small immersion cell or beaker on top of the lower filter. Pour in a little benzyl benzoate (just enough to cover the amethyst being examined). This is a refractive index liquid, available from schools such as GIA and many jewelry and chemical supply houses. It makes it easier to see what you're looking for. If none is available, use rubbing alcohol.

Place the amethyst in the liquid (you may need to use tweezers or a stone holder). Now, looking through the top filter, we'll find the optic axis of the amethyst. To do this, hold or place the stone in one position, for example, on its table facet (covered by the liquid), and then rotate it laterally while looking through the top filter. Be sure to *look through* the top filter only—*do not turn it.* Turn only the stone at this time.

If the stone stays dark as you rotate it a full 360 degrees, you've found the optic axis. If it goes bright and dark, you are not viewing it through the optic axis and must try again viewing the stone through a different direction. You might try holding it on end next. Repeat the procedure. Keep changing the direction in which you view the stone until you find the direction that stays dark as you turn it. When it stays dark, you are looking at the stone through its optic axis.

2. *View the amethyst through its optic axis.* Once you find its optic axis, *be sure to keep the stone in that position as you continue to view it.*

3. *Rotate the top filter.* Look through the top filter, and, *holding the stone still,* turn the filter until you find the bright position. What you see now will tell you whether or not the amethyst is genuine or synthetic.

If the stone looks smooth, even when viewed in this bright position, it is synthetic. If you see irregular lines (due to twinning, characteristic of all natural amethyst) you probably have a genuine stone.

We must caution you, however, that there is now a new synthetic amethyst that may also show the irregular lines characteristic of genuine. So, knowing for sure whether it is genuine may still pose a problem. *You can be sure it is synthetic if it has a nice smooth, even appearance. But you can't be sure it's genuine, even if it shows the characteristic irregular lines that indicate natural.*

The biggest mistake most people make in using the polariscope to separate synthetic and natural amethyst is not finding the optic axis of the amethyst first. In this case, one will not see the irregular lines observed in natural amethyst, and may erroneously conclude the stone is a synthetic when it may be genuine.

Using the Polariscope To Separate Jade and Chalcedony from Glass.

Jade is a polycrystalline substance. This means it is made up of numerous, small interwoven crystals. Chalcedony is cryptocrystalline (made up of numerous submicroscopic crystals). All polycrystalline and cryptocrystalline substances will stay "bright" when examined with the polariscope (using the procedure described in checking for single- and double-refraction). When rotated a full 360 degrees, these gems will not go dark/bright, dark/bright as in double-refracting stones. Nor will they stay dark, as in single-refracting gems and glass. They will remain bright.

Therefore, the polariscope can provide a very fast, simple test to separate stones such as carnelian or sard from glass imitations. If the stone goes dark, it is glass or some other imitation; if it stays bright, it's genuine. This can be especially useful when examining antique pieces that may be intricately carved and set, such as a Roman or Greek ring where one might as easily find glass as genuine.

The same holds true for jade. Jade will stay bright when examined with the polariscope. Anything that looks like jade *but goes dark with the polariscope* cannot be jade.

New *portable* RosGem polariscope with rotating lower filter for easier examination of stone. Works with standard maglite or portable diffused light unit, also made by RosGem.

12 / The electronic diamond tester

A portable diamond tester

More and more, people who are buying and selling diamonds are coming to depend on electronic diamond testers to determine genuineness. Many models are available today (see Chapter 2). Since they require no gemological skill, they make diamond testing both fast and easy—for anyone. They won't tell you what the stone is if it isn't a diamond, but, used properly, they can be very helpful, especially for the untrained. But they are not foolproof.

WHAT IS AN ELECTRONIC DIAMOND TESTER?

Most testers are small instruments that operate simply by reading the instructions, plugging them into the nearest electrical socket, and turning them on. Some also operate for a limited time by battery. They work by pressing a metal point against one of the stone's facets. The tester will then give a signal that indicates genuine or not genuine.

HOW TO USE THE DIAMOND TESTER

As we mentioned, using the electronic diamond tester is mostly a matter of reading and following instructions. But we've included a few pointers here that we feel will help optimize your use of the instrument. Some of these items are not included in the instructions so it is critical you read this chapter as carefully as you read the instructions.

153

1. *Stones must be cool.* The most important thing to understand about using electronic diamond testers is that the stone being tested must be cool. Even one's body temperature can warm a diamond sufficiently, just by wearing it. This will affect the reliability of the test. If a genuine diamond is too warm when tested, it may test not genuine. We recommend cooling the stone before testing by spraying it with an upside-down can of compressed air (to get freon), or placing it under cold water and wiping it dry prior to testing.

2. *Adjacent stones cannot be tested immediately.* It is important to understand that you cannot get a reliable reading if you consecutively test stones that are adjacent to one another (as in pieces using pavé or pieces such as wedding bands where stones are set closely together). Few realize that when the electrical charge goes through the pointer touching the stone, it heats the point. The heat from the point is then transmitted into the stone. The stone then transmits heat to the stones adjoining it. Therefore, since the adjacent stones are now warm, the tester may give a false reading. The adjacent stones may read not genuine when they are genuine because the temperature of the stones being tested is too high.

After testing the first stone, be sure to test stones that are not adjacent to it.

3. *Stones cannot be retested immediately.* If for some reason you immediately retest a diamond, you may get a different reading the second time for the same reason—overheating. After using the pointer to conduct the first test, the diamond will now be too warm and give a false reading for the second test.

4. *Be sure the pointer is not touching metal.* Electronic diamond testers will not work properly if the point is touching any metal, such as a bezel edge or a prong. Be sure the point is not in contact with metal. Some models have a "metal alert," to warn you of this problem.

5. *Keep the battery well charged.* If you are using a model that operates by battery as well as with a cord, be sure to check the battery and keep it properly charged so that you get a proper reading when not using the cord. It must be well charged or it will not work. Most now have an indictor that tells you if the battery is insufficiently charged, but remember to check.

6. *Beware of true diamond doublets.* Finally, there is one situation in which the diamond tester will always give you a false diagnosis— when testing a true diamond doublet (see Chapter 13). While we

haven't seen many of these recently, they still pop up from time to time, especially in antique and estate jewelry. A true diamond doublet is made by taking a genuine diamond top (crown) and gluing it to a genuine diamond bottom (pavilion). The diamond tester will indicate that the stone is genuine because the material being tested is diamond. This is why it's called a true doublet—it is actually made from genuine pieces of the stone it is imitating. The diamond tester cannot tell you it's a doublet. Again, review the section on doublets so you can make this determination yourself.

Increasingly we are finding reliable, well-made, portable equipment to aid in gem identification when one is away from the laboratory. With the instruments shown above, one has virtually everything needed for most gem identification. The components of this new RosGem system are interchangeable—the diffused-light unit illuminates the immersion cell and/or polariscope; the large maglite illuminates the dark-field loupe and/or the polariscope; the small maglite illuminates the refractometer and/or diffused light unit for immersion cell. The immersion cell can also be used with polariscope.

PART 5

ANTIQUE AND ESTATE JEWELRY

13 / *Antique and estate jewelry—true test of gem-identification skill*

More and more, jewelry lovers have begun to focus on antique and estate jewelry. It has become an important new profit center for many jewelry firms, as well as a growing passion for jewelry collectors. Retailers and gem enthusiasts alike are travelling greater distances and paying higher prices so they can add that unique piece to their collection.

Recent record-breaking sales at auction houses such as Christie's and Sotheby's reflect the trend. We have also noticed an increase in the number of retailers offering antique and estate jewelry, as well as more exhibitors of antique and estate pieces at international gem and jewelry exhibitions, antique shows, and flea markets.

We share the current enthusiasm for antique and period jewelry. But as we examine many of these pieces, we are reminded of the ingenuity of our predecessors—ingenuity not only in design, but in the art of creating pieces that *appear to be something they are not.*

For the gem "detective," antique and estate jewelry offers a real testing ground for your skill. Don't be surprised to find imitation stones in beautiful gold or platinum settings, and synthetic stones in pieces made prior to the production of synthetic gems. Never assume that because something is old, or belonged to the best of families or most endeared of relatives, that it is what it appears to be. As you will see, often this is not the case.

In this chapter we will discuss some of the imitation and alteration techniques frequently encountered in antique and period jewelry. Anyone identifying stones in old jewelry should be on the lookout for them.

ENHANCEMENT TECHNIQUES

Dyeing

Dyeing is one of the oldest techniques used to enhance stones for jewelry. It has been practiced since earliest times, particularly with the less expensive gemstone called chalcedony (a variety of quartz). Other stones frequently dyed are jade, opal, coral, lapis, and, to a lesser extent, poor-quality star rubies, star sapphires, and emeralds.

What follows is a list of stones often found dyed in antique jewelry (some of these stones have been subjected to dyeing for hundreds of years; others are of more recent vintage but find their way into antique pieces to replace lost or damaged stones).

Chalcedony. Dyed to produce stones that look like black onyx, banded agate, carnelian, and chrysoprase (which was often mistaken for jade). It is often found in antique jewelry.

Jade (Jadeite). Dyed to improve the color so that it resembles the beautiful emerald-green of imperial jade. It is also dyed colors other than green.

Coral and lapis. Dyed to deepen the color or create more uniform color.

Jasper. Dyed blue to resemble lapis and often sold as lapis, Swiss lapis, or German lapis.

Blackening

Blackening is a technique also used to alter color. It is done by starting a sugar-acid chemical reaction that produces carbon to blacken the color. This technique was used primarily with opal, to blacken it so it more closely resembled valuable black opal. This technique was also used on chalcedony to create "black onyx." Blackening of opal can be detected with the loupe or microscope because magnification reveals fine pinholes on the polished surface. With black onyx, however, there is no way to detect this treatment.

Smoking

Smoking is a technique used only for opal. An opal is wrapped in brown paper that is then charred. The charred paper deposits a thin dark brown coating on the opal to intensify its fire (the play of color that makes opal so desirable). This thin coating, however, eventually wears off. Normally such opals are easy to spot because they have a chocolate brown appearance not common to opal. If you suspect smoking, it can be detected simply by wetting the stone and observing the fire. In smoked opals the fire is diminished when wet, but returns when dry. Natural opals show essentially the same brilliance wet or dry.

Waxing

Waxing is a process used to enhance poor quality star rubies and, occasionally, star sapphires. It involves rubbing the stone with a tinted waxlike substance to hide surface cracks and blemishes and to improve color.

Waxing is detectable with a loupe or microscope.

Foil Backing and Diamond Jewelry

Foil backing is one of the most clever techniques from the olden days and, occasionally, even today. It was often used with stones that were set in closed-back settings (where you can't see the back of the stone). The technique simply involved lining the setting with a piece of colored metallic foil, and was used both for transparent cabochon stones and faceted stones. The foil was used to add brilliance and enhance or change the color.

Early diamond jewelry was sometimes foil backed to enhance the brilliance of the stones. Before diamond cutters perfected their art, diamonds lacked the brilliance we see today. By adding foil to the setting, the jeweler could add greater sparkle to the stones. Silver-foil backing was also used to mask the yellow in a diamond's body color, making the stone appear whiter.

In such pieces, the stones are genuine and the foil backing was used simply to enhance their beauty and desirability. When it comes to some of these early antique pieces, the diamond value is usually minimal, although it is really impossible to evaluate them properly without removing them from the setting. In most cases, however, removing them isn't advised because damage to the setting might reduce the value of the piece as a work of art. Careful consideration should always be given prior to removing stones from foil-backed settings.

Foil backing was not restricted to enhancement of genuine diamonds. It was more commonly used (and is still occasionally encountered in new jewelry) to create attractive imitations. When foil was placed behind glass or some other less valuable stone (such as colorless sapphire or topaz), it produced a clever imitation of diamond.

Several years ago, a young woman brought us a diamond ring inherited from her great-grandmother. It turned out, unfortunately, to be an excellent example of foil backing. As she unwrapped the ring from the handkerchief in which it was placed, she mentioned that one of its two diamonds had fallen out of the setting as she was cleaning it. Inside the setting she saw what she described as pieces of "tiny, mirror-like" fragments. She commented on how strange this was, but, unfortunately, it isn't as strange as most people think.

When we saw the ring we could immediately understand why she thought it was a fine heirloom. The ring was beautiful. Its design was classic. It held two "diamonds" appearing to be approximately one carat each. The ring mounting was finely worked platinum. But, alas, the stones were glass. The mirror-like fragments were pieces of silver foil. The foil acted as a mirror to reflect light back from the glass to the eye of the observer, causing the glass to appear brilliant enough to pass for genuine diamond!

Piggy-Backing—The Foil-Backing Master's Art

Sometimes the foil backing had a special touch—the addition of a genuine diamond table and culet. The cleverest fake of all used foil backing in combination with a genuine diamond top and bottom— *with nothing but foil in between the two parts*. This is called piggy-backing. It is a very ingenius device to create the illusion that a diamond is larger than it really is. There are two types of piggy-backing.

In the first type, a small genuine diamond is set into the top portion of a ring. The mounting is constructed with a wide box-like bezel or rim that begins at the girdle and follows what should be the contour of the diamond down the pavilion to a small opening through which the culet can be observed. The top portion of the diamond is genuine and the culet is also genuine. But there is nothing between the top piece of diamond and the bottom piece except foil lining the setting. It is hollow!

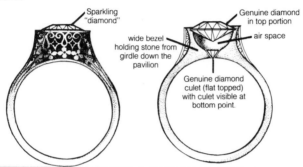

"Piggy back" diamond ring. As you can see from the cross-section, a *small* diamond sits in the very top, and a *small* diamond sits in the bottom, with only air in-between. Sometimes foil lines the inside of the bezel as well. An ingenious way to create a large diamond look!

The second method is often seen in jewelry using rose-cut diamonds and is also intended to make the stones appear deeper and heavier than they are. This method involves stamping the back of a closed-back setting with a *perfectly symmetrical facet pattern*. The back is painted with silver gilt. The diamond is mounted into the top of the setting—with nothing but air between it and the stamped back.

We recently examined an antique piece containing eight rose-cut diamonds. Keep in mind that there are different types of rose-cuts—some have a flat bottom (single-rose-cut); others have a bottom portion cut like the top portion (double-rose-cut). When we viewed this antique piece from the top, the diamonds all appeared to be lovely, large, *double-rose-cut* stones. However, they were not. What appeared to be depth—a bottom portion—was actually an optical illusion created by the gilt-covered, stamped back.

This latter method is easy to detect with a loupe. The first clue is the completely closed back. On careful examination of both the back facets and the top facets you will see something very curious. You will notice that *all* the back facets are *perfectly* symmetrical while the top

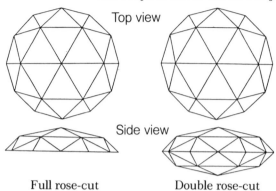

Full rose-cut   Double rose-cut

facets are more or less *asymmetrical.* This occurs because the back facets aren't really facets, but a gilt imprint resulting from the precise machine-stamping. This is why it's so perfectly uniform. The top facets, however, are done very sloppily (they didn't merit careful cutting). In the antique piece we examined, we could see that all the back facets, in each of the eight rose-cuts, were perfectly symmetrical while the top facets weren't symmetrical at all. In such pieces, this is always the case—sloppy symmetry on the top facets and perfect symmetry on the bottom facets.

Foil Backing and Colored Gems

Foil backing was not restricted to diamond jewelry. It was frequently used with colored gems (and occasionally still is). We actually see more examples of foil backing in colored gemstone jewelry than in diamond jewelry. It served essentially the same purpose—to enhance brilliance and color, and to create clever imitations.

Sometimes foil was used (silver and gold were both common) simply to increase the brilliance and sparkle of the stones, or, in some cases, to lighten the appearance of stones that looked too dark in the setting. But more often than not, in colored gemstone jewelry the foil itself was *colored.* Coloring the foil added greater depth of color to a stone that was too light, and, when used with a colorless gem, could create any color gemstone desired. In antique jewelry one can find examples of colored foil used with glass; colored foil used with pale stones to deepen color; and colored foil used with colorless stones to add color.

Several years ago we purchased an antique necklace from a New York auction gallery (see color photos in center of this book). The necklace was described in bold print as an "antique 22 karat gold and topaz necklace." In the further description of the piece, provided in small print, it stated the necklace dated about 1810 and contained "pink topaz."

Foil-backed pink topaz necklace

Notice the pink foil that has been removed and the *colorless* topaz alongside

In examining the stone, it gave all the indicators of genuine topaz. It was also obvious (as you will understand in a moment) that the piece was foil backed. The unanswered question was, What is the true color of the topaz? Of course, there was no way to answer the question without removing the stones, which was not possible under the circumstances. We purchased the necklace at a price we felt reflected the value of the gold, pearls, and workmanship and discounted the stones altogether.

After purchasing the necklace we removed one of the stones. The stones were topaz, but not rare, valuable "pink" topaz. They were common, very inexpensive, colorless topaz that appeared pink because pink foil had been placed behind each stone.

This is not always the case. We've seen magnificent closed-back pieces that contain rich, deeply colored pink topazes (and other gems as well) that are indeed natural color. The golden reflections from the closed backs sometimes brighten the stones, but often the setting simply reflects the style of the day.

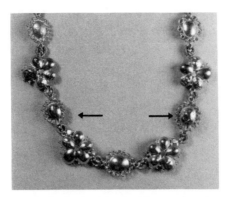

Notice the back of the necklace is *closed*—the gold completely conceals the backs of the stones themselves. Also, notice the gold on the back of the left-hand stone is smooth and unbroken while the gold on the back of the other stone has a "V"-shaped crack. The crack allows air to enter, which oxidizes the foil and causes it to change color.

Notice the stone on the left is a distinctly different shade of color than other stones in the necklace. This has resulted from oxidation.

Spotting a Foil-Backed Stone

This usually requires only a good eye. The first clue will be the fact that the back of the setting will be closed. While not all closed-back settings conceal some form of deception, many do. One should always examine stones set in closed-back settings with extreme care. While gently tilting the setting back and forth, carefully look through the stone at the back facets. Use a strong, direct light such as a fiber-optic light or penlight. It is usually easy to spot the light reflecting off the foil—it will look different from a stone's natural reflectivity. Also, where colored foil has been used, you may be able to observe slight variations in the color of the foil itself. Discoloration will take place if for some reason air has reached the foil and caused it to oxidize (if, for example, there is a hairline crack in the backing or in the bezel holding the stone). With a loupe, one can usually spot the foil immediately, as well as the reflectivity differences and color inconsistencies. However, sometimes it is necessary to use a microscope.

Once you determine the presence of foil backing, you must use your other gemological skills to determine whether the stone in question is glass or genuine, and, if genuine, whether it is the stone it appears to be or one from another gem family. Finally, you must determine whether the color has been enhanced by the foil. If the stone can't be removed without damage to the setting, this may pose a problem. A dichroscope can be useful in this situation (see Chapter 6). In the case of our pink topaz necklace, for example, the dichroscope could have told us immediately that it didn't contain pink topaz. Pink topaz will show two distinctly different shades of pink when examined with the dichroscope; colorless topaz will show only one.

The depth of color seen with the dichroscope can also be helpful. For example, if "emerald" is created by using *pale* emerald and deep green foil to enhance its color and value, the dichroism—the colors seen in the windows of the dichroscope—will be *weak*. However, genuine deep green emerald would have a strong dichroism—the colors seen in the dichroscope will be deeper. The depth of color seen with the dichroscope reflects the depth of the color in the gem being viewed. So, if the color seen in the piece is deep, but the colors seen with the dichroscope are weak, you should be immediately suspicious.

No one interested in buying and selling antique and estate jewelry can afford to make an assumption based on appearance and superficial examination!

COMPOSITE STONES–DOUBLETS AND TRIPLETS

Composite stones were used extensively prior to the introduction of synthetic material. Simply stated, a composite stone is exactly what its name implies, a stone composed or made up of more than one part. A composite stone is any stone created by the fusing or cementing together of two or more pieces of material. When two main pieces are joined together we call them "doublets," and when three pieces are joined together we call them "triplets."

There are, however, some differences in terminology. The soudé type composite is called a "doublet" in Europe and a "triplet" in America, probably because there is disagreement over whether or not the layer of colored gelatin or glass that lays across the girdle plane constitutes another part. Today the term "doublet" is generally applied to stones created by joining two pieces of material with a *colorless* bonding agent and the term "triplet" to stones created by joining together three pieces, or two pieces that are joined by a *colored* bonding agent.

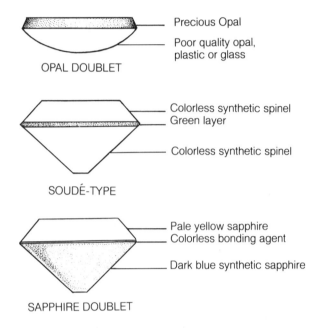

Composite stones (also called assembled stones)

Composites have been around for a long time. Doublets have been made since Roman times and used extensively through the Victorian period (until about 1900). They are also being made and sold today. Therefore, one must check for doublets not only in antique jewelry, but in new jewelry as well.

Two years ago, we met a young man in the diplomatic corps who thought he could make some extra money importing stones for which his country was famous. He had a "friend" in one of the mining districts who sent him a shipment of very fine aquamarine. He brought them to a local jeweler who brought them to us to examine because the price seemed too attractive. All were composites.

These "aquamarines" were made by taking colorless quartz tops and gluing them with blue glue to colorless quartz bottoms. It was easy to determine they were not aquamarine because they didn't exhibit the dichroism typical of aquamarine (see Chapter 6). Examination with the dichroscope told us immediately that there was something wrong—there was no dichroism.

Doublets and triplets should never be referred to as "genuine" stones (even if their respective parts are, in fact, genuine pieces of the stone they appear to be). Doublets and triplets generally were made for one of three reasons—to enhance the appearance of poor quality stones, to assemble small stones to create a larger stone, or to imitate more desirable, valuable gems. In the case of opal, the backing provided in a doublet or triplet serves to provide support for very thin opal that would break without such a backing.

Types of Composite Stones

There are many different types of composite stones. We will discuss some of the more common types.

Doublets. Doublets are the most frequently encountered type of composite stone. And the most commonly encountered doublet is a garnet-topped doublet, often referred to as a false doublet. The garnet-topped doublet consists of a thin portion of red garnet fused to glass. With the right combination, any gem could be simulated by this method, even diamond.

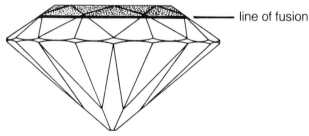

line of fusion

Garnet-topped doublet

Garnets were used for the top portion of these doublets because of their high luster, excellent durability, and easy availability. They wouldn't crack when fused with the glass, and, perhaps most important (and very difficult for anyone unfamiliar with these doublets to believe), even though red garnet was used, the red in its natural color did not affect the color seen in the final product. When one looks at a garnet-topped-glass "sapphire," for example, there will be no trace of red.

Garnet-topped glass doublets made excellent imitations of topaz, sapphire, emerald, ruby, and amethyst, and were used extensively in antique jewelry in the era prior to the availability of synthetic stones (the Verneuil process, the first commercial method for synthesizing gem material, was announced in 1902). Doublets are encountered extensively in Victorian jewelry as well as jewelry from earlier periods.

Another type of doublet is made by taking two parts of a gemlike material, usually colorless, and cementing or fusing it together in the middle with an appropriately colored glue. For example, a colorless synthetic spinel top and bottom held together in the middle (at the girdle) by red, green, or blue glue will make an excellent "ruby," "emerald," or "sapphire."

True Doublets. There are also doublets that are referred to as true doublets because they are made from two pieces of the genuine stone they are trying to create. Blue sapphire doublets are true doublets, composed of two parts of genuine sapphire. But the pieces are usually inexpensive, common *pale yellow* sapphire. The top and bottom are cemented with blue glue, so the resulting product is a "blue sapphire." These are especially convincing.

Another type of sapphire doublet is even more cleverly constructed and is particularly difficult to detect. This type is composed of a *genuine pale-yellow sapphire top fused to a synthetic blue sapphire bottom*. The result is a stone that appears to be a very fine *genuine blue sapphire*.

These can fool even a good gemologist because three different tests will all indicate that the stone is genuine when it is not. Normally the loupe, dichroscope, and refractometer would provide sufficient information to know what you have, but with this type of doublet they aren't enough. More important, if you stop after only these tests the information they provide may lead you to erroneously conclude such a doublet is genuine. Here's how. First, both the dichroscope and refractometer will give readings that indicate blue sapphire. A good gemologist, however, understands that these instruments can't separate natural sapphire from synthetic, so the next step would be examination with the loupe. With the loupe one can be easily misled by the inclusions *in the natural pale-yellow sapphire top*. The inclusions seen in the genuine, natural sapphire are indicative of natural rather than synthetic because the top portion *is* natural. So, in this case, the inclusions in the top portion of the doublet will lead one to conclude that the whole stone is genuine—genuine, fine *blue* sapphire.

Sometimes you can see the difference in color between the top and bottom if you are able to look across the stone, through the girdle. If the stone is set in a way that prevents this, the spectroscope can immediately tell you something is wrong. The microscope will also reveal telltale signs at the girdle. And, finally, if immersed in methylene iodide you will see immediately that you have a doublet because the entire top portion of the stone seems to disappear while in the liquid.

True-emerald-doublets and true-ruby-doublets are also encountered (although ruby doublets don't look as convincing). These are usually made by cementing together two pieces of pale or colorless beryl (for emerald) or corundum (for ruby) with the appropriate color glue. We've also seen true-emerald-doublets made from a piece of overly dark green emerald glued to a piece of pale or colorless beryl to create a larger "emerald."

Soudé-type. The soudé-type is often used to imitate emerald (and other stones less frequently). Here the "emerald" is created from two pieces of colorless stone, such as quartz or, today, synthetic colorless spinel, fused with a layer of green-colored gelatin (old type) or green glass (new type). Flawed stones are sometimes used to imitate emerald-like flaws. Colorless synthetic spinel also is used, and the spinel can be given a crackled effect to create a similar emerald-inclusion look.

We have a beautiful, large antique soudé-emerald ring that we use in lectures. Everyone goes "ooh" and "aah" the moment they see it. We then submerge it in methylene iodide and everyone gasps as the top and bottom portions of the stone *totally disappear* (after all, they are really colorless) leaving only a thin plane of dark green glue visible (which appears across the plane of the girdle)!

Sometimes pale genuine pieces of the stone being created are used, but the colored layer improves the color significantly. For example, a stone made with a crown and pavilion of *pale green* beryl with a layer of deep green glass or gelatin can make a very convincing fine, large deep-green emerald.

Diamond Doublets. One must also be attentive to the existence of diamond doublets, although they don't appear often. They are made by glueing together two pieces of diamond to create the appearance of one larger diamond. Sometimes the crown is a re-cut "old mine" or "old European" stone, glued to a pavilion made from another piece of diamond. Occasionally one may see a diamond doublet composed of a genuine diamond crown glued to another material such as synthetic sapphire or synthetic spinel. You might also encounter a stone with a genuine diamond crown, a genuine diamond culet, and, as we discussed with foil-backs, nothing but metallic foil in between.

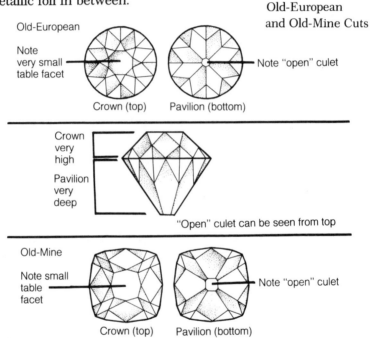

Old-European

and Old-Mine Cuts

Old-European

Note very small table facet

Note "open" culet

Crown (top)   Pavilion (bottom)

Crown very high

Pavilion very deep

"Open" culet can be seen from top

Old-Mine

Note small table facet

Note "open" culet

Crown (top)   Pavilion (bottom)

Side profile is similar in both. The Old-Mine cut has a higher crown and deeper pavilion than the Old-European, and is usually "cushion" shaped as illustrated here.

Opal Doublets and Triplets. There are also opal doublets. These usually consist of a thin top layer of genuine opal cemented to a base of poor quality opal or some other substance altogether.

The most commonly encountered opal doublets are those made to resemble the precious black opal. These are usually composed of a translucent or transparent top cemented with black cement to a bottom portion of cheap opal or other material that acts as a support.

The top of these "black opal" doublets is seldom genuine black opal, though they certainly do look like it.

Opal doublets can also be made by cementing a piece of fine opal to a larger piece of less fine opal to create a larger overall appearance. If the girdle can be observed, these doublets can be detected by noting the dark line where the cement joins the two pieces (the cement is usually black).

Triplets are frequently encountered in the opal market and have essentially replaced the opal doublet. These are similar to the opal doublet except a cabochon cap of colorless quartz (the third part) has been placed over the entire doublet, adding brightness and giving the delicate doublet greater protection from breakage.

Jadeite Triplets. Sometimes encountered, these are made by joining together three pieces of common white jadeite with a green cement that resembles mint jelly. They usually have a hollowed-out cabochon that is fitted onto another cabochon. A layer of green glue is inserted between the two, giving a green color to the whole stone. These can be very difficult to detect when set, but the abnormal pattern seen with the spectroscope can tell you immediately that you don't have natural green jadeite.

Composite Star Sapphire. This is a stone that has only recently entered the market. An excellent imitation of greyish-blue star sapphire, it is made by assembling star rose quartz, blue glass with a mirror on its underside, and dyed blue chalcedony to form the back. Some have also been made by "sputtering" a mirror-like substance to the back of star rose quartz.

The doublets and triplets we've covered here represent those that are most commonly encountered. Any stone can be imitated by doublets or triplets. Amethyst, topaz, even garnet itself can be created with composite stones. It is important to check for them particularly in antique jewelry, but never forget they are still being made today.

Detecting Doublets

Sometimes it is difficult to detect a well-made doublet or triplet, but most can be fairly quickly detected with a few simple tests, especially if the girdle and pavilion can be easily examined.

Examine with a Loupe.

1. *From the top* (Opals and Diamonds). When examining opals, first examine them from the top with the loupe, looking for the presence of any small telltale bubbles. Opal doublets and triplets usually reveal small bubbles when examined carefully with a loupe or higher magnification, evidence of more than one part being glued together (the bubbles in doublets or triplets are *flattened* air bubbles trapped in the cement between the two layers and will look more like flat discs than round bubbles). It is particularly important to examine opals carefully. Opal doublets and triplets are usually bezel-set so that the girdle can't be examined and, therefore, the line at the girdle where the parts are glued together can't be seen. When opals are bezel-set, one should be particularly cautious and alert to the possibility of a composite stone.

With black opals, also examine the stone from the back. Genuine black opals usually have a black or grayish-black back, whereas black opal doublets or triplets will not.

When examining diamonds, the use of a loupe with a strong light shining down on top of the stone will usually expose a diamond doublet. As we mentioned, diamond doublets may be made by glueing two pieces of genuine diamond (true doublets)—one piece forming the crown portion, one forming the pavilion portion—to make a larger diamond. Such stones are easy to detect. Examine the stone with the loupe, looking through the table at a slight angle, slowly tilting it back and forth. If the stone is a doublet, you will see a reflection of the table on the plane where the two parts are glued together. A normal diamond will not exhibit any such reflection.

 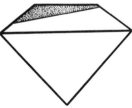 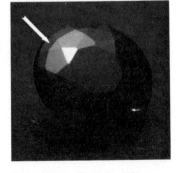

Garnet-topped doublet from top and side. Notice the garnet fused to the glass is not uniform in size or shape.

Right: A garnet-topped doublet examined with reflected light. Note the difference in the shininess (see arrow) where the garnet and glass appear side-by-side. This results from differences in reflectivity (the way they reflect light).

2. *From the side of the crown* (Colored Gems). First, examine the stone focusing on the side of the crown portion with a strong light shining from above. In garnet-topped doublets you should be able to see a difference in the reflectivity of the light where the garnet portion and the glass are joined. The garnet portion will be much *shinier* than the glass. You can easily spot the contrast between the two with a little practice. You should be able to observe this in any garnet-topped doublet. *Note*: The garnet top seldom constitutes the entire crown of the stone. It is usually an irregular section that includes the table and only a portion of the top part of the crown. Therefore, to detect this telltale contrast, you must rotate the stone, always keeping the light shining on the sloping area, to make sure you find where the glass and garnet are joined.

3. *From the girdle.* If the girdle is visible, examine it carefully and you will see where the stone has been fused or cemented together. If you can't see the girdle, examine the stone from the top and look for the characteristic disc-like inclusions (flattened air bubbles, all on the same plane, trapped where the parts have been fused together).

Examine with Liquid. This is the easiest and most positive way to detect many doublets or triplets. Immerse the stone or piece of jewelry in rubbing alcohol, using tweezers. Once immersed, many

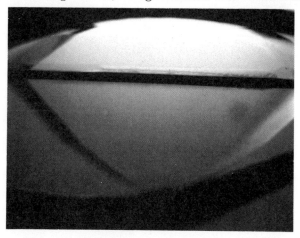

When some composite stones are immersed in *liquid* (such as alcohol or methylene iodide) one can often see two or three distinct parts. With soudé emeralds, the top and bottom may seem to disappear, leaving only a green plane visible across the girdle area. (Note: Immersion will not reveal garnet-topped doublets.)

doublets will exhibit a strange phenomenon—instead of seeing one stone, you will see two or three distinct parts. One or more of the parts may even seem to disappear (because they may actually be colorless). You can actually see the lines of demarcation showing where the parts have been fused or cemented together. *Note*: you will not see this phenomenon with garnet-topped doublets. If alcohol doesn't reveal anything, you may want to try immersing the piece in methylene iodide (diiodomethane). Methylene iodide often makes it easier to see. We frequently use it and have never had a negative reaction, but be careful not to leave the stone in the liquid for any extended length of time. The chemical may attack the glue or cement, weaken it, and alter the appearance of the stone.

Examine with a Dichroscope. Since most colored gems are dichroic, it is often possible to separate a doublet or triplet from the gem it is trying to imitate by using the dichroscope. This will work with all garnet-topped glass doublets and some false doublets. It will not be conclusive for true doublets or doublets such as the sapphire doublet we mentioned earlier (with the genuine pale yellow sapphire top and synthetic blue sapphire bottom).

With the dichroscope, one can usually tell in seconds if the stone is not what it appears to be. If the stone appears to be emerald, but is a false doublet, the dichroscope will not exhibit the colors that are appropriate for emerald. For example, a soudé-type emerald made with a synthetic white spinel or colorless quartz top and bottom, cemented with a layer of green glass or gelatin, will not exhibit the dichroic colors that would be exhibited by emerald. If it were emerald, green would be seen in one window of the dichroscope and bluish-green or yellowish-green in the second window. With the doublet, one will see only green; you will not be able to pick up a second color. The dichroscope may not tell you the stone is a doublet, but it will inform you it is not an emerald.

If you get only one color with the dichroscope, and the stone you're examining is supposed to show two colors, you will know that something is wrong, that the stone must be something else. In this case, other tests should tell you what you really have.

A word of warning is needed here. The dichroscope provides an immediate signal that a stone is not what it may appear to be only when you *DON'T see what you should*. The converse is not true. If you do see what you should see, you could still have a doublet—a true doublet. Other tests are required to know for sure.

Examine Against a White Surface. This is a simple test to use on unmounted stones. It will quickly reveal garnet-topped glass doublets if the stone it is imitating is *any color other than red*. Place the stone, table down, on a piece of white paper or other white background. Placing it table down on top of a few drops of water on a white ceramic surface works especially well, but simply placing it on any white background will also work. Look straight down on the stone. If you have a garnet-topped doublet you will see a red ring around the girdle. It may be weak or it may be distinct, but if it's there you have a doublet. Just remember, this test is only reliable for stones that are not red.

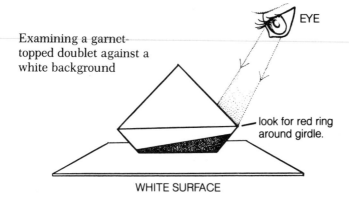

Examining a garnet-topped doublet against a white background

look for red ring around girdle.

WHITE SURFACE

Examine With A Spectroscope. Abnormal absorption spectra provide an immediate indicator that a stone is not what it appears to be. As in the case of jadeite triplets, the dye used in the green jelly causes an inappropriate spectral pattern to be seen. For stones that are set, the spectroscope can be fast and effective.

Failure To Be Thorough Can Cause Error

It is especially important to understand that you will not succeed in detecting certain types of doublets if you rely exclusively on inclusions, refractive index, or dichroism alone for positive ID. These tests can lead you to an erroneous conclusion.

For example, in the case of the sapphire doublet we mentioned earlier, the type made with a genuine pale yellow sapphire top and a dark blue synthetic sapphire bottom, these tests alone would lead you to conclude you were examining a genuine blue sapphire. Since the top is genuine sapphire (being yellow won't make any difference), you will see typical sapphire inclusions and since the bottom is dark blue (being synthetic won't make any difference) you would get the correct dichroism for blue sapphire. Also, because of the yellow sapphire top, you will also get the correct refractive index reading for sapphire.

When other tests indicate genuine, always be sure to examine carefully with the loupe or higher magnification for join lines, bubbles where the stone could be fused or cemented together, and differences in reflectivity between the different portions of a composite stone.

With a little practice one can learn to spot many doublets or triplets very quickly. As with all gem identification, however, it is usually easier to grasp if you spend a little time with a gemologist, focusing exclusively on composite stones. If there is a school that teaches gemology in your area (see Appendix), it might be possible to arrange to spend an hour or two studying composite stones from their teaching collection. If you can't locate anyone in your community, please write to us and we'll be happy to try to put you in touch with someone who might be helpful.

IMITATIONS AND SYNTHETICS ABOUND

We've already discussed numerous techniques used over the centuries to alter or enhance color and to imitate various stones, such as foil backing, piggy-backing, and the creation of composite stones. Now we will discuss imitations and synthetics to guard against whenever buying antique and estate jewelry.

Few realize how long humans have been imitating rare and beautiful gems. One of the earliest known imitations was turquoise. Highly prized by the Egyptians for both its beauty and magical powers, the Egyptians succeeded over 7,000 years ago in making a turquoise-colored ceramic material called faience that was used to make beads, amulets, pendants, and rings. They are also known to have produced beautiful glass, such as the lovely blue glass gems discovered in King Tut's tomb.

Glass has been used as a simulant for thousands of years. Most of us are aware of these fakes. We are also acutely aware of the use of synthetics today. But few think about synthetics when they examine old jewelry—especially very old jewelry. Few realize how long synthetics have been produced commercially. And fewer still are alert to the fact that often the original stones in a very old or antique piece have been damaged or lost and then replaced with a synthetic. Making assumptions because something is old can be very costly.

How Is a *SIMULANT* Different from a *SYNTHETIC*?

The terms "simulant" and "imitation" mean the same thing for our purposes, and can be used interchangeably. However, synthetic has a different, and very specific, meaning. These terms are confusing to many so, before we begin, we'd like to explain what each means.

A simulated gem is made by man. It's important to understand, however, that *a simulant has no counterpart found in nature.* For example, a brilliant green stone such as green YAG may have an emerald-green color and resemble an emerald, but it won't have any of the physical properties of real emerald. Nor will it have any physical properties of any other green gem that occurs in nature. It was not intended to duplicate a natural stone. YAG is a simulant or imitation. Glass is a simulant. Simulants are easy to distinguish from genuine gems of the same color since they are very different physically. Color is usually the only thing they have in common. The eye alone can often tell a simulant from the genuine—too much brilliance, not enough brilliance, etc. A few simple tests (often just the loupe) will quickly separate the simulant from the genuine.

A synthetic gem, however, while also made by man, has been scientifically developed *to duplicate a gem that occurs naturally.* It will, therefore, have virtually the same physical and chemical properties of the stone it appears to be. A synthetic stone may be easily confused with the genuine if one does not examine it carefully. Chatham emeralds are synthetic—they duplicate a substance found in nature and possess essentially the same physical and chemical characteristics. The Kashan ruby is a synthetic ruby, and was so close to the genuine that when it was first introduced it was mistaken by many for the genuine.

Synthetic gems have been produced commercially since the beginning of this century—synthetic ruby was being produced commercially in 1905 (although it was available earlier), synthetic blue spinel was introduced in 1908 (widely available after 1925), and synthetic blue sapphire in 1911.

In fact, many pieces of jewelry from the early part of the 20th century contained small synthetic gems to add color and accent other genuine gems. We have a beautiful natural seed pearl bracelet accentuated with genuine diamonds and *synthetic* blue sapphires. The sapphires are small, calibre-cut stones used to provide color. Given their small size, the fact that they're synthetic rather than genuine doesn't really affect the overall value of this beautiful piece. Nonetheless, it's important to know they're synthetic. If I sold this bracelet and neglected to point out that the sapphires are not genuine, my credibility and overall reputation would be seriously damaged if the buyer were to learn of it later.

Synthetic Stones in ANTIQUE Jewelry.

One must also be alert to the fact that synthetic stones may also appear in jewelry made long before synthetics were being produced—jewelry in which missing stones have been replaced.

We can't overemphasize the importance of carefully examining any stone that appears to be a fine gem. One cannot make assumptions based on the age of a jewelry piece, the reputation of the family to which it belonged, the beauty and detail in the workmanship, or the quality of diamonds used to enhance the main stone. In Geneva, Switzerland, at the auction of the magnificent jewels of the Duchess of Windsor, you may remember there was a strand of pearls that belonged to the Duchess. These pearls were listed in the catalogue as genuine, cultured pearls. They were not. They were fake! A serious mistake was made because someone *assumed*, given who the owner was, that they could only have been genuine. After all, who could have imagined the Duchess with a strand of fake pearls! Be careful not to make similar assumptions. (The auction house did announce the error prior to the start of bidding.)

We've seen examples of synthetic ruby, emerald, and sapphire used in magnificent, diamond-studded jewelry from the early part of this century. And we've seen much earlier jewelry that contains synthetic center stones, some complete with 18th- or 19th-century hallmarks, even enhanced by antique-cut diamonds appropriate to the age of the piece.

Even though synthetics may not yet have been produced at the time a given piece of jewelry was made, one must always be alert to the possibility of an original stone having been replaced with a synthetic. It is not unusual for a stone to be lost or damaged and then replaced with something less valuable than the original. Sad, but true.

Tremendous progress has been made in the area of synthesizing gems in recent decades. Synthetic emerald came on the scene in the 1930s, star ruby in the 1940s. In the 1970s, synthetic turquoise entered the market, as well as synthetic amethyst, synthetic alexandrite, and synthetic opal. In the 1980s, we find synthetic jadeite jade being produced (not yet commercially), and, most recently, the seemingly impossible has been achieved—gem-quality synthetic diamond has been produced (although currently only very small fancy-color yellow stones are being manufactured in any quantity).

Detecting Synthetics

Synthetic gems offer affordable alternatives to natural gems today. However, they also pose problems for today's jeweler and gem enthusiast because they are so difficult to distinguish from genuine. Although we've discussed how to identify synthetic stones in earlier chapters, we'd like to make a few additional comments here.

Today's synthetics present a real challenge. Some appear to be flawless when examined with the 10X loupe, and require very high magnification—sometimes up to 60X or more—to spot inclusions indicating synthetic. Others are being produced with visible inclusions to more closely imitate what one normally sees in the natural. We recommend very careful examination of any fine gem.

1. *Examine with a microscope.* Most gem enthusiasts today realize that flawless, gem-quality emeralds, sapphires, or rubies are so rare that such a stone is most likely synthetic. When a gem has typical looking inclusions, however, one is normally less suspicious. Yet inclusions now found in synthetic stones have been developed to better simulate the natural stone. Remember, careful examination

with the microscope (with at least 60X magnification) is essential for any gem that appears to be genuine.

2. *Examine with the spectroscope.* Old-type synthetics such as the Verneuil synthetic sapphire are also posing problems today: they are being heated to remove their telltale signs. Heat treatment of the Verneuil type synthetic blue sapphire can successfully remove the curved striae (curved lines) and color zoning. Even with the microscope it might be difficult to determine that one of these stones is synthetic. So, when examining blue sapphire with fine color—not too dark, not too light—it is essential to examine also with the spectroscope (see Chapter 10). If the stone is an old-type synthetic, no absorption line will be observed at 450 (4500). *Note: very dark* blue synthetic material may show a weak band at 450 (4500) and *very pale* natural blue sapphire may exhibit nothing.

3. *Examine with a polariscope.* There is a tremendous amount of synthetic amethyst currently on the market. Most of it is being properly represented as synthetic but some is being sold as genuine. So, careful examination with the polariscope is essential when examining fine, exceptionally clean, deep purple amethyst (see Chapter 11).

4. *Examine with a balance.* Synthetic lapis is a surprise to many. Lapis should also be tested, and there's an easy way to test it if you use a delicate balance. Weigh the piece of jewelry or unmounted stone and record the exact weight. Immerse it in clean water for about two minutes. Remove it and carefully wipe dry. Weigh it again. If it weighs more, it is synthetic. Synthetic lapis is very porous and readily absorbs water. Genuine lapis does not.

A Word About Turquoise.

Turquoise is a gem that requires particular attention today. One must be alert to the presence of numerous materials that look like turquoise—natural turquoise, synthetic turquoise, reconstituted (reconstructed) turquoise, and imitation turquoise. We are seeing tremendous misrepresentation of turquoise throughout the marketplace. Fine natural turquoise is very difficult to obtain. However, there is an abundance of reconstituted turquoise, often represented as natural. It is not. Also, reconstituted turquoise should not be confused with the synthetic turquoise now being produced. Reconstituted turquoise is not synthetic. Reconstituted turquoise is a product made by taking turquoise powder (made by pulverizing poor quality genuine stone) and mixing it with a binding agent (plastic) to form into solid pieces. It is something anyone dealing in turquoise should be aware of and on guard against.

Today's Synthetics

Manufacturers of synthetic gems have come a long way. Their products are beautiful. And they are, indeed, so good that they may easily be mistaken for the real thing.

Gemologists have also come a long way in learning how to identify and separate the natural from the synthetic and imitation. (See chart on next page.) Nonetheless, there are still some stones that, to be absolutely positive, require sophisticated testing and equipment not available to most. Infrared spectroscopy offers tremendous promise for the future . . . and for staying one step ahead of those who continue in their efforts to perfect the art of synthesizing. GIA is currently experimenting with the infrared spectroscope, and preliminary results lead them to believe this piece of equipment may well provide the means to separate, without question, any synthetic from the natural.

The world of gemstone synthesis is a dynamic one. The 20th century has seen the introduction and perfection of many synthetic gems. New developments are occurring constantly. Keeping on top of new developments may be the ultimate challenge to the jeweler and gem lover over the next few decades.

A Final Word About Antique and Estate Jewelry—Enjoy

We hope that we have not intimidated you with this discussion but, instead, enlightened you so that you can feel more confident about what you are seeing, buying, and selling. No doubt you'll encounter many of the techniques we've discussed here. We think they add interest to many pieces and can be fascinating in their own way. We hope you'll agree that the key to enjoying them is understanding and appreciating what you have.

Synthetic Gemstones and Man-Made Imitations

Color	Commercially Available	Method of Growth or Synthesis	Comments and Identification Characteristics
SYNTHETIC TYPES			
COLORLESS			
Sapphire	1910	Verneuil	1. No curved striae or coloration observed because stone is colorless. 2. Identifiable by exposure to ultraviolet radiation, which will produce a dull, deep blue fluorescence.
Spinel	1910	Verneuil	1. Can be easily identified by exposure to short-wave ultraviolet, under which it will fluoresce or glow a strong bluish-white. Inert under long-wave U. V. Also can be identified by the anomalous double refraction seen with the polariscope.
Rutile	1948	Verneuil	1. Too much "fire" or dispersion (seven times more than diamond). 2. Soft—can be scratched by a quartz gem such as amethyst, etc. The hardness on Mohs scale is 6 to 6.5. 3. Cloudy appearance if cut wrong (due to the strong doubling effect of its high birefringance—0.287). 4. Can be cut quite shallow without "leaking" light, due to its very high refractive index—2.616–2.903.
*Cubic Zirconia (CZ)	1973 (commercially 1976)	Skull furnace	1. Higher "fire" or dispersion than diamond—.060 versus .044 diamond. 2. Higher specific gravity. When compared to a one-carat round diamond, the CZ will weigh approximately 1.75 carats. 3. Hardness about 8.5 on Mohs scale. Can be easily scratched by a tungsten-carbide pen. 4. Fluoresce orangish-yellow under long-wave and stronger under short-wave ultraviolet though there are some that react just the opposite. 5. Negative reaction to diamond testing probes, needles or reflectometers. 6. Girdle reflections are slightly more "glassy" looking than that of diamond. 7. The readability test. In an unmounted CZ, placed table-facet down over a fine pen line or black print, you will be able to see some of the black line or print when viewed from above at a slight angle. With a well cut diamond you will not be able to read any print or see the black line.

* We have listed cubic zirconia as a synthetic since it has been *found in nature* as an inclusion. We consider it a simulant, however, since the stone is imitating is diamond, the properties of which differ significantly from CZ.

Gemstone	Date	Process	Characteristics
Sapphire	1911	Verneuil flame-fusion	1. Curved growth lines (curved striae) and color zoning. 2. Small spherical or pear-shaped bubbles. 3. Bluish-green to dull green usually exhibited by synthetic blue sapphire under short-wave ultraviolet radiation. 4. Heat treatment of synthetic blue sapphire can successfully eradicate the curved striations and color zoning. Therefore, examine with the spectroscope (See Chapter 10). 5. The dichroscope will *not* differentiate between natural and synthetic.
Spinel	1908 (in wide use after 1925)	Verneuil flame-fusion	1. Easily identified by observing the red coloration when examined with the Chelsea filter under incandescent light. 2. Anomalous double refraction seen under cross-polars when using the polariscope. 3. Proflated bubble inclusions. 4. Most fluoresce red under long-wave ultraviolet and most fluoresce orange, red or bluish-white under short-wave ultraviolet.
Turquoise	1972 (Gilson)	Methodology not revealed	1. Weak dull blue under long- and short-wave ultraviolet radiation. 2. Under microscopic examination seems to exhibit small angular crystalline pieces in a whitish groundmass. 3. With a loupe, one can sometimes see evenly distributed, small, whitish "cotton-puffs." 4. Synthetic turquoise can be even-colored or exhibit "spider-web" matrix design.
Lapis-lazuli	mid 1970s (Gilson)	Methodology not revealed	1. Easy to identify if you use a delicate balance. Weigh the jewelry piece or stone carefully on the balance and record the weight. Immerse in clean water for about two minutes and then carefully wipe dry. Weigh again. If it is synthetic it will weigh more. Synthetic lapis lazuli is porous and readily absorbs water. 2. If examined with a strong pen-light you will note that genuine lapis is slightly translucent and the Gilson synthetic is not. 3. It may or may not have pyrite inclusions.
GREEN Emerald	1934	Flux grown (I. G. Farben)	1. Very few were produced. 2. Wispy veils.
	1935	Flux grown (Chatham)	1. Wispy or veil-like feathery inclusions, liquid filled. 2. Phenacite crystal inclusions. 3. Gas bubbles. 4. Platinum crystal platelets, usually triangular shaped, but may be hexagonally shaped.

Synthetic Gemstones and Man-Made Imitations (*continued*)

Color	Commercially Available	Method of Growth or Synthesis	Comments and Identification Characteristics
SYNTHETIC TYPES			
Green continued			
			5. Strong red under Chelsea filter examination in incandescent light.
			6. Red fluorescence under long-wave ultraviolet radiation.
	early 1960s	Flux grown (Gilson)	1. Veil-like inclusions.
			2. Strong red under Chelsea filter.
			3. Red under long-wave ultraviolet.
			4. One (type N) does not fluoresce but has an absorption spectra at 4270 (427).
	1961 to 1970	Hydrothermal (Linde). Continued to be produced by Vacuum Ventures, Inc. of California and New Jersey. (Under license from Union Carbide)	1. Long, thin crystals that all point one way. Many are capped with a small ball and referred to as "nail-head" inclusions.
			2. Some of the lower grades made by Vacuum Ventures will show wispy inclusions.
			3. Strong red fluorescence under long-wave ultraviolet radiation.
	1960	Hydrothermal (Lechleitner)	1. A faceted beryl (aqua, emerald, etc.) on which a layer of hydrothermally grown synthetic emerald has been deposited. With a loupe, you can see easily that the surface of the facets are criss-crossed with a series of fine "fish-net" type cracks. The specific gravity of this type of stone will vary slightly, depending on the type of beryl coated.
	1986	Hydrothermal (Biron)	1. Can have "nail-head" type inclusions as seen in Linde synthetic.
			2. Two-phase inclusions.
			3. Gold platelets.
			4. Ghost lines—lines you see one moment, but which disappear when slightly tilted.
			5. Small whitish specks.
			6. Good red under the Chelsea filter.
			7. Non-fluorescent under ultraviolet (unusual for synthetic emerald).
			8. Exhibits a 4270 (427) absorption spectra like the synthetic Gilson "N" type II.
	1984	Flux grown (Seiko Japan)	1. Fluoresces green under ultraviolet.

...Maximum green in color.

			2. Synthetic spinels all exhibit anomalous double refraction under the polariscope. 3. They will not exhibit any dichroism. 4. Colorless spinel is used to make emerald colored doublets. The top and bottom will be colorless spinel, the two sections cemented together with green glue. (See chapter 13).
Jadeite Jade	1984	High Pressure Vice or Belt (made by General Electric)	1. Jadeite jade (including green and lavender) are not at this time being produced for commercial use. 2. These jades have a slightly higher hardness, 7.5 to 8, versus 7 for natural. 3. They appear to have a more granular texture and the colors are more blotchy or spotty. 4. The fluorescence, refractive indices and specific gravities are similar to natural jadeite. 5. The spectroscope is useful for separating from natural—the 4370 absorption line seen with natural stones is not seen in the fancy colored synthetic. 6. The Suwa Seikosha Co., Ltd. of Japan obtained a patent in 1985 for the production of synthetic jadeite. Who knows what the future for synthetic jadeite will hold.
Sapphire	1910	Verneuil	1. Same inclusions as seen in synthetic blue sapphire. 2. Shows reddish through the Chelsea filter (natural green stays dark).
RED Ruby*	Commercially 1905	Verneuil flame-fusion	1. Curved growth striations, curved color banding. 2. Small spherical, pear-shaped or tad-pole shaped bubbles. 3. Profilated gas bubble (a row of bubbles which, together, have a sausage-shaped outline). 4. Small black "dots" (excessive chromium oxide that did not melt or absorb during the synthesis). This is often observed in old ruby synthetics. 5. Strong red fluorescence when observed under long-wave ultra violet radiation. Burmese rubies also fluoresce strong red, but weaker than the synthetic.
	after 1920	Czochralski pulling method. Can produce very large crystals.	1. Very "clean" flaw-wise. May exhibit a weak layered or parallel color zoning. 2. Strong red fluorescence like the Verneuil.
	mid 1960's	Flux grown or diffusion	1. Small irregular-shaped, elongated bubbles. 2. A meshed net or veil in which the droplets are filled. Natural rubies could look similar but the droplets are not filled. The mesh holes are often hexagonally shaped in the Chatham synthetics.

* Synthetic rubies were being produced as early as 1885 (Geneva), but were not really commercially available until after 1900.

Synthetic Gemstones and Man-Made Imitations (*continued*)

Color	Commercially Available	Method of Growth or Synthesis	Comments and Identification Characteristics
SYNTHETIC TYPES			
Red continued			3. In some of the Kashan rubies you can observe irregular-shaped forms consisting of flux residues.
			4. Some Kashans are slightly cloudy from the presence of inclusions that resemble falling rain. They exhibit faint, light-colored straight lines that traverse the stone—you may think you are looking at a facet edge on the opposite side.
			5. Flux grown Kashans do not fluoresce as strong a red under the ultraviolet as those that are grown using the Vermeuil growth method.
			6. Chatham synthetics may contain small, usually triangular shaped, platinum platelets.
			7. In some Ramaura synthetic rubies, you may see nearly straight parallel growth bands that disappear as you tilt the stone slightly.
			8. Ramaura may show bluish under short-wave ultraviolet and also may fluoresce slightly yellow.
Star Ruby	1947	Vermeuil flame-fusion	1. Star is perfect, all 6 rays perfectly aligned.
			2. Linde-type will often show a poorly etched letter "L" on the back side of the cabochon.
			3. Many European grown will be more translucent and if examined carefully will exhibit curved striae or color zoning.
			4. A natural star stone will exhibit, to some degree, hexagonal cross-hatching, visible on the back side of the cabochon. This will not be observed in the synthetic stone.
			5. Some European stones will exhibit fine concentric circles on the back side of the cabochon.
Red Spinel	1930's	Vermeuil flame-fusion	1. The refractive index of these spinels is slightly higher than that of natural red spinels. Recently, however, some are being synthesized that have refractive indices comparable to natural stones.
			2. Under crossed-polars in the polariscope, these stones will exhibit anomalous double refraction (ADR).
			3. Natural and synthetic red spinels will fluoresce strong red under long-wave ultraviolet, though slightly weaker than the natural or synthetic rubies.

4. Ruby has good dichroism but red spinel and glass have none.
5. Genuine red spinel usually will show under magnification some small octagonally-shaped crystal inclusions not seen in synthetic.
6. Synthetic red spinel is often internally fractured (particularly earlier stones).

PURPLE Amethyst 1975	Hydrothermal autoclave	1. Fine deep purple, exceptionally "clean" synthetics are quite plentiful. 2. They can be identified by carefully examining with the polariscope (See chapter 11). The synthetic will not exhibit twinning lines seen in 99% of natural amethysts.
ALEXANDRITE TYPES Alexandrite 1973	Flux grown (Creative Crystals of California)	1. Veil-like patterns of interconnecting canals (healing feather types). 2. String-like arrangement of small bubbles. 3. Small brownish hexagonal platelets. 4. Flux type inclusions. 5. Platinum crystals, hexagonal or triangular in shape. 6. Strong red fluorescence under long-wave and short-wave ultraviolet.
Synthetic Spinel-Alexandrite type	Verneuil	1. No Dichroism. Spinel is single-refracting while alexandrite is triple-refracting. 2. Very good color change, green to red. 3. Gas bubbles. 4. Anomalous double refraction under polariscope not seen in natural. 5. Refractive index = 1.73.
Synthetic Corundum-Alexandrite type	Verneuil	1. Refractive index = 1.762–1.770 2. Strong red fluorescence long-wave and short-wave ultraviolet. 3. Some fluoresce orange under long-wave and short-wave ultraviolet. 4. Color change grayish-green to purple. 5. With the dichroscope this synthetic will show two colors while genuine or synthetic alexandrite will show three. The trichroism in genuine alexandrite varies slightly, depending on country of origin.

NOTE: Synthetic sapphires and spinels have been produced in many colors for experimental and scientific studies. We have not listed them all since most are not encountered in the trade.

Synthetic Gemstones and Man-Made Imitations (*continued*)

Color	Commercially Available	Method of Growth or Synthesis	Comments and Identification Characteristics
SIMULANTS AND IMITATION GEMSTONES (Simulants are not found naturally—synthetics duplicate gems that occur naturally.)			
COLORLESS Strontium titanate	1955	Verneuil	1. Very high "fire" or dispersion—more than four times that of diamond. 2. Very high specific gravity, (5.13), approximately 1.5 times higher than diamond (3.52). 3. Very soft, 6 to 6.5, and brittle. 4. Non-fluorescent. 5. To make the stone more durable and reduce the dispersion, it is made into a doublet with either a synthetic sapphire or spinel crown. 6. Sold as Wellington and Fabulite.
YAG (Yttrium Aluminum Garnet)	1969	Czochalski "pulling"	1. Dispersion is low (.028), nearly half that of diamond. 2. Has a good hardness, about 8.5 on Mohs scale. 3. Sold under the name "Diamonair" and "Diamonique." 4. Like strontium titanate, it has an R.I. that cannot be read on the normal refractometer. 5. Some fluoresce yellow under long- and weaker under short-wave ultraviolet. Some will fluoresce weak pink under long-wave ultraviolet. Some will not fluoresce under either long-wave or short-wave ultraviolet. 6. Since the R.I. is low, you can read print easily through the stone when trying the readability test. 7. Twisted drop-like inclusions, black square or triangular shaped crystals.
GGG (Gadolinium Gallium Garnet)	1975	Czochalski "pulling"	1. Dispersion nearly the same as diamond. 2. Specific gravity practically twice that of diamond, 7.02. 3. Hardness (7, same as the quartz gems) much lower than diamond, but durable. 4. Exposure to ultraviolet or sunlight will eventually turn GGG brown. The more exposure, the deeper the shade of brown. 5. Yellow fluorescence under long-wave and weaker under short-wave ultraviolet.
GREEN YAG (Yttrium Aluminum "Garnet")	1969	Czochalski "pulling"	1. Some fluoresce strong red under ultraviolet and are red under the Chelsea filter. Those that get their coloration from praseodymium are very weak under ultraviolet or Chelsea.

3. You can measure the R.I. of emerald but you cannot read the R.I. of YAG on your refractometer.

BLUE

Imitation Lapis — Germany — 1954

1. This was made from coarsely ground synthetic blue spinel, heated (but not melted) to form a solid mass. Sometimes gold specks were added.
2. Identifiable with the Chelsea filter (it exhibits a red coloration not seen in genuine).
3. Not many have been seen since 1954.

MULTICOLORED

Opal — Methodology kept secret. (Gilson) — 1972

1. Color patches are within boundaries and do not "blend" into the adjoining color patches.
2. Examination of stone's surface with 10X loupe will show patterns resembling "snake-skin," "chicken-wire," "honeycomb," or fine "wrinkles."
3. Immersed in chloroform, they will develop a colorless or clear envelope, a few millimeters thick, around the whole stone. When lifted out of the chloroform, clear envelope disappears. Make sure you do not inhale much chloroform!!
4. Gilson has stopped making opal and has turned over the synthesis to the Japanese.

Opal — Glass having a controlled precipitation. (J. L. Slocum) — 1977

1. Can be easily distinguished as imitation when examined with a 10X magnifier. Though there are many types of color configurations in Slocum opals, none resemble the genuine opal.
2. The specific gravity (2.40 to 2.50) is higher than that of natural opal (1.25 to 2.23).
3. The R.I. (1.49 to 1.50) is higher than natural (about 1.45).
4. The hardness is near 6 on Mohs scale.

Opal — Japanese (methodology complicated) — 1983

1. A plastic imitation that looks very realistic.
2. The specific gravity is low—1.18 to 1.20
3. The R. I. is a little higher—1.48 to 1.53.
4. The hardness is very low, about 2.5.
5. You can cut it with a sharp knife.
6. Mounted in a ring, it could fool you by resembling a precious opal that has a white groundmass.

YAG, GGG, and CUBIC ZIRCONIA can be produced in many colors—blue, yellow, red, etc. though not commonly seen. Recently a synthetic blue Russian sapphire turned out to be a blue CZ. None of these stones will exhibit dichroism and none are readable on the normal refractometer. Fluorescence and inclusions may help identify these "gems."

Glass is made in many colors to imitate many stones. The facet edges are usually not sharp. Any single reading on the refractometer from 1.50 to as much as 1.65 usually indicates the gem is glass. (Cryptocrystalline quartz such as chalcedony, amber and a few very rare gems are exceptions). Glass imitations will not exhibit any dichroism. The stones they are trying to imitate will usually have two readings on the refractometer.

APPENDICES

GEMSTONE PROPERTY TABLES

Frequently Encountered Transparent Gems By Color

RED AND PINK GEMSTONES AND THEIR LOOK-ALIKES

Transparent

Almandite garnet
Beryl (morganite)
Chrysoberyl (alexandrite)
Corundum (ruby & pink
  sapphire)
Diamond
Glass
Plastics
Pyrope garnet
Quartz (rose quartz)
Rhodolite garnet

Spinel
Spodumene (kunzite)
Synthetic corundum
Synthetic spinel
Topaz
Tourmaline
Zircon

Doublets
Triplets
Foil backs

BROWN AND ORANGE GEMSTONES AND THEIR LOOK-ALIKES

Transparent

Amber and pressed amber
Beryl
Chrysoberyl
Copal (and other natural
  resins)
Corundum
Diamond
Glass
Grossularite garnet
  (hessonite)
Opal (fire opal)
Plastics

Quartz
Chalcedony (carnelian and sard)
Sinhalite
Spinel
Synthetic corundum
Synthetic rutile
Synthetic spinel
Topaz
Tourmaline
Zircon

Doublets
Triplets

YELLOW GEMSTONES AND THEIR LOOK-ALIKES

Transparent

Amber
Beryl
Chrysoberyl
Corundum
Diamond
Glass
Grossularite garnet
  (hessonite)
Opal
Plastics
Quartz (citrine)

Spessartite garnet
Spodumene
Synthetic corundum
Synthetic rutile
Synthetic spinel
Topaz
Tourmaline
Zircon

Doublets
Triplets
Foil backs

GREEN GEMSTONES AND THEIR LOOK-ALIKES

Transparent

Andradite garnet (demantoid)
Beryl (emerald)
Chrysoberyl (including cat's
  eye and alexandrite)
Corundum (green sapphire)
Diamond
Glass
Grossularite garnet (tsavorite)
Peridot
Plastics
Quartz

Spinel
Synthetic corundum
Synthetic garnet (YAG)
Synthetic emerald
Synthetic spinel
Topaz
Tourmaline
Zircon

Doublets
Triplets

BLUE GEMSTONES AND THEIR LOOK-ALIKES

Transparent

Beryl (aquamarine)
Corundum (sapphire)
Diamond

Synthetic corundum
Synthetic rutile
Synthetic spinel

Blue continued

Glass	Tourmaline (indicolite)
Iolite (dichroite)	Zircon
Plastics	Zoisite (tanzanite)
Quartz (dyed)	
Opal	Doublets
Spinel	Triplets
Topaz	Foil backs

PURPLE AND VIOLET GEMSTONES AND THEIR LOOK-ALIKES

Transparent

Almandite garnet	Spinel
Chrysoberyl (alexandrite)	Spodumene (kunzite)
Corundum (sapphire)	Synthetic corundum
Diamond	Synthetic spinel
Glass	Topaz
Plastics	Tourmaline
Pyrope garnet	Zircon
Quartz (amethyst)	Zoisite (Tanzanite)
Rhodolite garnet	
	Doublets

BLACK GEMSTONES AND THEIR LOOK-ALIKES

Nontransparent

Andradite garnet (melanite)	Jet
Black coral	Nephrite jade
Chalcedony (black onyx)	Obsidian
Corundum (star sapphire)	Opal
Diopside (star)	Opal doublets
Diamond	Plastics
Glass	Psilomelane
Jadeite jade	Tourmaline
Hematite	

GRAY GEMSTONES AND THEIR LOOK-ALIKES

Nontransparent

Chalcedony (agate)   Jadeite jade
Corundum (star sapphire)   Labradorite feldspar
Hematite   Nephrite jade
Hemetine   Sintered synthetic corundum

WHITE GEMSTONES AND THEIR LOOK-ALIKES

Nontransparent

Alabaster   Jadeite jade
Chalcedony (chalcedony   Nephrite jade
  moonstone)   Onyx marble
Coral   Opal
Corundum   Opal doublets
Glass   Feldspar (moonstone)
Grossularite   Plastics

COLORLESS GEMSTONES AND THEIR LOOK-ALIKES

Transparent

Beryl
Corundum (white sapphire)   Spinel
Diamond   Strontium titanate
Glass   Synthetic corundum
Grossularite garnet   Synthetic rutile
Opal   Synthetic spinel
Feldspar (moonstone)   Topaz
Plastics   Tourmaline
Quartz (rock crystal)   Zircon (jargoon)

Hardness of Popular Gems

Diamond	10	Labradorite	6
Silicon carbide	9¼	Amblygonite	6
Corundum & Syn.	9	Hematite	5½–6½
Chrysoberyl	8½	Rhodonite	5½–6½
YAG	8¼	Opal	5–6½
Spinel & Syn.	8	Diopside	5–6
Topaz	8	Glass	5–6
Beryl & syn. emerald	7½–8	Strontium titanate	5–6
Zircon (high, medium)	7½	Lazulite	5–6
Almandite garnet	7½	Lazurite (lapis-lazuli)	5–6
Rhodolite garnet	7–7½	Turquoise	5–6
Pyrope garnet	7–7½	Sodalite	5–6
Spessartite garnet	7–7½	Sphene	5–5½
Tourmaline	7–7½	Obsidian	5–5½
Andalusite	7–7½	Bowenite (serpentine)	5–5½
Iolite	7–7½	Apatite	5
Grossularite garnet	7	Dioptase	5
Quartz & Syn.	7	Smithsonite	5
Chalcedony	6½–7	Syn. Turquoise	5
Peridot	6½–7	Syn. Opal	4½
Jadeite	6½–7	Fluorite	4
Andradite garnet (Demantoid)	6½–7	Rhodochrosite	3½–4½
Idocrase	6½	Malachite	3½–4
Scapolite	6½	Azurite	3½–4
Kornerupine	6½	Sphalerite	3½–4
Zircon (low)	6½	Coral	3½–4
Spodumene	6–7	Conch Pearl	3½
Sinhalite	6–7	Calcite	3
Epidote	6–7	Black Coral	3
Zoisite	6–7	Pearl	2½–4½
Rutile & Syn.	6–6½	Jet	2½–4
Albite-Oligoclase	6–6½	Serpentine	2–4
Orthoclase	6–6½	Amber	2–2½
Nephrite	6–6½	Copal	2
Pyrite	6–6½	Alabaster	2
Benitoite	6–6½	Steatite (soapstone)	1½–2½
Marcasite	6–6½		

Specific Gravity Table

Cassiterite	6.95 (±.08)	Kornerupine	3.30 (±.05)
Cubic Zirconia	5.80 (±.20)	Diopside	3.29 (±.03)
Strontium		Ekanite	3.28
titanate	5.13 (±.02)	Enstatite	3.25 (±.02)
Pyrite	5.00 (±.10)	Fluorite	3.18 (±.01)
Marcasite	4.85 (±.05)	Apatite	3.18 (±.02)
Zircon		Spodumene	3.18 (±.03)
(high)	4.70 (±.03)	Andalusite	3.17 (±.04)
(medium)	4.32 (±.25)	Euclase	3.10 (±.01)
Gahnite	4.55	Lazulite	3.09 (±.05)
YAG	4.55	Tourmaline	3.06 (−.05, +.15}
Smithsonite	4.30 (±.10)	Amblygonite	3.02
Rutile & Syn.	4.26 (±.02)	Danburite	3.00 (±.01)
Spessartite	4.15 (±.03)	Nephrite	2.95 (±.05)
Almandite	4.05 (±.12)	Phenakite	2.95 (±.01)
Sphalerite	4.05 (±.02)	Datolite	2.95
Gahnospinel	4.01 (±.40)	Brazilianite	2.94
Zircon (low)	4.00 (±.07)	Pollucite	2.92
Corundum		Prehnite	2.88 (±.06)
& Syn.	4.00 (±.03)	Beryllonite	2.85 (±.02)
Malachite	3.95 (−.70, +.15)	Conch pearl	2.85
Andradite	3.84 (±.03)	Turquoise	2.76 (−.45, +.08)
Rhodolite	3.84 (±.10)	Steatite	2.75
Azurite	3.80 (−.50, +.07)	Lazurite	
Pyrope	3.78 (−.16, +.09)	(lapis-lazuli)	2.75 (±.25)
Chrysoberyl	3.73 (±.02)	Beryl	2.72 (−.05, +.12)
Rhodochrosite	3.70	Labradorite	2.70 (±.05)
Syn. spinel	3.64 (−.12, +.02)	Calcite	2.70
Benitoite	3.64 (±.03)	Scapolite	2.68 (±.06)
Kyanite	3.62 (±.06)	Syn. emerald	
Grossularite	3.61 (−.27, +.12)	(hydroth.)	2.68 (±.02)
Taaffeite	3.61	(Gilson)	2.67 (±.02)
Spinel	3.60 (−.03, +.30)	(flux)	2.66
Topaz	3.53 (±.04)	Quartz & Syn.	2.66 (±.01)
Diamond	3.52 (±.01)	Syn. Turquoise	2.66
Sphene	3.52 (±.02)	Albite-	
Rhodonite	3.50 (±.20)	Oligoclae	2.65 (±.02)
Sinhalite	3.48	Coral	2.65 (±.02)
Idocrase	3.40 (±.10)	Iolite	2.61 (±.05)
Epidote	3.40 (±.08)	Chalcedony	2.60 (±.05)
Peridot	3.34 (−.03, +.14)	Serpentine	2.57 (±.06)
Jadeite	3.34 (±.04)	Orthoclase	2.56 (±.01)
Zoisite (tanzanite)	3.30 (±.10)	Microcline	2.56 (±.01)
Dioptase	3.30 (.05)	Variscite	2.50 (±.08)

Obsidian	2.45 (±.10)	Opal	2.15 (−.90, +.07)
Moldavite	2.40 (±.04)	Syn. Opal	2.05 (±.03)
Apophyllite	2.40 (±.10)	Coral (black)	1.37
Thomsonite	2.35 (±.05)	Jet	1.32 (±.02)
Alabaster	2.30	Plastics	1.30 (±.25)
Glass	2.3 to 4.5	Amber	1.08 (±.02)
Sodalite	2.24 (±.05)	Copal	1.06
Chrysocolla	2.20 (±.10)		

Refractive Index Tables
Single Refracting Gems

Gemstone	Refractive Index Reading
Diamond	2.417
Strontium titanate	2.409
Sphalerite	2.37
Cubic zirconia	2.15 (±.03)
Andradite garnet	1.875 (±.020)
YAG	1.833
Spessartite garnet	1.81 (±.010)
Gahnite (blue/blue green spinel)	1.80
Almandite garnet	1.79 (±.030)
Rhodolite garnet	1.76 (±.010)
Gahnospinel (blue spinel)	1.76 (±.02)
Pyrope garnet	1.746 (−.026, +.010)
Grossularite garnet	1.735 (+.015, −.035)
Synthetic Spinel	1.73 (±.01)
Spinel	1.718 (−.006, +.044)
Jet	1.66 (±.020)
Bakelite	1.61 (±.06)
Ekanite	1.597
Amber	1.540
Pollucite	1.525
Lazurite (lapis-lazuli)	1.500
Obsidian	1.500
Sodalite	1.483 (±.003)
Glass (normal)	1.48–1.70
(extreme)	1.44–1.77 (Most read between 1.45–1.65)
Moldavite	1.48
Opal	1.45 (−.080, +.020)
Synthetic opal	1.44
Fluorite	1.434

Refractive Index Tables
Double Refracting Gems

Gemstone	Low R.I. Reading	High R.I. Reading
Rutile & Syn.	2.616	2.903
Cassiterite	1.997	2.093
Zircon (high)	1.925	1.984
Scheelite	1.918	1.934
Sphene	1.900 ($\pm$.018)	2.034 ($\pm$.020)
Zircon (medium)	1.875 ($\pm$.045)	1.905 ($\pm$.075)
Zircon (low)	1.810 ($\pm$.030)	1.815 ($\pm$.030)
Corundum	1.762 ($-$.003, $+$.007)	1.770 ($-$.003, $+$.008)
Synthetic corundum	1.762	1.770
Benitoite	1.757	1.804
Chrysoberyl	1.746 ($\pm$.004)	1.755 ($\pm$.005)
Azurite	1.73 ($\pm$.010)	1.84 ($\pm$.010)
Rhodonite	1.73	1.74
Epidote	1.729 ($-$.015, $+$.006)	1.768 ($-$.035, $+$.012)
Taaffeite	1.719	1.723
Kyanite	1.716 ($\pm$.004)	1.731 ($\pm$.004)
Idocrase	1.713 ($\pm$.012)	1.718 ($\pm$.014)
Zoisite (Tanzanite)	1.691 ($\pm$.002)	1.704 ($\pm$.003)
Axinite	1.678	1.688
Diopside	1.675 ($-$.010, $+$.027)	1.701 ($-$.077, $+$.029)
Sinhalite	1.668 ($\pm$.003)	1.707 ($\pm$.003)
Kornerupine	1.667 ($\pm$.002)	1.680 ($\pm$.003)
Jadeite	1.66 ($\pm$.007)	1.68 ($\pm$.009)
Malachite	1.66	1.91
Spodumene	1.660 ($\pm$.005)	1.676 ($\pm$.005)
Enstatite	1.658 ($\pm$.005)	1.668 ($\pm$.005)
Dioptase	1.655 ($\pm$.011)	1.708 ($\pm$.012)
Peridot	1.654 ($\pm$.020)	1.690 ($\pm$.020)
Euclase	1.654 ($\pm$.004)	1.673 ($\pm$.004)
Phenakite	1.654 ($-$.003, $+$.017)	1.670 ($-$.004, $+$.026)
Apatite	1.642 ($-$.012, $+$.003)	1.646 ($-$.014, $+$.005)
Andalusite	1.634 ($\pm$.006)	1.643 ($\pm$.004)
Danburite	1.630 ($\pm$.003)	1.636 ($\pm$.003)
Datolite	1.626	1.670
Tourmaline	1.624 ($\pm$.005)	1.644 ($\pm$.006)
Smithsonite	1.621	1.849
Topaz	1.619 ($\pm$.010)	1.627 ($\pm$.010)
Prehnite	1.615	1.646
Turquoise	1.61	1.65
Lazulite	1.612	1.643

Double Refracting Gems—Continued

Gemstone	Low R.I. Reading	High R.I. Reading
Amblygonite	1.612	1.636
Nephrite	1.606	1.632
Brazilianite	1.602	1.621
Rhodochrosite	1.597	1.817
Synthetic turquoise	1.59	1.60
Beryl	1.577 (±.016)	1.583 (±.017)
Synthetic emerald (New Gilson)	1.571	1.579
Synthetic emerald (hydrothermal)	1.568 (±.02)	1.573 (±.02)
Synthetic emerald (flux)	1.561	1.564
Variscite	1.56	1.59
Serpentine	1.56 (−.07)	1.570 (−.07)
Coral, black (akabar)	1.56	1.57
Labradorite feldspar	1.559	1.568
Beryllonite	1.552	1.562
Agalmatolite (soapstone)	1.55	1.60
Scapolite	1.55	1.572
Quartz & Syn.	1.544 (±.000)	1.553 (±.000)
Iolite (dichroite)	1.542 (−.010, +.002)	1.551 (−.011, +.045)
Steatite (meerschaum)	1.54	1.590
Chalcedony	1.535	1.539
Apophyllite	1.535	1.537
Albite-oligoclase (moonstone)	1.532 (±.007)	1.542 (±.006)
Microcline (Amazonnite)	1.522	1.530
Orthoclase (Moonstone)	1.518	1.526
Thomsonite	1.515	1.540
Calcite	1.486	1.658
Coral	1.486	1.658

Table of Dispersion

The following figures represent the difference in the gem's refractive index for red light and blue-violet light.

Fluorite	.007	Peridot	.020
Silica glass	.010	Spinel	.020
Beryllonite	.010	Dioptase	.022
Kyanite	.011	Almandine garnet	.024
Orthoclase feldspar	.012	Rhodolite garnet	.026
Quartz	.013	Pyrope garnet	.027
Beryl	.014	Spessartite garnet	.027
Topaz	.014	Grossularite garnet	.028
Phenakite	.015	Epidote	.030
Chrysoberyl	.015	Zircon	.038
Euclase	.016	Benitoite	.044
Danburite	.016	Diamond	.044
Datolite	.016	Sphene	.051
Scapolite	.017	Andradite garnet	
Tourmaline	.017	(Demantoid)	.057
Spodumene	.017	Cassiterite	.071
Corundum	.018	Sphalerite	.156
Kornerupine	.019	Strontium titanate	.109
Idocrase	.019	Synthetic rutile	.280

Table of Birefringence of Gemstones

Apatite	.002–.006	Spodumene	.016
Syn. emerald (flux melt)	.003	Tourmaline	.018–.20+
		Euclase	.019
Zircon (low)	about .005	Brazilianite	.019
Beryl	.005–.009	Diopside	.026
Andalusite	.008–.013	Peridot	.036
Corundum	.008	Epidote	.039
Topaz	.008–.010	Sinhalite	.039
Zoisite (tanzanite)	.008	Datolite	.044
Chrysoberyl	.009	Benitoite	.047
Quartz	.009	Dioptase	.053
Beryllonite	.010	Zircon	up to .059
Enstatite	.010	Cassiterite	.096
Kornerupine	.013	Sphene	.134
Kyanite	.015	Calcite	.172
Phenakite	.015	Syn. Rutile	.287
Scheelite	.016		

Glossary

absorption spectrum—A term referring to the rainbow-like spectral picture of a gem produced by the spectroscope, characterized by dark lines or bars where some wavelengths of light have been absorbed by the gemstone as light passes through it. The areas of absorption appear in characteristic patterns for many gems and provide useful data for identification.

ADR (nomalous double refraction)—An optical effect resembling wiggly dark lines observed when using the polariscope with certain cubic or amorphous gems. It is caused by strain during crystal growth (see Chapter 11).

AGL—American Gemological Laboratory, a New-York based laboratory specializing in colored gemstone testing and detection of treatments. AGL also provides internationally recognized reports on colored gems.

amorphous—A term referring to substances that do not have crystalline properties, such as glass, amber, and opal.

anisotropic—Another term for gems that are double refracting.

antique jewelry—Jewelry that is at least 100 years old.

Art Deco jewelry—Jewelry exhibiting a decorative style popular from about 1920 to 1930. Derived from cubism, it is characterized by strong geometric design.

Art Modern (Retro)—Jewelry from about 1940, characterized by wide use of rose gold with both natural and synthetic ruby. Affordable colored stones such as citrine and aquamarine were popular. The style is typically large and bold.

Art Nouveau Jewelry—A style of jewelry popular from the early 1890s until about 1915, frequently mixing gemstones with more common materials (such as jet) regardless of intrinsic value. The style was flowing, with heavy use of enamelling. Baroque pearls with interesting shapes were often used. Themes evolved around nature, whimsical subjects, and mythology.

asterism—A star effect exhibited by some gems (natural and synthetic) when viewed under strong light. The star can be four- or six-rayed.

bezel facet—The facets in a brilliant-cut stone that slant upward from the girdle to the table (kite shaped).

bezel setting—A setting in which the stones are held along the girdle by a rim of metal rather than prongs.

birefringence—A measurement of the strength of a gem's double refraction; a value obtained for double-refracting gems that reflects the difference in its highest and lowest refractive index (see Chapter 8).

blackening—a technique using a sugar-acid chemical reaction to introduce carbon into a stone to blacken it. Most "black onyx" and some "black opal" is created by this technique.

brilliance—The intensity or vividness of color, or the degree of brightness, resulting from the reflection of light from the back facets back to the eye.

bubble—A type of inclusion that resembles a bubble. Bubbles provide important clues to gem identification (see Chapters 4 and 9).

carat—A unit of weight (one-fifth of a gram) by which gemstones are weighed.

cabochon—A cutting style that produces a stone with a smooth, polished, rounded, or convex surface. It lacks the tiny, flat faces (facets) seen in most gems, such as diamond, to enhance their brilliance.

CG or CGA—Certified Gemologist or Certified Gemologist Appraiser, highly respected titles awarded by the American Gem Society to those who pass stringent examinations. One of the most prestigious titles awarded to gemologists and gemologist appraisers in the U.S.

chatoyancy—An optical phenomenon exhibited by some gems such as "cats-eye chrysoberyl," whereby an "eye" effect is seen as the stone is tilted under a strong light.

clarity—The term that refers to a stone's freedom from inclusions. Sometimes referred to as the "flaw grade."

cleavage—A plane of weakness along which some gems will split apart, leaving a fairly smooth surface where it has split rather than a jagged edge (as seen in most cracks or fractures). Cleavage planes occur in certain definite directions, and some gems have a tendency to break along these planes.

closed back setting—A type of setting that completely encloses the back of the stone so that it can't be seen from the back side. Used often in antique jewelry to add brilliance, this type of setting was also used to deceive (see Chapter 14).

composite stone—A stone created by gluing or fusing together two or three parts (see Chapter 14).

crown—The top portion of any faceted stone; the part above the girdle.

cryptocrystalline—A gemstone composed of innumerable small crystals that are so small they can't even be detected with most high power microscopes (they are visible with the powerful, highly sophisticated electron microscope).

cubic system—A crystal system (also called isometric) in which several gems crystallize. These gems are single refracting and their properties do not change when examined from various directions.

culet—A tiny flat facet that runs parallel to the girdle and is located at the very tip of the pavilion of a faceted stone (it is so small that to most people it looks like a "point").

dendritic—A pattern having a root- or branch-like design.

density—The weight of a substance compared to the weight of an equal volume of water; or, how many times heavier a substance is than the same amount of water. The term "density" is usually used for liquids and the term "specific gravity" for solids.

depth of field—The limited distance or range in which objects are in focus while being viewed under a magnifier such as a loupe or microscope (see Chapters 4 and 9).

dichroism—The property of a stone that causes two colors or shades of the same color to be visible when examined with the dichroscope. These are called dichroic stones (see Chapter 6).

dispersion—The extent to which a transparent gem splits white light into the seven colors of the spectrum and displays "fire"—the flashes of color reflected from the internal facets of the cut stone. Diamond has a high dispersion and synthetic rutile has the highest.

doublet—A stone *created by man* by fusing or cementing two pieces of material together (doublet); when three pieces are used, it is called a "triplet."

doubling—A phenomenon that resembles "seeing double" when looking through some stones to the back facet edges with a magnifier. When viewing certain stones with a loupe or microscope from different directions, through at least one direction the edges of the back facets will appear doubled, like railroad tracks.

double refracting—A property found in most gems whereby single rays of light entering the stone are split into two rays (see Chapters 6 and 8).

emerald filter—Another name used for the Chelsea color filter since it was originally used to separate genuine emeralds from their lookalikes.

facet—A polished, flat plane on the surface of a cut gem.

faceted—A cutting style that consists of placing small, flat, polished "faces" around a stone at varying angles to one another, usually in a repeated, geometric pattern. It is normally used for transparent gems, to influence the way light travels through the stone so that maximum brilliance and fire are obtained. Faceting is an art form that has only been fully developed in the 20th century.

fancy—(1) A colored diamond; (2) an unusual cut or cutting style. A diamond dealer specializing in "fancies" either specializes in natural colored diamonds or in diamonds cut in special or unusual cuts/shapes.

FGA—Fellow of the Gemmological Association of Great Britain, a designation awarded to individuals who have passed examinations given by this association. The FGA title is considered one of the most prestigious titles awarded to gemologists anywhere in the world.

fire—The variety and intensity of rainbow colors seen in a gem. Another word for "dispersion."

fluorescence—A property found in some diamonds and colored gems that causes them to appear one color when viewed in normal light and to glow a different color when viewed under ultraviolet light. As a result of fluorescence, some diamonds can appear whiter than they actually are in certain lights. Whether or not a stone fluoresces, and the particular color it may fluoresce, can provide an important clue to identification (see Chapter 7).

fluorescent light—Light produced by the fluorescence of phosphors inside a glass tube (these are what you have in a fluorescent lamp).

foil backing—A technique used for jewelry in which the setting is lined with a sheet of metallic foil. Foil backing was used for both transparent faceted stones and cabochons to add brilliance and enhance or change the color (see Chapter 14).

GG—Graduate Gemologist, the highest title awarded by the Gemological Institute of America, to persons who have passed the required examinations administered by the GIA. Internationally recognized.

GIA—Gemological Institute of America, an organization that offers educational programs in gemology and related fields; also operates the Gem Testing Laboratory (New York and Santa Monica) that issues reports on diamonds, colored gems and pearls.

girdle—The edge of the stone that forms its perimeter; the point (border) at which the top portion meets the bottom portion of the stone—its "dividing line." The portion usually grasped by the setting.

immersion microscopy—Microscopic examination of a stone that is immersed in a liquid (normally with a high refractive index). This often enables one to more easily see inclusions, color banding, striae, twin lines, and other phenomena.

incandescent light—Light such as that produced by an ordinary light bulb or candle (see Chapter 3).

imitation stone—Materials such as glass or plastic that resemble a genuine stone in appearance but do not possess the chemical, physical, or crystal properties of the stone it is trying to imitate.

inclusion—Something that is "included" inside the gemstone—any foreign body enclosed within it. It can be a gas, liquid, or solid. Inclusions provide important clues for gem identification (see Chapters 4 and 9).

inert—A gem that shows no change under testing procedures. For example, a stone that shows no color change when examined with the Chelsea filter is inert; a stone that shows no color change when examined under the ultraviolet lamp is inert.

iridescence—A rainbow-like effect that usually occurs when light hits a fracture (crack) in a stone (especially noticeable when the crack breaks the surface).

irradiation—The bombardment of gems by atomic particles or exposure to radioactive radiation to change or enhance their color.

isotropic—Amorphous materials (opal, amber, glass, plastic) and gems that crystallize in the cubic system. Such gem materials are single refracting and will exhibit the same optical properties from any direction.

luster—The intensity and quality of reflected light from the *surface* of a stone. Luster varies among different gemstone families as a result of different physical characteristics and can be described as adamantine (bright luster as seen in diamond), vitreous (shiny or glassy), resinous, and pearly. Most gems have vitreous luster.

Master Gemologist Appraiser(MGA)—The highest title awarded to gemologist appraisers of the American Society of Appraisers, to those
passing very stringent examinations given by the Accredited Gemologists Association. One of the most prestigious gemologist appraiser titles
available in the United States.

monochromatic light—A light source that produces only one color of the
visible spectrum. Monochromatic yellow light is often used for gem
testing (see Chapter 3).

metamict—A gemstone (such as zircon) that has had its internal structure
disrupted by radioactive exposure causing it to lose its original crystal
structure and become amorphous.

Mohs hardness scale—A scale ranging from 1 to 10 that is used to indicate
relative hardness. The value of 1 indicates the softest (talc) and 10
indicates the hardest (diamond).

oiling—A gem enhancement technique used to hide or seal cracks in a stone
and, in some cases, to improve a stone's color.

Old European cut—a round, brilliant-cut developed in the 1880s and
characterized by its small table facet, high crown, and large (open) culet.
It was replaced by the modern brilliant-cut, after 1919.

Old mine cut—an early brilliant-cut that evolved from the rose cut, probably
in the 18th century, and continued into the 19th century until the
development of the old European cut. It can be either round or cushion-
shape (roundish, but slightly squared or rectangular), has an even
higher crown than the old European, and, usually an even larger culet
and smaller table.

opaque—A term used for gemstones such as lapis or malachite through
which light cannot travel; stones through which you can't see any light
at all.

paste—A term loosely applied to all glass imitation gemstones.

pavilion—The bottom portion of a stone; the portion below the girdle.

phosphorescence—The property of some gems that have been exposed to
radiation such as ultraviolet to continue to glow after the radiation has
been turned off (see Chapter 7).

pleochroism—A general term embracing dichroism and trichroism (see
Chapter 6).

polycrystalline—A term describing gems that are made up of aggregates of very small crystals. Jadeite is a very good example.

reflected light—Light shining off a polished surface is reflected light. Gems having a high refractive index tend to reflect light more strongly than those with a lower refractive index.

refraction—The amount a light ray bends as it passes through a gem.

refractive index—A measurement of the angle at which light is bent as it travels through a stone (see Chapter 8).

rough—Uncut gem material.

sheen—An effect resembling luster that is caused by the reflection of light from fine inclusions or structural texture *inside* a gem. Luster is light reflected from the surface of a gem and sheen is light reflected from something within the gem.

silk—Fine, intersecting, needlelike crystal inclusions that exhibit a silky sheen in reflected light.

simulant—A gem material that is manmade and has not been found to occur naturally.

single refracting—A gem material that allows a single ray of light to enter it and continue through as a single ray (see Chapter 8).

soudé-type composite—A stone created by fusing together two pieces of gem material such as colorless quartz or synthetic colorless spinel with an appropriate coloring agent in the center. There are many soudé-type emerald doublets.

specific gravity—See *density*

species—A term used to designate a gem family. Quartz is a species that has varieties called rose quartz, amethyst, citrine, smoky quartz, praseolite, aventurine, chalcedony, jasper, and so on; beryl is a species that has varieties called emerald, aquamarine, heliodor, and morganite.

synthetic—A manmade stone *that has essentially the same physical, chemical, and optical properties of the genuine stone it is trying to imitate.* Some of the newest synthetics are extremely difficult to distinguish from the genuine. Care must be taken to verify that a gem is genuine and not synthetic. Do not confuse with "imitation," a term that refers to manmade stones that may look like something they aren't but are very easily distinguished from the genuine because their physical and chemical properties are completely different.

table—The large, flat, horizontal facet at the very top of a faceted stone. The table is the largest facet.

transmitted light—Light shining through a stone from the bottom or sides.

translucent—Transmitting light imperfectly so that one cannot see through the material clearly. With the exception of translucent material such as star ruby, star sapphire, or precious cats-eye, most is suitable only for cabochons, beads, or carvings.

treated stone—A stone that has been dyed, stained, heated, and/or irradiated to enhance color or improve clarity; also, gems that have had cracks filled with glass to conceal them or to enhance color.

trichroism—A property exhibited by some stones that causes three colors or shades of the same color to be visible—two at a time—when viewed with the dichroscope. These are called trichroic gems (see Chapter 6).

triplet—A stone created by joining together three pieces of some gemlike material; a type of composite stone like the doublet but composed of three pieces rather than two (see Chapter 14).

variety—Different types and colors of a gem within a species. See *species*.

Verneuil—The name of the first commercial method for making synthetic gems. Starting in 1902, this flame-fusion method was used to produce synthetic ruby and spinel.

Victorian jewelry—Jewelry made from about 1837 to 1901.

waxing—A process in which the stone is rubbed with a tinted waxlike substance to hide surface cracks or blemishes and improve color.

vitreous luster—Luster with a shiny, glassy appearance. Most gems exhibit this glass-like luster.

zoned—A term used to describe *uneven* distribution of color. In such stones, zoning usually occurs in parallel planes (zones) with a zone of color laying parallel to a colorless zone. When viewed from the top, the stone may *appear* to have uniform color. Zoning can be most easily seen viewing the stone *through the side* (against a flat white background, if possible) rather than from the top.

Recommended Reading

Books

Anderson, B. W. *GEM TESTING*. 9th Edition. London: Heywood & Co., 1971

Fully updated and revised. Essential for the serious gemologist.

Arem, Joel E. *COLOR ENCYCLOPEDIA OF GEMSTONES*. New York: Van Nostrand, Reinhold, 1977.

Excellent color photography makes this book interesting for anyone, but it is of particular value for the gemologist.

Ball, S. H. *A ROMAN BOOK ON PRECIOUS STONES*. Los Angeles: Gemological Institute of America, 1950.

A ROMAN BOOK ON PRECIOUS STONES is very interesting from a historical perspective, especially for the knowledgeable student of gemology

Bauer, M. *PRECIOUS STONES AND MINERALS*. Translated by L. J. Spencer. Rutland, Vt.: C. E. Tuttle Co., 1971.

A comprehensive book recommended for the advanced student.

Bruton, E. *DIAMONDS*. 2nd Edition. London: Northwood, 1977.

An excellent, encyclopedic, well-illustrated book, good for both amateur and professional gemologist.

Cavenago-Bignami Moneta, S. *GEMMOLOGIA*. Milan: Heopli, 1965.

One of the most extensive works on gems available. Excellent photography. Available in the Italian language only. Recommended for advanced students.

Gaal, R. A. P. *A DIAMOND DICTIONARY*. Los Angeles: Gemological Institute of America, 1977.

Gubelin, Edward. *INCLUSIONS AS A MEANS TO GEMSTONE IDENTIFICATION*. Los Angeles: Gemological Institute of America, 1953.

————. *INTERNAL WORLD OF GEMSTONES*. Woburn, Mass.: Butterworth, 1979.

Gubelin, Edward and J. L. Koivula. *PHOTOATLAS OF INCLUSIONS IN GEMSTONES*. Zurich: ABC Editions, 1986.

All are recommended for the serious student of gemology. Best and most comprehensive collection of photographs of inclusions ever assembled.
Important for learning to recognize the indicators of treatments and synthetics—especially new-type synthetics.

Liddicoat, R. T. *HANDBOOK OF GEM IDENTIFICATION*. Los Angeles: Gemological Institute of America, 1987.

Excellent textbook for the student of gemology.

Matlins, A. and A. Bonanno. *JEWELRY & GEMS: THE BUYING GUIDE*. So. Woodstock, Vermont, Gemstone Press, 1988.

Well reviewed for its discussion of factors affecting quality and value, what to look for and look out for. Covers diamonds, pearls and colored gemstones. Includes comparative price charts.

Nassau, Kurt. *GEMSTONE ENHANCEMENT*. Woburn, Mass.: Butterworths, 1983.

Possibly the most comprehensive, up-to-date, and understandable book available on gem enhancement.

———. *GEMS MADE BY MAN*. Philadelphia: Chilton & Co., 1980.

Important work on synthetics. A primary reference source.

Pagel-Theisen, V. *DIAMOND GRADING ABC*. New York: Rubin & Son, 1980.

Highly recommended for anyone in diamond sales.

Pough, F. H. *THE STORY OF GEMS AND SEMIPRECIOUS STONES*. New York: Harvey House, 1969.

Good for beginning and amateur gemologists.

Schumann, W. *GEMSTONES OF THE WORLD*. Translated by E. Stern. New York: Sterling Publishing Co., 1977.

This book has superior color plates of all of the gem families and their different varieties and for this reason would be valuable to anyone interested in gems.

Shipley, R. M. *DICTIONARY OF GEMS AND GEMOLOGY*. Los Angeles: Gemological Institute of America, 1951.

For the student of gemology.

Sinkankas, John. *GEMSTONE AND MINERAL DATA BOOK*. London: Northwood, 1982.

A great collection of information for the serious gem enthusiast.

Spencer, L. J. *KEY TO PRECIOUS STONES*. London: Blockie & Co., 1959.

Good for the beginning student of gemology.

Webster, R. *GEM IDENTIFICATION*. New York: Sterling Publishing, 1975.

————. *GEMOLOGIST'S COMPENDIUM. 5th Edition. London: Northwood, 1970.*

————. *GEMS*. London: Butterworth & Co., 1970. (4th Edition, revised by B. W. Anderson).

————. *GEMS IN JEWELRY*. London: Northwood, 1975.

————. *PRACTICAL GEMOLOGY*. 6th Edition. London: Northwood, 1976.

All of the above are highly recommended for the serious student of gemology, especially *GEMS*.

Journals

AUSTRALIAN GEMMOLOGIST. Published by the Gemmological Association of Australia, P.O. Box 35, South Yarra, Victoria 3141, Australia.

BULLETIN. Published by the Canadian Gemmological Association, P.O. Box 1106, Station Q, Toronto, Ontario, Canada M4T 2P2

GEMOLOGIA. Published by the Associacao Brasileira de Gemologia e Mineralogia, Departmento de Mineralogia e Petrografia, Sao Paulo University, Brasil.

GEMMOLOGY. Also entitled *JEMOROJI*. Published by Zenkoku Hoseigaku Kyokai, Tokyo, Japan.

GEMS & GEMOLOGY. Published by the Gemological Institute of America, Santa Monica, CA. Quarterly; containing many technical articles on gems and gem treatments.

JOURNAL OF GEMMOLOGY. Published by the Gemmological Association of Great Britain, London. Quarterly; containing many technical articles on gems and gem treatments.

JOURNAL OF THE GEMMOLOGICAL SOCIETY OF JAPAN. 1974—Also entitled *HOSEKI GAKKAISHI*. Published by the Society, Sendai, Tohoku University.

REVUE DE GEMMOLOGIE. Published by the Association francaise de gemmologie, 162 rue St. Honore, 75001 Paris, France.

ZEITSCHRIFT. Published by Deutsche Gemmologische Gesellschaft, Postfach 12 22 60, D-6580 Idar-Oberstein, FRG.

Magazines

ASIAN JEWELRY. Published by Myer Publishing Ltd., Wanchai, Hong Kong.

AURUM. Published by Aurum Editions S.A., Geneva, Switzerland.

GZ (GOLDSCHMIEDE UND UHRMACHER ZEITUNG). Published by Ruhle-Diebener-Verlag GmbH & Co. KG, Stuttgart, West Germany.

HONG KONG WATCH & JEWELLERY REVIEW. Published quarterly by Brilliant-Art Publishing Ltd., Wanchai, Hong Kong.

JEWELERS' CIRCULAR-KEYSTONE. Published by Chilton, Radnor, PA. Monthly; readable, business oriented review of events within the U.S. jewelry industry.

JEWELLERY NEWS ASIA. Published in Central Hong Kong.

JQ (JEWELRY & GEM QUARTERLY). Published by JQ Magazine, Sonoma, California.

LAPIDARY JOURNAL. Published by Lapidary Journal, Inc., San Diego, CA. Monthly; very readable magazine for gem cutters, collectors, and jewelers.

MODERN JEWELER. Published by Vance Publishing, Lincolnshire, ILL. Monthly; especially good for its monthly "Gem Profiles."

UHREN JUWELEN SCHMUCK. Published in Konigstein, West Germany.

NATIONAL JEWELER. Published by Gralla, N.Y., 24 issues per year; readable, business oriented review of events and issues within the U.S. jewelry industry.

RETAIL JEWELLER. Published by Knightway House, 20 Soho Square, London, W1V 6DT. U.K.

Sources of Price Information

PRECIOUS STONES MARKET MONITOR. Gemological Appraisal Association, 666 Washington Road, Pittsburgh, Pennsylvania, 15228.

THE DIAMOND REGISTRY. 30 West 47th Street, New York, New York, 10036.

DIAMOND INSIGHT. Tryon Mercantile Inc., 50 East 66th Street 2A, New York, NY 10021.

THE GUIDE. (Quarterly—diamonds and colored gems). Gemworld International, Inc., 5 South Wabash, Chicago, Illinois, 60602.

RAPAPORT'S DIAMOND REPORT. 15 West 47th Street, New York, New York.

GEMSTONE PRICE REPORTS. (diamonds; colored gems) UBIGE S.P.R.L., 26/08 Avenue General De Gaulle, B-1050 Brussels, Belgium.

MICHELSEN GEMSTONE INDEX. (diamonds; colored gems) Gem Spectrum, 1401 South Dixie Highway East, #5, Pompano Beach, Florida 33060.

Where To Go For Additional Gemological Training

Some of the organizations listed below offer formal training, others offer short courses or workshops. GIA periodically offers extension courses in cities throughout the U.S. For specific information regarding course offerings, duration and costs, contact organization directly.

UNITED STATES

Alabama

Holland School for Jewelers
231 Broad Street
Box 882
Selma, AL 36701

Arizona

International Gemological
  Services
4160 North Scottsdale
Scottsdale, AZ 85251

California

Gemological Institute of America
Santa Monica Campus
1660 Stewart Street
Santa Monica, CA 90404

Institute of Jewelry Training
3901 Norwood Ave.
Suite B
Sacramento, CA 95838

Jewelry Tech Institute, Inc.
12831 Western Ave.
Suite H
Garden Grove, CA 92641

Revere Academy of Jewelry Arts
760 Market #939
San Francisco, CA 94102

District of Columbia

(see Maryland listing)

American Society of Appraisers
Box 17265
Washington, DC 20041

Florida

Keno Gemological Bureau
2000 E. Sunrise Blvd.
Ft. Lauderdale, FL 33304

Georgia

Art Institute of Atlanta
3376 Peachtree Rd. N.E.
Atlanta, GA 30326

Atlanta Foundation For Jewelry
  Studies
110 E. Andrews Drive, #203
Atlanta, GA 30305

Emory University
Evening at Emory
Atlanta, GA 30322

Oglethorpe University
4484 Peachtree Rd. N.E.
Atlanta, GA 30319

Illinois

Parkland College
2400 W. Bradley Ave.
Champaign, IL 61820

Louisiana

International Gemological School
3100 Ridgelake Drive
Suite 301
Metairie, LA 70002

Maryland

Columbia School of Gemology
8600 Fenton Street
Silver Spring, MD 20910

Missouri

Diamond Council of America
9140 Ward Parkway
Kansas City, MO 64114

New York

Fashion Institute of Technology
227 West 27th Street
New York, NY 10001

Gemological Institute of America
New York Campus
580 Fifth Avenue
New York, NY 10036

Yeshiva University
Midtown Center
245 Lexington Ave.
New York, NY 10033

Texas

Paris Junior College
2400 Clarksville St.
Paris, TX 75460

Wisconsin

Milwaukee Area Technical College
1015 N. Sixth Street
Milwaukee, WI 53203

Northeast Wisconsin Technical Institute
2470 W. Mason
Green Bay, WI 54303

OTHER COUNTRIES

Australia

Gemmological Association of Australia
Queensland Branch
20 Rosslyn Street
East Brisbane 4169
Queensland, Australia

Gemmological Association of Australia
South Australian Branch
G.P.O. Box 5133 AA
Melbourne, 3001

ACT Institute of TAFE
Gemmology Department
P.O. Box 273
Civic Square ACT 2608

Belgium

European Gemological Laboratory
Rijfstraat 3
Antwerpen, Belgium

HRD Institute of Gemmology
Diamond High Council
Antwerp, Belgium

State University Antwerpen
Middlelheimlaan 1
2020 Antwerpen, Belgium

Brasil

Universidade Federal De Ouro
  Preto
Escola De Minas
Praca Tirandentes, 20
35400
Ouro Preto, MG, Brasil

Canada

Carleton University
Office of Admissions
Ottawa, Ontario
Canada K1S 5B6

George Brown College of Applied
  Arts & Technology
Box 1015
Station B
Toronto, Ontario
Canada M5T 2T9

Pacific Institute of Gemology
P.O. Box 69024
Vancouver, BC
Canada V5K 4W3

England

Department of Mineralogy
British Museum (Natural History)
Cromwell Road
London SW7 5BD

Gemmological Association of
  Great Britain
2 Carey Lane
London EC2

Gemmological Laboratory (Sun-
  derland Polytechnic)
Dept. of Applied Geology
Benedict Building
St. George's Way
Stockton Road
Sunderland, SR2 7BW

Huddlestone Gemmological
  Consultants LTD
Suite 221
100 Hatton Garden
London EC1N 8NX

France

Institut National de Gemmologie
1 rue Saint-Georges
75009 Paris

Institut de Gemmologie (ING)
2 Place de la Bourse
Paris 2

European Gemological Laboratory
9, Rue Buffault
75009 Paris

Hong Kong

The Hong Kong Institute of
  Gemmology
1104 Blissful Building
247 Des Voeux Road Central
Hong Kong

The Gemmological Association of
  Hong Kong
TST P.O. Box 89711
Kowloon, Hong Kong

Israel

E.G.L. Gemological Institute for
  Precious Stones
Noam Bldg.
Bezalel Str. 52
Ramat Gan, Israel

Gemmological Association of Israel
1 Jabotinsky St.
Ramat Gan, 52520
Israel

Italy

Istituto Gemmologico
  Mediterraneo
Via Marmolaia 14
38033 Cavalese, Italy

School of Gemology: Gemval s.n.c.
Istituto Analisi Gemmologiche
Via Sassi, 44
15048 Valenza (AL)
Italy

Japan

Association of Japan Gem Trust
2-3F Okachimachi Cy Bldg.
5-15-14 Ueno, Taito-ku
Tokyo, Japan T110

Gemological Institute of America
c/o Yoshiko Doi
Shimizu Building
3-19-4, Ueno
Taito-Ku, Tokyo

Central Gem Laboratory
Taiyo Bldg., 15–17
5-chome, Veno, Taito-Ku
Tokyo 110, Japan

Gemmological Association of
  All Japan
Tokyo-bihokaikan
1–24, Akashi-cho, Chuo-ku
Tokyo 104, Japan

Mrs. Anne C. Paul, F.G.A.
Apt. 101, Azabu Parkside
5-8-3 Minami Azabu
Minato-ku, Tokyo, Japan 106

Korea

Mi-Jo Gem Study Institute
244-39, Huam-dong Yongsan-ku
Seoul, Korea 140-190

Netherlands

Netherlands Gem Laboratory
Hooglandse Kerkgracht 17
2312HS Leiden
The Netherlands

Singapore

International Gemological
  Laboratory (S) Pte. Ltd.
402, Orchard Road, #03–07
Delfi Orchard
Singapore, 0923

South Africa

Gem Education Centre
P.O. Box 28940
Sandringham 2192
South Africa

  also at:
508 Medical Arts Building
220 Jeppe Street
Johannesburg 2001
South Africa

University of Natal
P.O. Box 375
Pietermaritzburg, Natal

University of Stellenbosch
Stellenbosch 7600
Cape Province
South Africa

Independent Coloured Stones
  Laboratory
P.O. Box 1354
Randburg 2125
South Africa

Sri Lanka

Dept. of Mining & Minerals
Engineering
University of Moratuwa
Katubedde, Sri Lanka

Petrological Laboratory
Geological Survey Dept.
48, Sri Jinaratana Road
Colombo 2, Sri Lanka

State Gem Corporation
Research & Development Unit
24 York Street
Colombo 1, Sri Lanka

Sweden

Rolf Krieger, F.G.A.
Kungsgatan 32 VI
S 111 35 Stockholm
Sweden

Switzerland

Gemmologie Laboratoire
  Service S.A.
Rue de Bourg 3
1003 Lausanne, Switzerland

Swiss Foundation for the
  Research of Gemstones
Lowenstrasse 17
CH-8001 Zurich
Switzerland

Thailand

Asian Institute of
  Gemological Sciences
987 Silom Rd
Rama Jewelry Bldg., 4th Floor
Bangkok 10500
Thailand

West Germany

Deutsche Gemmologische
  Gesellschaft
  (German Gemmological
  Association)
Prof.-Schlossmacher-Str. 1
P.O. Box 12 22 60
Idar–Oberstein, West Germany
D6580

Zimbabwe

Gem Education Centre of
  Zimbabwe
Founders House
15 Gordon Avenue
Harare, Zimbabwe 707580

Laboratories That Provide
Internationally Recognized Reports
of Genuineness and Quality

American Gemological Laboratory
580 Fifth Avenue, 12th floor
New York, NY 10036
(Services available to the jewelry
   trade and to the public)

GIA Gem Trade Laboratory
Gemological Institute of America
580 Fifth Avenue
New York, NY 10036
(Only to the jewelry trade)

Colored Diamond Laboratory
   Services, Inc.
15 West 47th Street
New York, New York 10036
(Issuing reports on colored dia-
   monds only)

GIA Gem Trade Laboratory
Gemological Institute of America
1660 Stewart Street
Santa Monica, Ca. 90404
(Only to the jewelry trade)

Hoge Raad voor Diamant (HRD)
Hoveniersstraat, 22
B-2018 Antwerp, Belgium

Gemmological Lab. Gubelin
Denkmalstrasse, 2
Ch-6006 Luzern, Switzerland
(Only to the jewelry trade)

Schweizerische Stiftung
   fur Edelstein-Forschung
   (SSEF)
Lowenstrasse, 17
Ch-8001 Zurich, Switzerland

International List of Gem Testing Laboratories and Gemologists

The following has been compiled from the International Colored Gemstone Association membership, the American Gem Society, the Accredited Gemologist Association, and the American Society of Appraisers. We hope it will aid you in locating laboratories and gemologists to assist you with gem identification or to offer guidance in developing your own proficiency.

An asterisk has been placed by labs we know to be accredited or recognized by a respected gem or jewelry industry association. CGA indicates a Certified Gemologist Appraiser is on staff. MGA indicates a Master Gemologist Appraiser is on staff.

For an up-to-date listing of CGAs in your area, contact the American Gem Society, 5901 West 3rd Street, Los Angeles, CA 90036-2898 (Tel. 213-936-4367). For MGA's, contact the American Society of Appraisers, Box 17265, Dulles International Airport, Washington, DC 20041 (Tel. 703-478-2228).

Australia

ACT Institute of T.A.F.E
Gemmology Dept.
P.O. Box 273
Civic Square,
ACT, 2608 Australia
Tel. 451798

Australian Gemmologist
P.O. Box 35
South Yarra, Victoria 3141
Australia

*Gemm'l. Assoc. of Australia—

Queensland Div.
20 Rosslyn St.
East Brisbane, Queensland
Australia 4169
Tel. (07) 3915

S. Australia Div., Box 191
Adelaide, S. Australia 5001

Western Australia Div.
P.O. Box 355
Nedlands, West Australia

Austria

*Austrian Gemmological Research
Institute (Erste Osterreichische
Gemmologische
Gesellschaft-EOGG)
Salesianergasse, 1
A-1030 Vienna, Austria
Tel. (222) 71168, Ext. 318 or 260

Belgium

European Gem'l. Laboratory
Rijfstraat, 3
2018 Antwerp, Belgium
Tel. 233 82 94

Hoge Raad voor Diamant (HRD)
Hoveniersstraat, 22
B-2018 Antwerp, Belgium

227

Canada

Brodman Gem'l. Lab., Inc.
1255 Phillips Square #1105
Montreal, Quebec,
  Canada H3B 3G1
Tel. (514) 866-4081

*De Goutiere Jewellers, Ltd.
2542 Estevan Avenue
Victoria, British Columbia
Canada V8R 2S7
(604) 592-3224
A. De Goutiere, (CGA)

*Ernest Penner Inc.
53 Queen Street
St. Catherines, Ontario
Canada L2R 5G8
(416) 688-0579
Ernest Penner (CGA)

Gem Service Lab
Harold Weinstein Ltd.
55 Queen St. E. 1301
Toronto, Ontario, Canada M5C 1R6
Tel. 366-6518

*The Gold Shop
345 Quellette Avenue
Windsor, Ontario
Canada N9A 4J1
(519) 254-5166
Ian M. Henderson (CGA)

Kinnear d'Esterre Jewellers
168 Princess Street
Kingston, Ontario
Canada K7L 1B1
(613) 546-2261
Erling Alstrup (CGA)

*Nash Jewellers
182 Dundas Street
London, Ontario
Canada N6A 1G7
(519) 672-7780
John C. Nash (CGA)

England

British Museum (Natural History)
Dept. of Mineralogy
Cromwell Road
London SW7 5BD, England
Tel. (01) 938-9123

*The Gem Testing Laboratory
27 Greville Street
Saffron Hill Entrance
London EC1N8SU, England

   (Not available to the public.
   Identification/verification can
   be requested by a jeweler or gem
   dealer on behalf of customer).

*Sunderland Polytechnic
  Gemmological Laboratory
Dept. of Applied Geology,
Benedict Bldg., St. George's Way
Stockton Rd.
Sunderland, SR2 7BW, England
Tel. (091) 567-9316

Huddlestone Gemmological
  Consultants LTD
100 Hatton Garden, Suite 221
London EC1N 8NX, England
Tel. 01-404-5004

France

*European Gemological
  Laboratory
9, Rue Buffault
75009 Paris, France
Tel. (1) 40-16-16-35

*Laboratoire Public De Controle
  des Pierres Precieuses de la
  Chambre De Commerce (C.C.I.P.)
2, Place De La Bourse
75002 Paris, France
Tel. 40268312

Germany

*Deutsches Diamant Institut
Poststrasse 1
Postfach 470
D-7530 Pforzheim, Germany
Tel. 07231/32211

*Deutsches Edelstein
Testinstitut (only gemstones)
Mainzerstrasse 34
D-6850 Idar-Oberstein, Germany

*Deutsche Gemmologische
Gesellaschaft EV
Prof.-Schlossmacher-Strasse 1
D6580 Idar-Oberstein 2, Germany
Tel. 6781/4-30-11

German Foundation of Gemstone
   Research (DSEF)
Prof.-Schlossmacher-Str. 1
D-6850 Idar Oberstein, Germany
Tel. 6781/4-30-13

Hong Kong

*Yang Mulia Gem Technological
   Consultancy and Laboratories
1103, Blissful Bldg.
247 Des Voeux Road Central
Hong Kong
Tel. 5-8152705

India

Gem Identification Laboratory
372 Gopal Ji Ka Rasta
Jaipur 302003, India
Tel. 47528

Gem'l. Inst. of India
29 Gurukul Chambers,
187 Mumbadevi Rd.
Bombay 400 002, India

Gem Testing Laboratory
Rajasthan Chamber.
Mirza Ismail Rd.
Jaipur, India

Israel

Gem'l. Inst. for Precious Stones
52 Bazalel St., 1st Floor
Ramat Gan 52521, Israel

*Nat'l. Gem'l. Inst. of Israel
52 Bazalel St.
Ramat Gan 52521, Israel
Tel. 751-7102

Italy

Analisi Consulenze
   Gemmologiche
Via Tortrino, 5
15048 Valenza (Alessandria)
Italy
Tel. 0131-953161

Centro Analisi Gemmologiche
Viale Vicenza 4/D
15048 Valenze, Italy

*Cisgem-External Service for
   Precious Stones/Chamber of
   Commerce of Milan
Via Brisa/Via Ansperto, 5
20123 Milano, Italy
Tel. 02/85155499

Instituto Analisi Gemmologiche
Via Sassi, 44
15048 Valenza, Italy
Tel. 0131-946586

Instituto Gemmologico Italiano
Viale Gramsci, 228
20099 Sesto San Giovanni
Milano, Italy
Tel: (02) 2409354

also at:
Via Appia Nuova, 52
00183 Roma, Italy
(06) 7575685

*Laboratorio Scientifico
Professionale di Controllo di
Diamanti, Pietre Preziose e
Perle della CONFEDORAFI
Via Ugo Foscolo 4
1-20121 Milano, Italy

Holland

*Nederlands Edelsteen
  Laboratorium
  (only gemstones)
Hooglandse Kergracht 17
2312 HS Leiden, Nederland
Tel: (31) 071-143844

*Stichting Nederlands Diamant
Instituut (only diamonds)
Van de Spiegelstraat 3
Postbus 29818
NL-2502LV's-Gravenhage,
Nederland
Tel. 070-469607

Japan

Central Gem Lab
Taiyo Bldg. 15–17, 5 Chome,
Ueno, Taito-Ku
Tokyo 110, Japan
Tel. 03-836-3131

*CIBJO Institute of Japan (only
  diamonds)
Tokyo-Bihokaikan 1–24,
Akashi-Cho
Chuo-Ku, Tokyo, Japan
Tel. 03-543-3821

Kenya

Mr. P. Dougan
P.O. Box 14173
Nairobi, Kenya

*Ruby Center of Kenya Ltd.
Fedha Towers, Second Floor
Muindi Mbingu Street
Nairobi, Kenya (East Africa)
Tel. 335261, 334299

Korea

Mi-Jo Gem Study Institute
244-39, Huam-dong Youngsan-ku
Seoul, Korea 140-190
Tel. 754-5075, 0642

Republic of South Africa

European Gemological Laboratory
Paulshop Bldg.
Corner Plein & Twist Streets
Johannesburg, South Africa
Tel. 29-9647

*Gem Education Center
508 Medical Arts Bldg.
220 Jeppe Street
Johannesburg, 2000, South Africa
Tel. 337-3457, 3458

Independent Coloured Stones Lab.
5 Hengilcon Avenue
Blairgourie, Randburg
Transvaal,
Rep. of South Africa
2194
Tel. (011) 787-3326

Singapore

International Gemological Lab,
  (S) Pte. Ltd.
402 Orchard Road
#03-07, Delfi Orchard
Singapore 0923
Tel. 732-7272/ 732-3636

Spain

*Instituto Gemologico Espanol
Victor Hugo, 1, 3e
Madrid-4, Spain

*Laboratorio Oficial de la
Association Espanola de
Gemologia AEG
Pseo. de Gracia 64 entr. 2a
Barcelona-7, Spain
Tel. 2 15 43 12

Sri Lanka

Gem'l. Assoc. of Sri Lanka
Professional Center
275/75 Bauddhalokka Mawatha
Colombo 7, Sri Lanka

*Gemmology   Laboratory/Depart-
  ment of Mining & Minerals
  Engineering
University of Moratuwa,
Katubedde, Sri Lanka
Tel. Colombo 505353

Petrological Laboratory
Geological Survey Dept.
48, Sri Jinaratana Rd.
Colombo 2, Sri Lanka
Tel. 29014/15

State Gem Corporation
Gem Testing Laboratory
24, York Street
Colombo 1, Sri Lanka
Tel. 28701

State Gem Corporation
No. 92/4A, Templars Road
Mount Lavinia, Sri Lanka

Sweden

Swedish Inst. For Gem Testing
P.O. Box 3021
S-12703 Stockholm, Sweden

Rolf Krieger
Kungsgatan 32 VI
S 111 35 Stockholm, Sweden
Tel. 8/ 10-13-65

Switzerland

*Gemgrading
4, Rue Albert-Gos
1206 Geneva, Switzerland
Tel. (022) 46-60-61

*Gemmological Lab Gubelin
Denkmalstrasse, 2
Ch-6006 Luzern, Switzerland

*Gemmologie Laboratoire Service
Rue de Bourg, 3
1003 Lausanne, Switzerland
Tel. (021) 20-49-77

*Schweizerische Stiftung
fur Edelstein-Forschung (SSEF)
Lowenstrasse 17,
CH-8001 Zurich, Switzerland
Tel. 01/211 24 71

Thailand

*Asian Institute of Gemmological
  Science
987 Silom Rd.,
Rama Jewellery Bldg., 4th Floor
Bangkok 10500, Thailand
Tel. 233-8388/9, 235-1254/5

Zimbabwe

Gem Education Centre of
  Zimbabwe
Founders House
  15 Gordon Avenue
Harare, Zimbabwe 707580

UNITED STATES

Alabama

*Jimmy Smith Jewelers
Southland Plaza Shopping Center
Decatur, AL 35602
(205) 353-2512
Jimmy Ray Smith (CGA)

*Mason Jewelers
3011 South Parkway
Huntsville, AL 35801
(205) 883-2150
Ronnie Robbins (CGA)
  and at
5901-73 University Drive
Madison Square Mall
Huntsville, AL 35806
(205) 830-5930
Emily White Ware (CGA)

*Mickleboro's of Montgomery
3003-C McGehee Road
Montgomery, AL 36111
(205) 281-6597
Amy J. Michaels (CGA)

*Ware Jewelers
111 So. College Street
Auburn, AL 36830
(205) 821-7375
Stanley Arington (CGA)
  and at
Village Mall
162 Opelika Road
Auburn, AL 36830
(205) 821-3122
Ronnie Ware (CGA)

Arizona

*Ambassador Diamond Brokers
4668 E. Speedway Blvd.
Tucson, AZ 85712
(602) 327-8800
Stewart M. Kuper (MGA)

*Caldwell Jewelry Corp.
7225 N. Oracle Rd.
Tucson, AZ 85704
(602) 742-3687
Brenda J. Caldwell (MGA)

*Dennis D. Naughton Jewelers
129 Park Central Mall
Phoenix, AZ 85013
(602) 264-2857
Net T. Burns (CGA)

*Grunewald & Adams Jewelers
Biltmore Fashion Park
2468 E. Camelback
Phoenix, AZ 85016
(602) 955-8450
Sandra Overland (CGA)

*Jim Anderson Jewelers
2112 N. Fourth Street
Flagstaff, AZ 86004
(602) 526-0074
James R. Anderson (CGA)

*Joseph M. Berning Jewelers
130 E. University Drive
Tempe, AZ 85281
(602) 967-8917
Patricia Berning (CGA)

*Marshall's Artistry in Gold, Inc.
4811 E. Grant Road, #113
Tucson, AZ 85712
(602) 325-9955
Richard G. Marshall (CGA)

*Michelle Hallier (MGA)
1250 East Missouri St.
Phoenix, AZ 85014
(602) 277-9780

*Molina Fine Jewelers
1250 E. Missouri St. #3
Phoenix, AZ 85014
(602) 265-5001
Alfredo J. Molina (MGA)

*Ouellet and Lynch
5743 W. St. Johns Road
Glendale, AZ 85308
(602) 264-3210
Craig A. Lynch (MGA)

*Paul Johnson Jewelers
1940 E. Camelback Road
Phoenix, AZ 85016
(602) 277-1421
Thomas Hergenroether (CGA)

*Paul Johnson Jewelers, Inc.
6900 E. Camelback Rd.
Scottsdale, AZ 85251
(602) 994-0133
Michael Holmes (CGA)

*Peterson's Jewelry
209 W. Gurley Street
Prescott, AZ 86301
(602) 445-3098
James Lamerson (CGA)

*Schmieder & Son Jewelers
Park Central Mall West
Phoenix, AZ 85013
(602) 264-4464
Carl Schmieder (CGA)

*Schmieder & Son Jewelers
10001 W. Bell Road
Sun City, AZ 85351
(602) 974-3627
Robert Delane Cloutier (CGA)

*Setterberg Jewelers
Campana Square
9885 West Bell Rd.
Sun City, AZ 85351
(602) 972-6130
Wendell Setterberg (CGA)

Arkansas

*Stanley Jewelers
3422 John F. Kennedy Blvd.
North Little Rock, AK 72116
(501) 753-1081
Loyd C. Stanley (CGA)

*Underwood's Jewelers
611 W. Dickson
Fayetteville, AK 72701
(501) 521-2000
William G. Underwood (CGA)

California

*A.L. Jacobs & Sons Jewelers
675 B. Street
San Diego, CA 92101
(619) 232-1418
Christopher Jacobs (CGA)

*The Altobelli Jewelers
4419 Lankershim Blvd.
North Hollywood, CA 91602
(818) 763-5151
Cos Altobelli (CGA)

*American Jewelry Co.
Oak Park Tower #500
3200 21st St. at Oak
Bakersfield, CA 93301
(805) 325-5023
Carl M. Saenger (CGA)

*Azevedo Jewelers & Gemologists
210 Post Street #321
San Francisco, CA 94108
(415) 781-0063
Kathleen Beaulieu (CGA)

*Balzan's Gemological Lab.
P.O. Box 6007
San Rafael, CA 94903
(415) 924-1201
Cortney G. Balzan (MGA)

*Barrett W. Reese-Goldsmith
499 No. Central Ave.
Upland, CA 91766
(714) 981-7902
Barrett W. Reese (CGA)

Brewsters
6052 Magnolia Avenue
Riverside, CA 92506
(714) 686-1979
Frank A. Wright

*Bubar's Jeweler
216 Santa Monica Place
Santa Monica, CA 90401
(213) 451-0727
Basil Marnoff (CGA)

*Cardinal Jewelers
1807-L Santa Rita Road
Pleasanton, CA 94566
(415) 462-6666
James A. Kuhn (CGA)

*Charles H. Barr Jewelers
1048 Irvine Avenue
Westcliff Plaza
Newport Beach, CA 92660
(714) 642-3310
Donna H. Blackman (CGA)

*Chase Jewelers, Inc.
20442 Redwood Road
Castro Valley, CA 94546
(415) 581-0632
Edward A. Chase (CGA)

*Currie & Underwood
3957 Goldfinch Street
San Diego, CA 92103
(619) 291-8850
Thom Sorensen Underwood
   (MGA)

*Dudenhoeffer Fine Jewelry, Ltd.
118 E. Main Street
El Cajon, CA 92020
(619) 588-9001
Roy Dudenhoeffer (CGA)

*Dudenhoeffer Fine Jewelry, Ltd.
123 Horton Plaza
San Diego, CA 92101
(619) 236-0316

*European Gemological
   Laboratory
608 S. Hill Street, Ste. 1013
Los Angeles, CA 90014
(213) 623-8092
Thomas Tashey (MGA)

*Finley-Gracer
5112 E. Second Street
Long Beach, CA 90903
(213) 434-4429
Warren Finley (CGA)

*Frederic H. Rubel Jewelers
167 Central City Mall
San Bernardino, CA 92401
(714) 889-9565
Gary W. Rubel (CGA)

*Frederic H. Rubel Jewelers
560 Main Place
2800 N. Main Street
Santa Ana, CA 92701
(714) 558-9144
David A. Rubel (CGA)

*The Gem Connection
9227 Haven Avenue
Rancho Cucamonga, CA 91730
(714) 941-4500
Ronald L. Base (MGA)

*Gem Profiles
416 West Santa Ana
Fresno, CA 93705
(209) 229-7361
Bob Praska

*George Carter Jessop & Co.
1025 Second Avenue
Westgate Mall
San Diego, CA 92101
(619) 234-4137
James C. Jessop (CGA)

*Gleim the Jeweler
119 Stanford Shopping Ctr.
Palo Alto, CA 94304
(415) 325-3533
David C. Loudy (CGA)

*Grebitus & Son Jewelers
Country Club Centre
3332 El Camino
Sacramento, CA 95821
(916) 487-7853
Robert Grebitus (CGA)

*Grebitus & Son Jewelers
511 L. Street
Sacramento, CA 95814
(916) 442-9081
J. Marlene White (CGA)

*G M E
1600 Howe Ave.
Sacramento, CA 95825
(916) 925-6711
Alison LeBaron (MGA)
G. Marilyn Thomas (MGA)

*Hammond's Jewelry, Inc.
16 N. Tower Square
Tulare, CA 93274
(209) 686-9224
Richard Hammond (CGA)

*The Hardware Store, Fine Jewelry
11621 Barrington Court
Los Angeles, CA 90049
(213) 472-2970
Gary M. Murray (CGA)

*Harlequin Jewelry Design
3158 Jefferson Street
Napa, CA 94558
(707) 255-2121
Mark London (CGA)

*Harwin Jewelers
110 S. Hope Avenue
Santa Barbara, CA 93105
(805) 682-8838
Joel S. Harwin (CGA)

*Houston Jewelers
4454C Van Nuys Blvd.
Sherman Oaks, CA 91423
(818) 783-1122
Richard Houston (CGA)

*Int'l Gemological Lab.
650 S. Hill St., Ste. 229
Los Angeles, CA 90014
(213) 688-7837
Andrew Y.K. Kim (MGA)

*J.C. Humphries Jewelers
1835 Newport Blvd. #D152
Costa Mesa, CA 92627
(714) 548-3401
Joseph C. Humphries (CGA)

Jack E. Rich Jewelers Inc.
338 Merchant Street
Vacaville, CA 95688
(707) 448-4808
Dale S. Rich (CGA)

*Jewels by Stacy
458 Morro Bay Blvd.
Morro Bay, CA 93442
(805) 772-1003
Nancy Frey Stacy (MGA)

*Johnson & Co. Jewelers
111 Stanford Shopping Ctr.
Palo Alto, CA 94304
(415) 321-0764
Steven Graham (CGA)

*Johnson Jewelers
16727 S. Bellflower Blvd.
Bellflower, CA 90706
(213) 867-4420
Russell Sowell (CGA)

*Lee Frank Mfg. Jewelers
2200 Shattuck Avenue
Berkeley, CA 94704
(415) 843-6410
Angie Dang (CGA)

*Lynn's Jewelry
2434 E. Main Street
Ventura, CA 93003
(805) 648-4544
Robert A. Lynn (CGA)

*Marshall Adams Gems
2364 N. Del Rosa Ave., #8
San Bernardino, CA 92404
(714) 883-8463
Marshall A. Adams (MGA)

*Montclair Jewelers
2083 Mountain Blvd.
Oakland CA 94611
(415) 339-8547
David J. Coll (CGA)

*Morgan's Jewelers, Inc.
311 Del Amo Fashion Center
Torrance, CA 90503
(213) 542-5925
Marshall Varon (CGA)

*Shoemake's
  Jeweller/Gemmologist
1323 J. St.
Modesto, CA 95454
(209) 577-3711
Otto R. Zimmerman (CGA)

*Sidney Mobell Fine Jewelry
141 Post Street
San Francisco, CA 94108
(415) 986-4747
Philip Chen (CGA)

*Sidney Mobell Fine Jewelry
Lobby Fairmont Hotel
San Francisco, CA 94106
(415) 421-4747

*Smith Jewelers
704 San Ramon Valley Blvd.
Danville, CA 94526
(415) 837-3191
Laurence James Smith (CGA)

*Morton Jewelers, Inc.
212 N. Santa Cruz Avenue
Los Gatos, CA 95030
(408) 395-3500
Sue Maron-Szuks (CGA)

*Nielsen Jewelers Inc.
1581 W. Main Street
Barstow, CA 92311
(619) 256-3333
Carl G. Nielsen (CGA)

*Norman Mahan Jewelers
2211 Larkspur
  Landing Circle
Larkspur, CA 94939
(415) 461-5333
Nancy Mahan-Weber
  (CGA)

*Robann's Jewelers
125 S. Palm Canyon Dr.
Palm Springs, CA 92262
(619) 325-9603
Roger Kerchman (CGA)

*San Diego Gemological
  Laboratory
3957 Goldfinch St.
San Diego, CA 92103
(619) 291-8852
Thom Underwood (MGA)

*Stucki Jewelers
148 Mill Street
Grass Valley, CA 95945
(916) 272-9618
George M. Delong (CGA)

*Timothy Fidge & Co.
27 Town & Country Village
Palo Alto, CA 94301
(415) 323-4653
Patricia Rickard (CGA)

*Troy & Company
527 South Lake Ave., #105
Pasadena, CA 91101
(818) 449-8414
Troy B. Steckenrider (CGA)

United States
Gemological Services
14080 Yorba St, #237
Tustin, Ca. 92680
(714) 838-8747
David Ascher

*The Village Jeweler
1014-8 Westlake Blvd.
Westlake Village, CA 91361
(805) 497-4114
James W. Coote (CGA)

*Wickersham Jewelers
3320 Truxtun Avenue
Bakersfield, CA 93301
(805) 324-6521
John C. Abrams, (CGA)

*Wight Jewelers
207 N. Euclid Avenue
Ontario, CA 91762
(714) 984-2745
P. Donald Riffe (CGA)

Colorado

*Merritt Sherer, Gemologist
Southmoor Park Center
6448 East Hampden Ave.
Denver, CO 80222
(303) 691-9414
Merritt Sherer (CGA)

*Molberg's Jewelers–
  Gemologists Inc.
University Hills Shopping Ctr.
2700 S. Colorado Blvd.
Denver, CO 80222
(303) 757-8325
Leonard J. Molberg (CGA)

*Purvis Jewelers Inc.
9797 West Colfax Ave., #2G
Lakewood, CO 80215
(303) 233-2798
John Purvis III (CGA)

*Walters & Hogsett
  Fine Jewelers
2425 Canyon Blvd.
Boulder, CO 80302
(303) 449-2626
William Lacert (CGA)

*Zerbe Jewelers, Inc.
118 N. Tejon Street
Colorado Springs, CO 80903
(719) 635-3521
Charles J. Zerbe (CGA)

Connecticut

*Addessi Jewelry Store
207 Main Street
Danbury, CT 06810
(203) 744-2555
Doreen A. Guerrera (CGA)

*Craig's Jewelry Store
394 Main Street
Ridgefield, CT 06877
(203) 438-3701
William D. Craig (CGA)

*Lux Bond & Green
Somerset Square
Glastonbury, CT 06033
(203) 659-8510
Cynthia L. Konney (CGA)
  and at
15 Pratt Street
Hartford, CT 06103
(203) 278-3050
John A. Green (CGA)
  and at
46 La Salle Road
West Hartford, CT 06107
(203) 521-3015
Marc A. Green (CGA)

*M.B.A. Associates
99 Pratt Street
Hartford, CT 06103
(203) 527-6036
Neil H. Cohen (MGA)

*Michaels Jewelers
127 Bank Street
Waterbury, CT 06702
(203) 754-5154
Ernest Bader (CGA)

*Michael's Jewelers
926 Chapel St.
New Haven, CT 06510
(203) 865-6145

*Michaels Jewelers, Inc.
80 Main Street
Torrington, CT 06790
(203) 482-6553
Edward Bush (CGA)

*Neil Cohen Gemologist
99 Pratt Street
Hartford, CT. 06103
(203) 247-1319
Neil Cohen (MGA)

Delaware

*Continental Jewelers
1732 Marsh Road
Graylyn Shopping Center
Wilmington, DE 19810
(302) 478-7190
Paul S. Cohen (CGA)

District of Columbia

(see "Maryland" and "Virginia")

Florida

*Antares & Co., Gems & Jewelry
5613 University Blvd., W.
Jacksonville, FL 32216
(904) 737-8316
B. Young McQueen (MGA)

*Bechtel Jewelers, Inc.
226 Datura Street
West Palm Beach, FL 33401
(407) 655-8255
Robert L. Bechtel (CGA)

*Burt's Jewelers
1706 N.E. Miami Gardens Drive
Miami, FL 33179
(305) 947-8386
Lloyd Aaron (MGA)

*Carroll's Jewelers, Inc.
915 E. Las Olas Blvd.
Ft. Lauderdale, FL 33301
(305) 463-3711
Robert B. Moorman Jr. (CGA)

*Gause & Son Oaks Mall
6663 Newberry Road
Gainesville, FL 32605
(904) 374-4417
Albert Seelbach (CGA)

*Gemological Lab Service
   Corporation
22 N. W. 1st Street, Ste. 101
Miami, FL 33128
(305) 371-6437
David M. Levison (MGA)

*Gemstone Corp. of America
7507 S. Trail
Sarasota, FL 34231
(813) 921-4214
Carol M. Daunt (MGA)
John J. Daunt III (MGA)

*Griner's Jewelry Haven, Inc.
850 Cypress Gardens Blvd
Winter Haven, FL 33880
(813) 294-4100
Randall M. Griner (CGA)

*Harold Oppenheim (MGA)
633 N.E. 167th St., Rm. #1023
North Miami Beach, FL 33162
(305) 652-1319

*Indep. Gem Testing, Inc.
2455 E. Sunrise Blvd. #501
Fort Lauderdale, FL 33304
(305) 563-2901
William C. Horvath (MGA)

*J.B. Smith & Son
   Jewelers, Inc.
900 E. Atlantic Ave., Suite 21
Delray Beach, FL 33483
(407) 278-3346
James T. Smith (CGA)

Jaylyn Gemologists Goldsmiths
30 S.E. 4th Street
Boca Raton, FL 33432
(305) 391-0013
James O'Sullivan

*Jos. W. Tenhagen
  Gemstones, Inc.
36 NE First Street, Suite 419
Miami, FL 33132
(305) 374-2411
Joseph Tenhagen (MGA)

*Kempf's Jewelers, Inc.
236 Fifth Avenue
Indialantic, FL 32903
(407) 724-5820
Gale M. Kempf (CGA)

*Lee Jewelry
1823 East Colonial Dr.
Orlando, FL 32803
(407) 896-2566
Robert A. Lee (CGA)

*Mayor's Jewelers, Inc.
283 Catalonia Avenue
Coral Gables, FL 33134
(305) 442-4233
Bruce Handler (CGA)

*Moon Jewelry Company
536 N. Monroe
Tallahassee, FL 32301
(804) 224-9000
Jeff Hofmeister (CGA)

*The Oak's Keepsake
  Diamond Gallery
The Oaks Mall A-13
Gainesville, FL 32605
(904) 331-5337

*P.J. Abramson, Inc.
180 N. Park Ave., Suite 4D
Winter Park, FL 32789
(407) 644-3383
Pamela J. Abramson (MGA)

*Paul J. Schmitt Jeweler
765 Fifth Ave. S.
Naples, FL 33940
(813) 262-4251
Paul J. Schmitt (CGA)

*Paul J Schmitt Jeweler
4321 Tamiami Trail
Naples, FL 33940
(813) 261-0600
James T. Merkley (CGA)

*Peter Bradley, Inc.
13499 US 41 S.E.
Fort Myers, FL 33907
(813) 482-7550
Peter F. Bradley (MGA)

*Roger Hunt & Son
Div. Maison D'Or, Inc.
232 S. W. 10th Street
Ocala, FL 32671
(904) 629-1105
Roger E. Hunt (CGA)

*Suncoast Accredited Gem. Lab.
Bayshore Office Bldg.
6221 14th St. West, Suite 105
Bradenton, Fl. 34207
(813) 756-8787

*Wells Jewelers, Inc.
4452 Hendricks Avenue
Jacksonville, FL 32207
(904) 730-0111
Laurence Bodkin (CGA)

Georgia

*Ford, Gittings & Kane Inc.
312 Broad St.
Rome, GA 30161
(404) 291-8811
Jan J. Fergerson (CGA)

Hawaii

*Hallmark Jewelers
2242 Ala Moana Ctr.

Oahu, Honolulu
Hawaii, 96814
(808) 949-3982
Yoshimasa Ishihara (CGA)

Illinois

*Denney Jewelers
51 Central Park Plaza South
Jacksonville, IL 62650
(217) 245-4718
Shane S. Denney (CGA)

*Doerner Jewelers
9201 North Milwaukee Avenue
Niles, IL 60648
(312) 966-1341
Michael Doerner (CGA)

*Fey & Company Jewelers, Inc.
1156 Fox Valley Center
Aurora, IL 60505
(312) 851-8828
Edgar H. Fey III (CGA)

*Franz Jewelers, Ltd.
1220 Meadow Road
Northbrook, IL 60062
(312) 272-4100
Frank E. Pintz (CGA)

*Rand Jewelers, Inc.
2523A Waukegan Rd.
Bannockburn Green Shop. Ctr.
Bannockburn, IL 60015
(312) 948-9475
William E. Rand (CGA)

*Samuels Jewelers, Inc.
4500 16th Street
South Park Mall
Moline, IL 61265
(309) 762-9375
Corey James England (CGA)

*Stout and Lauer
1650 Wabash-The Yard
Springfield, IL 62704
(217) 793-3040
Deborah Lauer-Toelle (CGA)

Indiana

*Droste's Jewelry Shoppe, Inc.
4511 First Avenue
Evansville, IN 47710
(812) 422-4351
Gregory Scott Droste (CGA)

*Philip E. Nelson Jeweler, Inc.
22 E. Main Street
Brownsburg, IN 46112
(317) 852-2306
Jeffrey R. Nelson (CGA)

*Troxel Jewelers, Inc.
7980 Broadway
Merrillville, IN 46410
(219) 769-0770
Donald Troxel (CGA)

*Williams Jewelry Inc.
114 N. Walnut
Bloomington, IN 47408
(812) 339-2231
Mark A. Thoma (CGA)

Iowa

*Becker's Jewelers
123 West Monroe
Mt. Pleasant, IA 52641
(319) 385-3722
William D. Becker (CGA)

*Gunderson's Jewelers
Terra Center
600 Fourth St.
Sioux City, IA 51101
(712) 255-7229
Brian Gunderson (CGA)

*Josephs Jewelers
320 6th Ave.
Des Moines, IA 50309
(515) 283-1961
William J. Baum (CGA)

*Mark Ginsberg (MGA)
110 E. Washington St.
Iowa City, IA 52240
(319) 351-1700

*Samuels Jewelers, Inc.
320 W. Kimberly
Northpark Mall
Davenport, IA 52806
(319) 391-4362
Peggy K. Friederichs (CGA)

*Thorpe & Company Jewellers
501 4th Street
Sioux City, IA 51101
(712) 258-7501
Bruce C. Anderson (CGA)

Kansas

*Donaldson's Jewelers, Inc.
Seabrook Center
2001 S.W. Gage Blvd.
Topeka, KS 66604
(913) 273-5080
Tracie E. Forkner (CGA)

*Jewelry Arts, Inc.
8221 Corinth Square
Prairie Village, KS 66208
(913) 381-8444
Ryudy Giessenbier (CGA)

*Lavery's Jewelry
404 Delaware
Leavenworth, KS 66048
(913) 682-3182
Evelyn J. Chapman (CGA)

*Riley's Jewelry Inc.
6116 Johnson Dr.
Mission, KS 66202
(913) 432-8484
William A. Riley (CGA)

Kentucky

*Bernard Lewis & Co.
313 Broadway
Paducah, KY 42001
(502) 442-0002
(800) 327-4056
Bernard G. Lewis (CGA)

*Brundage Jewelers
141 Chenoweth Lane
Louisville, KY 40207
(502) 895-7717
William E. Brundage (CGA)

*Cortland Hall Jewelers, Inc.
133 St. Matthews Avenue
Louisville, KY 40207
(502) 897-6024
Mark L. Redmon (CGA)

*Farmer's Jewelry
821 Euclid Avenue
Lexington, KY 40502
(606) 266-6241
William L. Farmer (CGA)

*Merkley Jewelers
400 Old East Vine
Lexington, KY 40507
(606) 254-1548
Kimberley S. Hall (CGA)

*Merkley-Kendrick Jewelers Inc.
138 Chenoweth Lane
Louisville, KY 40207
(502) 895-6124
Donald J. Merkley (CGA)

*Miller & Woodward, Inc.
115 West Short Street
Lexington, KY 40507
(606) 233-3001
Russell Pattie (CGA)

*Seng Jewelers
453 Fourth Avenue
Louisville, KY 40202
(502) 585-5109
Lee S. Davis (CGA)

Louisiana

*Champions Jewelers—
  Gemologists
1123 North Pine Street
Park Terrace Shopping Ctr.
De Ridder, LA 70634
(318) 463-7026
John Cunningham (CGA)

*Clarkes Jewelers, Inc.
3916 Youree Drive
Shreveport, LA 71105
(318) 865-5658
Gary L. Clarke (CGA)

*Simon Jeweller
  Gemmologist, Inc.
941 E. 70th Street
Shreveport, LA 71106
Horace Simon (CGA)

Maine

*Brown Goldsmiths & Co., Inc.
One Mechanic Street
Freeport, ME 04032
(207) 865-4126
W. Stephen Brown (CGA)

*Etienne & Company
20 Main Street
Camden, ME 04843
(207) 236-9696
(800) 426-4367
Peter Theriault (CGA)

*J. Dostie Jeweler
4 Lisbon Street
Lewiston, ME 04240
(207) 782-7758
Linda Chamberlain (CGA)

Maryland

*Colonial Jewelry Inc.
9 W. Patrick St., P.O. Box 674
Frederick, MD 21701
(301) 663-9252
Jeffrey I. Hurwitz (MGA)

*National Gem Appraising Lab.
8600 Fenton Street
Silver Spring, MD 20910
Antonio C. Bonanno (MGA)
Karen J. Ford (MGA)

*Tilghman Company
44 State Circle
Annapolis, MD 21401
(301) 268-7855
Thomas O. Tilghman (CGA)

Massachusetts

*Andrew Grant Diamond Center
144 Elm Street
Westfield, MA 01085
(413) 562-2432
Robert K. Grant (CGA)

*Appraisal Associates
7 Kent Street
Brookline Village, MA 02146
(617) 566-1339
Nancy A. Smith (MGA)

*Kenyon A. Carr, Jeweler
422 Main Street
Hyannis, MA 02601
(617) 775-1968
William F. Carr (CGA)

*La France Jeweler
763 Purchase Street
New Bedford, MA 02740
(508) 993-1137
Paul R. Rousseau (CGA)

*Romm & Co.
162 Main Street
Brockton, MA 02401
(508) 587-2533
Dean B. Learned (CGA)

*Sharfmans, Inc.
164 Worcester Center
Worcester, MA 01608
(508) 791-2211
(800) 451-7500
Nancy R. Rosenberg (CGA)

*Shreve, Crump & Low
330 Boylston Street
Boston, MA 02116
Joseph P. Pyne (CGA)

*Swanson Jeweler, Inc.
717 Massachusetts Ave.
Arlington, MA 02174
(617) 643-4209
Robert Swanson (CGA)

*Wyman Jewelers Inc.
18 Wyman Street
Stoughton, MA 02072
(617) 344-5000
Philip Minsky (CGA)

Michigan

*Birmingham Gemological
  Services
251 Merrill Street
Birmingham, MI 48011
(313) 644-8828
James Krol (MGA)

*Dobie Jewelers
14600 Lakeside Circle #205
Lakeside Mall
Sterling Heights, MI 48078
(313) 247-1730
Edmund P. Dery (CGA)
  and at
500 S. Washington St.
Royal Oak, MI 48067
(313) 545-8400
Joseph M. Cayuela (CGA)

*Everts Jewelers, Inc.
109 E. Broadway
Mount Pleasant, MI 48858
(517) 772-3141
Lawrence W. Everts (CGA)

*F.A. Earl Jewelers
156 E. Front Street
Traverse City, MI 49684
(616) 947-7602
Brad Shepler (CGA)

*Haffner Jewelers
3204 Rochester Rd.
Royal Oak, MI 48073
(313) 588-6622
David Williamson (MGA)

*J. F. Reusch Jewelers
427 E. Mitchell Street
Petoskey, MI 49770
(616) 347-2403
John F. Reusch (CGA)

*Jules R. Schubot Jewellers
3001 W. Big Beaver Rd., #112
Troy, MI 48084
(313) 649-1122
Brian T. Schubot (CGA)

*Losey's Fine Jewelry
133 East Main Street
Midland, MI 48640
(517) 631-1143
Roger E. Schmidt (CGA)

*Milkins Jewelers
13 Washington St.
Monroe, MI 48161
(313) 242-1023
Bruce A. Milkins (CGA)

*Mosher's Jewelers, Inc.
336 Huron Ave.
Port Huron, MI 48060
(313) 987-2768
William A. Mosher (CGA)

*Siegel Jewelers
Amway Grand Plaza Hotel
Pearl & Monroe
Grand Rapids, MI 49503
(616) 459-7263
B. Miller Siegel (CGA)
  and at:
28 Woodland Mall
3135 28th S.E.
Grand Rapids, MI 49508
(616) 949-7370
James W. Siegel (CGA)

Minnesota

*Bockstruck Jewelers
27 W. Fifth St.
St. Paul, MN 55102
(612) 222-1858
DeWayne Amundsen (CGA)

*Korst & Sons Jewelers
3901 W. 50th Street
Edina, MN 55424
(612) 926-0303
William Korst Jr. (CGA)

*R.F. Moeller Jeweler
2073 Ford Parkway
St. Paul, MN 55116
(612) 698-6321
Mark Moeller (CGA)

*Stadheim Jewelers
215 S. Broadway
Albert Lea, MN 56007
(507) 373-3440
Beth S. Ordalen (CGA)

Mississippi

*Way-Fil Jewelry
1123 W. Main Street
Tupelo, MS 38801
(601) 844-2427
Patricia A. Witt (CGA)

Missouri

Clayton Gemological
  Services, Inc.
Bemiston Tower. Suite 800
231 South Bemiston
St. Louis, MO 63105-1914
(314) 862-4005
Therese S. Kienstra

*Elleard B. Heffern, Inc.
7777 Bonhomme Ave.
Suite 1800
St. Louis, MO 63105
(314) 863-8820
Christopher E. Heffern (CGA)

*Frank Gooden Co., Inc. Gemlab
1110 Grand Avenue
Kansas City, MO 64106
(816) 421-0281
Ricki Kendall Gooden

*Tivol, Inc.
220 Nichols Rd.
Kansas City, MO 64112
(816) 531-5800
J. Michael Tracy (CGA)

Montana

*Blacks' Jewelers
211 Third Ave.-Box 869
Havre, MT 59501
(406) 265-2522
(800) 843-3564
Richard J. Growney (CGA)

*Chaussee Precious Gems &
  Fine Jewelry
228 N. Higgins
Missoula, MT 59802
(406) 728-8639
Yvette I. Clevish (CGA)

*Crown Jewelry, Inc.
419 Central Ave.
Great Falls, MT 59401
(406) 453-5312
E.W. O'Neil (CGA)

*William Sargent, Jeweler
20 N. Main
Kalispell Center Mall
Kalispell, MT 59901
(406) 752-7464

Nebraska

*Karl's Jewelry
84 West 6th
Box 710
Fremont, NB 68025
(402) 721-1727
Karl Rasmussen IV (CGA)

*Michael's Jewelry of
  Fremont, N.E. Inc.
540 N. Main Street
Fremont, NB 68025
(402) 721-7300
Dolores Dunker (CGA)

*Sartor-Hamann Jlrs.
3404 W. 13th
Grand Island, NB 68803
(308) 382-5850
Bennett Murphy, Jr. (CGA)
    and at:
1150 "O" Street
Lincoln, NB 68508
(402) 226-2917
Robert H. Fixter (CGA)

Nevada

*Huntington Jewelers, Inc.
3661 S. Maryland Parkway #19N
Las Vegas, NV 89109
(702) 732-1977
Richard C. Huntington (MGA)

New Hampshire

*A.E. Alie & Sons, Inc.
1 Market Street
Portsmouth, NH 03801
(603) 436-0531
Stephen R. Alie (CGA)

*Beacon Hill Jewelers, Inc.
42 Hanover St.
Manchester, NH 03101
(603) 627-7338
Judith Fineblit (CGA)

*Harrington's Jewelers
New London Shopping Center
New London, NH 03257
(603) 526-4440
Douglas J. Lantz (CGA)
    and at:
33 Main St.
Newport, NH 03773
(603) 863-1662
Douglas J. Lantz (CGA)

*Sawyers Jewelry
Downtown Laconia Mall
Laconia, NH 03246
(603) 524-3309
Richard Beauregard (CGA)

New Jersey

*Earth Treasures
Circle Plaza Shopping Center
Eatontown, NJ 07724
(201) 542-5444
Paul Bischoff

*Hamilton Jewelers
2542 Brunswick Pike
Lawrenceville, NJ 08648
(609) 771-9400
Hank B. Siegel (CGA)

*The Jewel Shop
436 Main Street
Metuchen, NJ 08840
(201) 549-1490
Andrew H. Zagoren (CGA)

*Martin Jewelers
12 North Avenue West
Cranford, NJ 07016
(201) 276-6718
Ellen R. Ramer (CGA)
    and at
125 Quimby St.
Westfield, NJ 07090
(201) 232-6718
Davia Sue Freeman (CGA)

*Rose City Jewelers-Gemologists
Corner of Waverly &
Main Streets
Madison, NJ 07940
(201) 377-2146
Joseph Falco Jr. (CGA)

*Simms Jewelers, Inc.
17 Mine Brook Road
Bernardsville, NJ 07924
(201) 766-4455
Arthur Sockolof (CGA)

New Mexico

*Butterfield Personal
  Service Jewelers
2411 San Pedro, N.E.
Albuquerque, NM 87110
(505) 884-5747
Larry D. Phillips (CGA)

*J.A. May Jewelers, Inc.
112 West Main Street
Farmington, NM 87401
(505) 325-5102
William D. McGraw (CGA)

*Larry D. Phillips (MGA)
801 Marie Park NE
Albuquerque, NM 87123
(505) 884-5747

*Shelton Jewelers, Ltd.
7001 Montgomery Blvd., N.E.
Albuquerque, NM 87109
(505) 881-1013
Eric M. Shelton (CGA)

New York

*American Gemological Lab.
580 Fifth Avenue, Suite 1211
New York, NY 10036
(212) 704-0727
C.R. "Cap" Beesley (MGA)

*Castiglione Gem Jewelers Inc.
25 N. Main Street
Gloversville, NY 12078
(518) 725-1113
Louis J. Castiglione (CGA)

*Cornell Jewelers
Dutchess Mall, Rt. 9
Fishkill, NY 12524
(914) 896-8950
Thomas F. Kavanagh (CGA)

and at:
119 Newburgh Mall
1067 Union Avenue
Newburgh/Beacon, NY 12550
(914) 564-5100
Charles T. Kavanagh (CGA)

*Freedman Jewelers
345 New York Ave.
Huntington, NY 11743
(516) 423-2000
Eric M. Freedman (CGA)

*Lights Jewelers & Gemologists
Plattsburgh Plaza
Plattsburgh, NY 12901
(518) 561-6623
Andre Thomas Light (CGA)

*Lourdes Gemological Lab.
Rt. 6 & Hill Blvd.
Jefferson Valley, NY 10535
(914) 245-4676
Howard N. Biffer (MGA)

*Reyman Jewelers, Inc.
16 W. First Street
Mount Vernon, NY 10550
(914) 668-9281
Mark Reyman (CGA)

*Ruby & Sons Jewelers
6 Washington Avenue
Endicott, NY 13760
(607) 754-1212
Leonard Levine (CGA)

*Schneider's Jewelers, Inc.
290 Wall St.
Kingston, NY 12401
(914) 331-1888
Thomas W. Jacobi (CGA)

*T.H. Bolton Jeweler Inc.
16 East Main Street
Rochester, NY 14614
(716) 546-7074
E. Jean Bolton (CGA)

*Van Cott Fine Jewelry
Oakdale Mall
Johnson City, NY 13790
(607) 729-9108

*William Scheer Jewelers Inc.
3349 Monroe Ave., Pittsford Plaza
Rochester, NY 14618
(716) 381-3050
Jack Monchecourt (CGA)

North Carolina

*Arnold Jewelers
305 Overstreet Mall
Southern National Center
Charlotte, NC 28202
(704) 332-6727
Frank V. Taylor (GCA)

*Bailey's Fine Jewelry
117 Winstead Ave.
Rocky Mount, NC 27804
(919) 443-7676
(800) 338-7676
Clyde C. Bailey (CGA)

*Bisanar Jewelers
226 Union Square
Hickory, NC 28601
(704) 322-5090
J. Timothy Cline (CGA)

*Green's Jewelers
106 N. Main St.
Roxboro, NC 27573
(919) 599-8381
Sam B. Green (CGA)

*Henry J. Young's Diamonds
and Fine Jewelry
257 N. Hills Mall
Raleigh, NC 27609
(919) 787-1422
Henry J. Young (CGA)

*Johnson's Jewelers, Inc.
309 Fayetteville St.
Raleigh, NC 27602
(919) 834-0713

*Karat Gold Corner, Inc.
1809 Pembroke Road
Greensboro, NC 27408
(919) 272-2325
Lorraine D. Dodds (CGA)

*McCormick Jewelers
9015-1 J.M. Keynes Drive
Charlotte, NC 28213
(704) 547-8446
James G. McCormick (CGA)
    and at:
3716 MacCorkle Ave. S.E.
Charleston, WV 25304
(304) 925-3435
James R. McCormick (CGA)

*NC Gem Lab
107 Hunter's Ridge Road
Chapel Hill, NC 27514
(919) 966-2227
William Benedick (MGA)

*Parker-Miller Jewelers
100 S. Main St.
Lexington, NC 27292
(704) 249-8174
Christopher L. Bramlett (CGA)

*T. William Benedict (MGA)
107 Hunter's Ridge Road
Chapel Hill, NC 27514
(919) 929-9179

*Wick & Greene Jewelers
121 Patton Ave.
Asheville, NC 28801
(704) 253-1805
Michael E. Greene (CGA)

Ohio

*Argo & Lehne Jewelers
20 So. Third St.
Columbus, OH 43215
(614) 228-6338
Shannon F. Patterson (CGA)

*David Baker Creative
  Jewelers, Inc.
37 West Bridge Street
Dublin, OH 43017
(614) 764-0068
David M. Baker (CGA)

*E.M. Smith Jewelers, Inc.
668 Central Ctr.
Chillicothe, OH 45601
(614) 774-1840
Robert J. Smith (CGA)

*Grassmuck & Lange
  Jewelers, Inc.
441 Vine Street
Carew Tower Arcade
Cincinnati, OH 45202
(513) 621-1898
William F. Grassmuck (CGA)

*Henry B. Ball, West
2291 W. Market St.
Pilgrim Square
Akron, OH 44313
(216) 867-9800
Mary Ball Gorman (CGA)
  and at:
5254 Dressler Rd. N.W.
Belden Village
Canton, OH 44718
(216) 499-3000
Robert A. Ball (CGA)

*Jack Siebert, Goldsmith & Jeweler
1623 W. Lane Ave. Ctr.
Columbus, OH 43221
(614) 486-4653
Jack Siebert (CGA)

*John Gasser & Son Jewelers
205 Third Street, N.W.
Canton, OH 44702
(216) 452-3204
Gerald D. Blevins (CGA)

*O'Bryant Jewelers & Gemologists
101 E. Wayne Street
Maumee, OH 43537
(419) 893-9771
James P. O'Bryant (CGA)

*Raymond Brenner, Inc.
7081 West Blvd., Route 224
Youngstown, OH 44512
(216) 726-8816
Raymond Brenner Jr. (CGA)

*Thomas Jewelers, Inc.
409 S. Main St.
Findlay, OH 45840
(419) 422-3775
James L. Thomas (CGA)

*Wendel's
137 S. Broad Street
Lancaster, OH 43130
(614) 653-6402
Stuart Palestrant (CGA)

*Wm. Effler Jewelers
7618 Hamilton Ave.
Cincinnati, OH 45231
(513) 521-6654
Mark T. Andrus (CGA)

*Yeager Jewelers, Inc.
14814 Madison Ave.
Lakewood, OH 44107
(216) 521-6658
Jack Yeager (CGA)

Oklahoma

*B.C. Clark, Inc.
101 Park Avenue
Oklahoma City, OK 73102
(405) 232-8806
Paul C. Minton (CGA)

Oregon

*Deuell Jewelers, Inc.
1327 Main Street
Philomath, OR 97370
(503) 929-3422
JoAnne Hansen (CGA)

*Gayer Jewelers
300 E. Second Street
The Dalles, OR 97058
(503) 298-GEMS
Scott Gayer (CGA)

*The Gem Lab
20776 St. George Court
Bend, Oregon 97702
(503) 389-6790
Jim "Fritz" Ferguson

*Hart Jewelers
235 S.E. 6th Street
Grants Pass, OR 97526
(503) 476-5543
Thomas R. Hart Sr. (CGA)

Pennsylvania

*Bill Lieberum Fine Jewelers &
  Gemologists
Centre Pointe Place Shopping Ctr.
872 West Street Rd
Warminster, PA 18974
(215) 443-8000
William R. Lieberum (CGA)

*D.A. Palmieri Co., Inc.
666 Washington Road
Pittsburgh, PA 15228
(412) 344-0300
Susan G. Bower (MGA)
Donald Palmieri (MGA)

*D. Atlas & Co., Inc.
732 Sansom Street
Philadelphia, PA 19106
(215) 922-1926
Michael Jordan (MGA)
Edward R. Skinner Jr. (MGA)

*David Craig Jewelers, Ltd.
Summit Square Shopping Ctr.
Langhorne, PA 19047
(215) 968-8900
David C. Rotenberg (CGA)

*Futer Bros. Jewelers
Continental Square
York, PA 17401
(717) 845-2734
J.H. Eigenrauch III (CGA)

*Gemological Appraisal
  Associates, Inc.
666 Washington Road
Pittsburg, PA 15228
(412) 344-5500
Donald Palmieri (MGA)

*John M. Roberts & Sons Co.
429-431 Wood Street
Pittsburgh, PA 15222
(412) 281-1651
Maureen F. O'Brien (CGA)

*Joseph A. Rosi Jewelers
4636 Jonestown Road
Harrisburg, PA 17109
(717) 652-8477
Joseph A. Rosi Jr. (CGA)

*M.A.B. Jewelers
1162 Baltimore Pike
Olde Sproul Village
Springfield, PA 19064
(215) 554-4656
Samuel S. Bruner (CGA)

*N.B. Levy's
120 Wyoming Ave.
Scranton, PA 18503
(717) 344-6187
Seymour H. Biederman (CGA)

*Yardley Jewelers
JBD Studio – 2 So. Main Street
Yardley, PA 19067
(215) 493-1300
Jon Barry DiNola (CGA)

Rhode Island

*Tilden-Thurber Corp.
292 Westminster St.
Providence, RI 02903
(401) 421-8400
Robert Quinn (CGA)

South Carolina

*Cochran Jewelry Company of
   Greenville, Inc.
211 North Main Street
Greenville, SC 29601
(803) 233-3641
Walter S. Morris (CGA)

Tennessee

*Alexander & Co., Inc.
5050 Poplar, #634
Memphis, TN 38157
(901) 767-4367
William A. Mathis (MGA)

*Fischer Evans Jewelers
801 Market Street
Chattanooga, TN 37402
(615) 267-0901
Mrs. Taylor M. Watson (CGA)

*Helm's Jewelry
100 W. 7th Street
Columbia, TN 38401
(615) 388-7842
Debbie Nelson Wells (CGA)

*M.M. Schenck Jewelers, Inc.
3953 Hixson Pike
Chattanooga, TN 37415
(615) 877-4011
Mrs. Mary Schenck (CGA)

*Mackley & Co., Inc.
8906 Kingston Pike, Suite 214
Knoxville, TN 37923
(615) 693-3097
Joseph Mackley (MGA)
Emily White Ware (CGA)

*Sites Jewelers, Inc.
206 Franklin Street
Clarksville, TN 37040
(615) 648-0678
William C. Sites (CGA)

Texas

Ann Hawken Gem Laboratory
603 West 13th, Suite 312
Austin, TX 78701
(512) 288-3590
Ann Hawken

*Anna M. Miller (MGA)
P.O. Box 1844
Pearland, TX 77588
(713) 485-1606

*Antique Appraisal Service
P.O. Box 27903
Houston, TX 77227
(713) 665-8245
Christine W. York (MGA)

*Barnes Jewelry, Inc.
2611 Wolflin Village
Amarillo, TX 79109
(806) 355-9874
Vess Barnes Jr. (CGA)

*C. Kirk Root Design
6418 B Westside Drive
Austin, TX 78731
(512) 338-0360
Charles K. Root (MGA)

*Crowell Jewelers, Inc.
2417 West Park Row
Arlington, TX 76013
(817) 460-1962
C.G. Crowell, Jr. (CGA)

*Duncan & Boyd, Jewelers
113 West 8th Street
Amarillo, TX 79101
(806) 373-1067
Ronald Boyd (CGA)

*I. David Clark & Associates
305 21st St.
Galveston, TX 77551
(409) 762-3229
Irving D. Clark (CGA)

*Jewelry Forest
9100 N. Central/Park Lane
185 Caruth Plaza
Dallas, TX 75231
(214) 368-5352
Jerry Forrest (CGA)

*Lacy & Co.
River Oakes Shopping Village
3301 So. 14th
Abilene, TX 79605
(915) 695-4700
Ellen W. Lacy (CCA)

*Nowlin Jewelry, Inc.
145 Oyster Creek Dr.
Lake Jackson, TX 77566
(409) 297-7252
John F. Nowlin (CGA)

Utah

*John's Jewelry
3920 Washington Blvd.
Ogden, UT 84403
(801) 627-0440
John Christiansen (CGA)

*Robert L. Rosenblatt
2736 Commonwealth Ave.
Salt Lake City, UT 84109
(801) 364-3667

*Spectrum Gems
1615 S. Foothill Drive
Salt Lake City, UT 84108-2742
(801) 266-4579
Dana Lynn Richardson (MGA)

*Sutton's of Park City
Park City Resort Village
Park City, UT 84060
(801) 649-1187
Keith M. Sutton (CGA)

Virginia

*Carreras, Ltd.
150 Sovran Plaza
Richmond, VA 23277
(804) 780-9191
Mark A. Smith (CGA)

*Cowardin Jewelers
Chesterfield Towne Center
Rt. 60 and Rt. 147
Richmond, VA 23235
(804) 794-4478
Ronald L. Cowardin (CGA)

*Everhart Jewelers, Inc.
6649 Old Dominion Dr.
McLean, VA 22101
(703) 821-3344
William R. Everhart II (CGA)

*Fauquier Gemological Laboratory
P.O. Box 525, Main Street
Marshall, VA 22115
(703) 364-1959
Jelks H. Cabaniss (MGA)

*Frank L. Moose Jeweler
207 1st St. S.W.
Roanoke, VA 24011
(703) 345-8881
F. Geoffrey Jennings (CGA)

*The Greenhouse
P.O. Box 525
Marshall, VA 22115
(703) 364-1959
Jelks Cabaniss (MGA)

*Hardy's Diamonds
4212 Virginia Beach Boulevard
Wayside Village, VA 23452
(804) 486-0469
George B. Hardy (CGA)

*Marvin D. Miller Gemologists
3050 Covington St.
Fairfax, VA 22031
(703) 280-2169
Marvin D. Miller (MGA)

*Schwarzchild Jewelers, Inc.
Broad at Second St.
Richmond, VA 23219
(804) 644-1941
B. Harton Wolf (CGA)

*Thomas P. Hartnett (MGA)
11344 Links Drive
Reston, VA 22090
(703) 437-7108

*Van Doren Jewelers
6025-D Burke Center Pkwy.
Burke, VA 22015
(703) 978-2211
Christian W. Lietwiler (MGA)

Washington

*Ben Bridge Jeweler
1101 Pike
Seattle, WA 98111
(206) 628-6879
Jane Ann Buescher (CGA)
and at
1119 Tacoma Mall
Tacoma, WA 98409
(206) 473-1227
Cathy Hall (CGA)

*Blessing's Jewelers
225 W. Meeker St.
Kent, WA 98032
(206) 852-3455
Leslie S. Thomas (CGA)

*Button Jewelers, Inc.
2 S. Wenatchee Ave.
Wenatchee, WA 98801
(509) 663-4654
Douglas D. Button (CGA)

*Carroll's Fine Jewelry
1427 Fourth Avenue
Seattle, WA 98101
(206) 622-9191
Patricia M. Droge (CGA)

*Fox's Gem Shop
1341 Fifth Ave.
Seattle, WA 98101
(206) 623-2528
Sandra L. Ordway (CGA)

*Gemological Training
  Corporation
1425 4th Avenue, Ste. 502
Seattle, WA 98101
(206) 625-0105
David W. Hall (MGA)

*Henry Gerards Jewelers, Inc.
W. 714 Main
River Park Square Skywalk
Spokane, WA 99201
(509) 456-8098
Janis Ann Gerards (CGA)

*Pavilion Gemological
  Laboratories
19415 Pacific Hwy. So., Ste. 414
Seattle, WA 98188
(206) 824-9132
Joseph V. Paul (MGA)

*S.O. Hawkes & Son Jewelers Inc.
123 E. Yakima Ave.
Yakima, WA 98901
(509) 248-2248
Kathy Hawkes Smith (CGA)

West Virginia

*Calvin Broyles Jewelers
4833 McCorkle Ave. S.W.
Spring Hill, WV 25309
(304) 768-8821
Don C. Broyles (CGA)

*McCormick Jewelers, Inc.
3716 MacCorkle Ave. S.E.
Charleston, WV 25304
(304) 925-3435
James R. McCormick (CGA)

*R.D. Buttermore & Son
623 Market St.
Parkersburg, WV 26101
(304) 422-6401
R.D. Buttermore Jr. (CGA)

Wisconsin

*Gemstone Goldsmiths
100 Main Street
Stone Lake, WI 54876
(715) 865-2422
David R. Neilson (CGA)

*J. Vander Zanden & Sons Ltd.
217 N. Washington St.
Green Bay, WI 54305
(414) 432-3155
Peter Vander Zanden (CGA)

*Midwest Gem Lab of Wisc., Inc.
1335 S. Moorland Rd.
Brookfield, WI 53005
(414) 784-9017
James S. Seaman (MGA)

*Rasmussen Jewelry
3119 Washington Ave.
Racine, WI 53405
(414) 633-9474
William E. Sustachek (CGA)

*Schwanke-Kasten Co.
324 E. Silver Spring Dr.
Milwaukee, WI 53217
(414) 964-1242
James E. Brown (CGA)

Wyoming

*Wiseman Jewelers
501 Ivinson Avenue
Laramie, WY 82070
(307) 745-5240
Scott Alan Wiseman (CGA)

Associations

United States and Canada

Accredited Gemologists Assoc.
1615 South Foothill Drive
Salt Lake City, Utah 84108
(801) 581-9000 or 364-3667
Dana Richardson, Editor

American Gem Trade Association
#181 World Trade Center
2050 Stemmons Expressway
Dallas, Texas 75207
(214) 742-4367 (800) 972-1162
Peggy Willett, Exec. Director

American Society of Appraisers
Box 17265
Washington, DC 20041
(703) 478-2228
Shirley Belz, PR Director

Appraisers Association of America
60 East 42nd St.
New York, NY 10165
(212) 867-9775
Victor Wiener, Exec. Director

Association Professionelle des
  Gemmologists du Quebec
6079, Boul. Monk
Montreal, Quebec
Canada H4E 3H5
(514) 766-7327

Association of Women Gemologists
P.O. Box 1844
Pearland, Texas 77588
(713) 485-1606
Anna Miller, Director

Canadian Gemmological Assoc.
P.O. Box 1106, Station Q
Toronto, Ontario
Canada M4T 2P2

Warren Boyd
(416) 652-3137

Canadian Jewellers Institute
Canada Trust Tower, Suite 1203
20 Eglinton Ave. W., Box 2021
Toronto, Ontario
Canada M4R 1K8
(416) 480-1424

Diamond Council of America Inc.
9140 Ward Parkway
Kansas City, MO 64114
(816) 444-3500
Jerry Fogel, Executive Director

Diamond Dealers Club Inc.
580 5th Avenue
New York, NY 10036
(212) 719-4321
Abe Shainberg, Exec. Director

International Colored Gemstone
  Association
22643 Strathern St.
West Hills, CA 91304
(818) 716-0489
Maureen Jones, Exec. Director

Jewelers of America, Inc.
1271 Avenue of the Americas
New York, New York 10020
(212) 489-0023
Michael D. Roman,
  Chairman and Exec. Director

National Association of Jewelry
  Appraisers
4210 North Brown Avenue
Suite "A"
Scottsdale, AZ 85251
(602) 941-8088
Richard E. Baron,
  Executive Director

Associations: Other Countries

Austria

Bundesgremium Des Handels Mit
  Juwelen
P.O. Box 440
A-1045 Vienna
Austria
Karl M. Heldwein

Australia

Gemmological Association of
  Australia
P.O. Box 184
East Brisbane, Queensland 4169
Australia

Gemmological Association of Aust.
  also at:
G.P.O. Box 5133 AA
Melbourne, 3001
Australia
Mr. Franz Thrupp

Australian Gem Ind. Assoc.
P.O. Box 104, Bondi Beach
New South Wales
Australia
Joy Clayton

Brazil

ABGM
Rue Barao de Itapetininga
No. 255 – 12 Andar
CEP 01042 – Sau Paulo – SP
Brazil

Ajorio – Sindicato National
Do. Com. Atacadista de Pedras
  Preciosas
Av. Graca Aranha
19/40 Andar Sala 404
CEP 20031
Brazil

Associacao Brasileria de
  Gemologiae
Mineralogiae Rue Alvarez
Machado
41,18000/801 501
Sao Paulo

IBGM
Rua Teixeira Da Silva, No. 654
CEP 04002 – Paraiso
Sao Paulo – SP
Brasil

Instituto Brasileiro de Gemas e
  Metais Preciosos
Av. Rio Branco
135 Sala 1018
CEP 20040
Brasil

Burma

Gem & Jade Corporation
86, Kala Aye Pagoda Road
P.O. Box 1397 Rangoon

Dubai

Institute of Goldsmithing &
  Jewellery
Sikat Al Khail Road
P.O. Box 11489
Dubai, U.A.E.

England

De Beers Consolidated Mines Ltd.
40 Holborn Viaduct
London ECIPIAJ

Gemmological Association of Great
  Britain
Saint Dunstan's House
Carey Lane
London, EC2V 8AB

Jewellery Information Centre
44 Fleet Street
London, ECA

Finland

Gemmological Society of Finland
P.O. Box 6287
Helsinki, Finland

France

French Diamond Association
7 Rue de Chatesudun
Paris 75009
France
Claude Varnier

Service Public Du Controle
2, Place de la Bourse
Paris 75002
France
Mr. Poirot

Syndicat des Maitres Artisans
    bijoutiers-joailliers
3, Rue Sainte-Elisabeth
75003 Paris
France

Association Francaise de
    Gemmologie
1 Rue Saint Georges
Paris 75009
France

Germany

Deutsch Gemmologische Gesell-
    schaft EV
(German Gemmological Society)
Prof.-Schlossmacher-Str. 1
Postfach 122260
6580 Idar-Oberstein 2
West Germany

Diamant - und Edelsteinborse,
    Idar-Oberstein E.V.
Mainzer Str. 34
D-6580 Idar-Oberstein
West Germany

Hong Kong

The Gemmological Association of
    Hong Kong
TST P.O. Box 97711
Kowloon
Hong Kong

Hong Kong Gemmologists' Assoc.
P.O. Box 74170
Kowloon Central Post Office
Hong Kong

India

The All India Jewellers' Assoc.
19 Connaught Place
New Delhi
India

Andhra Pradesh Gold, Silver, Jew-
    ellery and Diamond Merchants
    Association
Secunderabad
India

Bangiya Swarna Silpi Samitee
162 Bipin Behari Ganguli Street
Calcutta 12
India

Bombay Jewellers Association
308 Sheikh Memon Street
Bombay 400 002

The Cultured & Natural Pearl
    Association
1st Agiary Lane, Dhanji Street
Bombay 400 003
India

Gem & Jewellery Information
Centre of India
A-95, Jana Colony
Journal House
Jaipur 302 004

Gujarat State Gold Dealers and
    Jewellers' Association
2339-2, Manek Chowk
Ahmedabad
India

Jewellers' Association
Nagarthpet
Bangalore 560 002
India

Tamil Nadu Jewellers Federation
(also The Madras Jwlers. & Dia.
Merch. Assoc.)
11/12 Car St.
Netaji Subhaschandra Road
Madras 600 001

Indonesia

L.G. Tampubolon
Indonesian Gemstone & Jewellery
Assoc.
J1. Teuku Umar 53
Jakarta 10310
Indonesia

Israel

Gemmological Association of Israel
1 Jabotinsky St.
Ramat-Gan
5250, Israel

Israel Precious Stones Exchange
Maccabi Building
1 Jabotinsky Street
Ramat-Gan 52520
Israel
Yehuda Kassif

Italy

CIBJO
Lungo Tevere Osali Anguillarh 9
Roma 00153
Italy
Dr. Amirante

Instituto Gemmologico Italiane
Piazzale Gambrare, 7/8
20146 Milano, Italy

Japan

CIBJO of Japan
Chuo-Jiho Bldg. 3.1-3 Shintomi
2 Chome, Chuo-ku, Tokyo
Japan

Gemmological Association of All
Japan
Tokyo Biho Kaikan
24 Akashi-chu, Chuo-ku,
Tokyo 104 Japan

Kenya

Kenya Gemstone Dealers Assoc.
P.O. Box 47928
Nairobi
Kenya
Dr. N.R. Barot

Malaysia

Malaysian Institute of Gemmolog-
ical Sciences
Lot 3, 76-3, 78 3rd Floor
Wisma Stephens
Jalan Caja Chulma
Kuala Lempur

Netherlands

CIBJO-International   Confedera-
tion of Jewellery, Silverware, Di-
amonds, Pearls and Stones
Van de Spiegelstratte #3
P.O. Box 29818
The Hague, Netherlands
2502LV
Dr. Bernard W. Buenk,
President

Pakistan

All Pakistan Gem Merch. & Jwlrs.
Association
1st Floor, Gems & Jewellery Trade
Centre
Blenken Street
Saddar Karachi-3
Pakistan

Singapore

Singapore Gemologist Society
3, Lengkok Marak
Singapore-1024

South Africa

Gem'l Assoc. of South Africa
P.O. Box 4216
Johannesburg 2000
South Africa
A. Thomas

Sri Lanka

Gemmologists Association of Sri
 Lanka
Professional Centre, 275-76
Baudhaloka Mawatha
Colombo-7
Sri Lanka

Sweden

Swedish Association of
 Gemmologists
Birger Jarlsgatan 88
S-114 20 Stockholm
Sweden
Ake Gewers

Swedish Geological Society
c/o SGU, Box 670
S-751 28 Uppsala
Sweden

Switzerland

The Swiss Society of Gemmology
Kanagase 6,
Biel, Switzerland

Scheweizerische
Gemmologische
Gesellschaft
St. Gallen, Switzerland

Swiss Gem Trade Association
Nuschelerstr. 44
8001 Zurich
Switzerland
Dr. Christoph Kerez

Thailand

Asian Institute of Gemmological
 Sciences
987 Silom Road
Rama Jewellery Building
4th Floor, Bangkok 5

Thai Gems and Jewelry Assoc
33/85 Surawongse Road
17th Floor
Bangkok 10500
Thailand
 and
942/152 Charn Issara Tower
15th Floor
Rama 4 Road, Bangkok 10500
Thailand

Zambia

Zambia Gemstone & Precious
 Metal Association
P.O. Box 31099, Room 17
Luangwa House
Cairo Road, Lusaka
Zambia

Zimbabwe

Gem Education Centre of
 Zimbabwe
Founders House
15 Gordon Avenue
Harare, Zimbabwe 707580
Lesley Faye Marsh, F.G.A.

Selected List of
Gem Identification Equipment Suppliers

Albert Froidevaux & Sons/USA
Albert Froidevaux et Fils S.A.,
　Switzerland
11449 Randall Dr.
Lenexa, KS 66215
913-338-3131 Fax. 913-338-3144

B. Jadow & Sons, Inc.
Vigor/Jemeter (Vigor tools and
　equipment available from dis-
　tributors)
53 W. 23rd St.
New York, NY 10010
212-807-3800 Fax. 212-645-8637

Berco Watch & Jewelers Supply
29 East Madison
Chicago, ILL. 60602
312-782-1050 Fax. 312-982-4441

Borel & Frei
712 S. Olive St.
Los Angeles, CA. 90014
213-689-4630 Fax. 213-488-0485

Bourget Bros.
1636 11th St.
Santa Monica, CA. 90404
213-450-6556

Carl Zeiss, Inc.
One Zeiss Drive
Thornwood, NY 10594
914-747-1800

Cas-Ker Co.
2121 Spring Grove Ave.
P.O. Box 14069
Cincinnati, OH 45214
513-241-7073 Fax. 513-241-5848

· Colmans-Borel
812 Huron Rd., Ste. 600
Cleveland, OH
216-771-2343 Fax. 216-771-7304

Columbia School of Gemology
8600 Fenton Street
Silver Spring, MD 20910
301-588-7770

The Contenti Co.
123 Stewart St.
Providence RI 02903
800-343-3364 or 401-421-4040

Dallas Jewelry Supply House
9979 Monroe Dr.
Dallas, TX 75220
214-351-2263 or 800-346-5397

S. Fargotstein & Sons
P.O. Box 111049
2505 Poplar Ave.
Memphis, TN
901-452-8475 Fax. 901-452-2600

Findco, Inc.
5444 Westheimer Rd., Ste. 635
Houston, TX 77056
713-995-8380

Gemlab, Inc.
P.O. Box 6333
Clearwater, FL 34618
813-447-1667 Fax. 813-442-1221

Gemmological Instruments Ltd.
St. Dunstan's House
Carey Lane
London EC2V 8AB England
01-726-4374 Fax 01-726-4837

Gemological Products
  Corporation
2834 Colorado Blvd., #14
Santa Monica, CA 90404
213-398-2567

Gemstone Press
P.O. Box 276
South Woodstock, VT. 05071
802-457-4000/800-962-4544
Fax 802-457-4004

GIA Gem Instruments
Gemological Institute of America
P.O. Box 2110
1660 Stewart St.
Santa Monica, CA 90406
213-829-2991 Fax. 213-828-0247
  and:
580 Fifth Avenue
New York, NY 10036
212-221-5858

Goldberg & Co., Inc.
725 Sansom St.
Philadelphia, PA 19106
215-922-0664

Hammel, Riglander & Co.
750 Washington Avenue
Carlstadt, NJ 07072
(201) 935-0100

Hanneman Gemological
  Instruments
P.O. Box 2453
Castro Valley, CA 94546
414-847-4391

Jewelers Equip. & Tools Corp.
5 North Wabash St., #818
Chicago, ILL 60602
312-263-8221

I. Kassoy, Inc.
28 W. 47th St.
New York, NY 10036
212-719-2290 Fax. 212-575-1883

Sy Kessler Sales, Inc.
2263-C Valdina St.
Dallas, TX 75207
214-630-2563 Fax. 214-632-2568

Leeds Precision Instruments
801 Boone Ave. N.
Minneapolis, MN 55427
612-546-8575 Fax 612-546-4369

J.F. McCaughin Co.
2628 N. River Ave.
Rosemead, CA 91770
818-573-5781, 213-623-6210
Fax. 818-307-6912

Nikon Inc., Instrument Division
623-T Stewart Avenue
Garden City, NY 11530
516-222-0200

Otto Frei-Jules Borel Co.
P.O. Box 796
126 2nd St.
Oakland, CA 94604
415-832-0355

Page & Wilson, Ltd.
330 W. Pender St.
Vancouver, BC
Canada V6B 3K2
604-685-8257

Nebula
P.O. Box 3356
Redwood City, CA 94064
415-369-5966

Norman Press, Inc.
18345 Ventura Blvd., Ste 305
Tarzana, CA 91356
818-343-4655

Raytech Industries
P.O. Box 6
Stafford Springs, CT. 06076
203-684-4273

Roseco, Inc.
8111 LBJ, Ste 840
Dallas, TX 75271
214-437-9129

Rosenthal Jewelers Supply Corp.
138 N.E. 1st Ave.
Miami, FL 31132
305-371-5661 Fax. 305-577-8275

Rubin & Son Diamond & Jewelry
  Supplies/USA
96 Spring St.
New York, NY 10012
212-966-6300 Fax. 212-966-6354

Sarasota Instruments, Inc.
Jemeter
1960 Main St.
Sarasota, FL 34236
813-366-4646

Spectronics Corporation
956-T Brush Hollow Road
Westbury, NY 11590
516-333-4840

Swest, Inc.
P.O. Box 540938
10803 Composite Dr.
Dallas, TX 75354
214-350-4011 Fax. 214-357-9664

Transcontinental Tool Co.
21 Dundas Sq. #605
Toronto, ON
Canada M5B 1B7
416-363-7251

Tulper & Co.
2223 E. Colfax St.
Denver, CO 80206
303-399-9291

Vibrograf USA Corp.
504 Cherry Ln.
Floral Park, NY 11001
516-437-8700

INDEX

Gem Identification (Webster), 25
Gemlab
  Fiberscope 2
  microscope, 16
  Gem Spectroscope, 20
Gemmological
  Instruments Ltd., 17
Gemologist's Compendium (Webster), 25
Gems (Webster), 146
Gems & Gemology, 25
Gemscope Model 2 microscope, 17
Gem Spectroscope, 20
Gemstone Press, 12
Gepe, 13
GGG, 101, 103, 105
ghost lines, 129
GIA, 150, 183
  dichroscope, 11, 14
  Discan spectroscope, 20
  Duplex II refractometer, 15, 94, 96
  Gemscope Model 2 microscope, 17
  Illuminator Polariscope, 20
  loupe, 13
  Pocket Diamond Tester, 21
  Short-wave/Long-wave Ultraviolet Lamp, 15
  Specific Gravity Liquid Set, 25
  utility lamp, 28-30, 95
  ultra-violet lamp, 82
  viewing cabinet, 16
G.I.A. laboratory, 123
Gilson synthetics, 85-86, 127
girdle fringes (bearding), 48
girdle roughness, 49
glass, 162, 164, 169, 171, 173, 177, 179
  Chelsea filter and, 55, 61, 62, 72
  dichroscope and, 65, 67, 68, 71, 72, 176
  inclusions in, 124
  loupe and, 72, 175
  microscope and, 118
  polariscope and, 147, 151
  refractometer and, 99, 101, 103, 105

spectroscope and, 144
growth (grain) lines, 48
Gubelin, Edward, 25, 47, 115, 12

halogen lamp, 95
halo (disc-like) inclusions, 52, 123, 128-130
Handbook of Gem Identification (Liddicoat), 23, 25, 145-146
Hanneman Gemological Instruments
  Diamond Beam/the Diamond Eye diamond tester, 21
  filter set, 13
  video spectroscope, 20
Hastings loupe, 39
healing-feather (liquid-filled) inclusions, 51, 122, 123, 128, 129
hiddenite (spodumene)
  Chelsea filter and, 61
  inclusions in, 52
horse-tails, 130

Illuminator Polariscope, 20
immersion cell, 20
incandescent light, 22, 27, 31, 56
inclusions in colored gems
  learning to spot, 117-122
  types of, 50-53, 61, 122-125
inclusions in diamonds
  learning to spot, 46-47
  types of, 47-49, 123
Internal World of Gemstones (Gubelin), 47, 115
invisible light, 32-33
iron pyrite, 126
isopropyl (rubbing alcohol), 20, 22, 42, 116, 148, 150, 175-176
ivory, 105

jade, 160, 181
  Chelsea filter and, 56, 58-59, 61, 145
  polariscope and, 147, 151

refractometer and, 96, 103
spectroscope and, 59, 136, 145, 173, 177
jasper, 88, 160
Jemeter refractometer, 15, 94, 96, 100, 105
jet, 105
Jewelry & Gems: The Buying Guide (Matlins and Bonanno), 25
Journal of Gemology, 25

Kassoy
  loupe, 13
  #MIC611 microscope, 17
  #MIC631 microscope, 17
  #MIC631Z microscope, 17
knaat, 48
knaat (twin) lines, 49
Koivula, John L., 25, 47, 115
kunzite, inclusions in, 52

lapis, 160, 182
  refractometer and, 96
  ultraviolet lamp and, 88
laser-hole, 123
laser line, 48-49, 126
lath-like inclusions, 123, 127, 130
Lechleitner synthetics, 50, 127
Liddicoat, Richard T., 23, 25, 145-146
lighting
  Chelsea filter and, 56-57
  daylight, 22, 27, 31, 56
  dichroscope and, 68-69
  flashlight, 22
  fluorescent, 27, 31-32, 56-57
  halogen lamp, 95
  importance of proper, 27, 115
  incandescent, 22, 27, 31, 56
  intensity of, 27, 28
  invisible, 32-33
  loupe and, 44-45
  microscope and, 114, 115, 117-120